CHINA'S FINANCIAL STABILITY

Inherent Logic and Basic Framework

CHINA'S FINANCIAL STABILITY

Inherent Logic and Basic Framework

DEXU HE

Chinese Academy of Social Sciences, China

社会科学文献出版社
SOCIAL SCIENCES ACADEMIC PRESS (CHINA)

World Scientific

Published by

World Scientific Publishing Co. Pte. Ltd.

5 Toh Tuck Link, Singapore 596224

USA office: 27 Warren Street, Suite 401-402, Hackensack, NJ 07601

UK office: 57 Shelton Street, Covent Garden, London WC2H 9HE

Library of Congress Cataloging-in-Publication Data
Names: He, Dexu, author.
Title: China's financial stability : inherent logic and basic framework /
Dexu He (Chinese Academy of Social Sciences, China).
Description: New Jersey : World Scientific, 2016. | Includes bibliographical references.
Identifiers: LCCN 2016008383 | ISBN 9789813109056 (hc : alk. paper)
Subjects: LCSH: China--Economic policy--2000- | Monetary policy--China. |
Economic stabilization--China.
Classification: LCC HC427.95 .H4 2016 | DDC 339.50951--dc23
LC record available at https://lccn.loc.gov/2016008383

British Library Cataloguing-in-Publication Data
A catalogue record for this book is available from the British Library.

Sponsored by the Innovation Project of CASS

《中国金融稳定: 内在逻辑与基本框架》
Originally published in Chinese by Social Sciences Academic Press (China)

Desk Editors: Dr. Sree Meenakshi Sajani/Dong Lixi

Typeset by Stallion Press
Email: enquiries@stallionpress.com

Preface

Triggered by the USA subprime mortgage crisis of 2007, the Financial Tsunami is the most serious global financial crisis since the Great Depression. It had enormous impact on the real estate and credit markets, the financial sector and the real economy in both developed and developing countries, and the global economic and financial systems in general.

Before the Crisis, the financial sector held an important position in the economic growth of developed countries. In the United States, for example, after the burst of the Internet bubble, sectors such as finance, real estate, and automobile were critical components of the economy and were a key driving force for economic growth. The finance sector was at the time characteristically highly leveraged and risky. When the global financial crisis broke out, financial institutions, related businesses, and the household sector were forced to deleverage, becoming smaller, less profitable, and less influential. Global trade and financial interactions were hard hit, and the global economy went into a slump. All this plunged the global financial system into considerable chaos.

First, the financial system was hit in its basic functions. As the crisis spread, USA government-sponsored enterprises, large insurance companies, and leading commercial banks were all swept up. The Top five USA investment banks either went bankrupt or transformed into a bank holding company. The market-oriented and bank-dominated financial system was also seriously affected, which revealed its vulnerability. Secondly, deficiencies in financial regulation that had since gone unnoticed became evident. The worsening crisis helped to expose obvious financial regulatory shortcomings in the United States: the existing system could not keep pace with changes in the economic and financial systems; the absence of a single, authoritative regulator made it impossible to eliminate systemic risks or prevent systemic crisis; functional overlaps among different regulatory agencies resulted in blind spots, reducing regulatory effectiveness, as was exemplified by the lack of effective regulation over financial holding companies; the compartmentalized financial regulatory system ill-suits the needs of mixed business models in the market. Problems with the financial regulatory system became an important cause of the global financial crisis. Once again, financial innovation came with higher risks, and there is no doubt they helped to trigger the global financial crisis. Financial innovations in the United States, such as adjustable rate mortgage (ARM), subprime mortgage securitization, the "mark to market" bookkeeping method employed by some financial institutions, risk value-based asset-liability management (ALM) and excessive leverage helped spawn the global financial crisis. In some sense, the crisis amounted to a liquidation of excessive financial innovations. Third and last, the mismatch between the regulatory models of the financial sector and the prevailing business model was an institutional factor that led to the global financial crisis. In 1999, the United States replaced the Glass-Steagall Act with the Financial Services Modernization Act. Financial institutions in the United States went from providing a single type of service to providing a variety of services. Thus, the United States, the United Kingdom, Japan, and other countries formed the multi-service institution camp. At the beginning, the model, showing greater flexibility and efficiency than the single-service model long-established in Germany, Switzerland, France, and other countries, became a template for the development of the financial sector in Latin American countries and some emerging economies. The seriousness of the problem was attributable to the mismatch between the prevailing business and regulatory models in the United States, which resulted in a large number of regulatory loopholes.

The global financial crisis has yet to end. The global economy remains jittery and full recovery illusory, and the financial markets have not yet emerged from their doldrum. Debt problems caused by deficits remain prominent, job growth is slow, global trade and global economic growth are sluggish. It is important at a time like this to accelerate the development of the financial regulatory system, promote the improvement of financial innovation mechanisms, and maintain healthy and stable financial markets. Also, financial restructuring is needed for building a solid financial foundation for the further development of the global economy and for the finance sector to become a powerful force in support of growth.

According to its internal logic, financial restructuring involves the following aspects:

First, the market system must match risk management. Both the United States, which is representative of countries that adopt the capital market-driven model of financial market, and Germany, representative of countries in which the bank-dominated model prevails must establish a risk management mechanism that applies to its own specific needs. The scope of the mechanism must cover financial authorities, financial institutions, investors, and other financial market participants. The key is that the financial regulatory authorities must introduce appropriate regulatory policies for effective supervision to ensure the stability and security of the entire financial market system; in the process of risk management, financial institutions must focus on risk management rules such as capital adequacy ratio (CAR), leverage ratio, on-/off-balance sheet items, on-/off-exchange transactions, risk-based pricing and debt maturity; individual investors must understand and assess the risk-return tradeoffs of financial products, as well as their risk preferences/tolerance and capacity for dealing with risks; for a capital market-driven financial market system, in particular, large financial institutions should be subject to more stringent regulations, so they won't generate serious moral hazards and systemic risks by becoming too big to fail

Second, financial innovations must be coordinated with financial risks. While they can help optimize financial resource allocation and are as such conducive to financial development and economic growth, financial innovations may also cause uncertainties in capital flows, financial system fragility, the spread of financial crises and systemic risks. Therefore, it is necessary to balance them against risk management. This requires improving transparency for information related to financial innovations (e.g., implementing mandatory disclosure of information by the originator of financial innovation) strengthening risk management for new financial products (e.g., requiring financial institutions to perform asset impairment loss accounting by factoring in different types of risks, such as those related to market, credit, operations, and liquidity), designing a scientifically sound and effective regulatory system to address the security, liquidity, and profitability of financial innovations and the CAR, asset quality, and on-/off-balance sheet items of financial institutions. Even as we try to strengthen risk management, we must nonetheless continue to support and encourage financial innovations, because it is the main approach to avoiding or reducing financial risks and ensuring financial security.

Third, financial system reform must be deepened and institutional contradictions eliminated. As we all know, every financial market system, business model or regulatory regime has its historical background, institutional basis, and is to some degree rational and adaptable. However, with changes in the economic environment and the development of the financial industry, defects in the system itself will become increasingly evident. Institutional contradictions are in some sense inevitable. Take the compatibility of financial regulations with business models as an example. Despite the introduction of a new financial regulatory system reform plan in the United States, the problem of the incompatibility of the regulatory model, which is compartmentalized, with a mixed business model remains. Therefore, it is especially important for purpose of financial restructuring to improve the fit among different parts of the financial industry, such as between risk management and the market system and between the regulatory system and business operations model, promote cooperation among different levels in the industry in order to ensure coherence in risk management throughout the hierarchy, establish a firewall system that would prevent the spread of crises among different markets, and optimize financial innovation mechanisms in order to try to balance innovation against risks.

Fourth, it is time for the financial economy (or virtual economy) to become reintegrated with the real economy. With gradual recovery of both the economy and the functions of the financial market in many places, financial institutions and the household sector may have begun to re-leverage. For example, the real estate bubble risk in emerging markets is increasing, and the virtual economy is again showing signs of deviating from the real economy, even though it is one of the basic functions of the financial sector to serve the needs of the latter. The main objectives of financial restructuring are to deleverage financial institutions and the household sector, prevent excessive expansion or deviation of the virtual economy, and avoid "new and bigger crises". In sum, both the importance and urgency of financial restructuring have been increasing in terms of risk management, institutional improvements, market development, functional maturation, and the coordinated development of the real economy and the financial sector. Since financial restructuring is a difficult and systemic project, relevant economic entities and policymakers must take long-term and powerful actions, including those that address such issues as market model, business model, regulatory efficiency, financial innovation, and institutional improvement. This process will involve dramatic socioeconomic changes quite different from the ones caused by the previous financial crises. In addition, there will be uncertainties about the future, as the whole world seems to be at a critical moment in institutional transition and reordering. In contrast with these uncertainties, financial stability has become more important than ever, as have studies of how to achieve it in today's world.

We were honored to receive support from the National Social Science Fund of China (NSSFC) for the research project titled, "Understanding how to build a mechanism for sustaining long-term financial stability through an economic analysis of the USA financial crisis". Major output of the investigation is presented in this book: China's Financial Stability: Inherent Logic and Basic Framework. On the basis of a thorough review of existing literature on this topic, drawing in particular on lessons learned from the most recent financial crisis in the United States, we present our own understanding and analysis of financial stability in terms of its determining factors, causal mechanisms, and institutional requirements.

We focus in our economic analysis of the latest USA financial crisis on its causes and evolutionary trajectory. Efforts by governments of western countries in the areas of financial regulations, monetary policies, and reconfiguration of government functions in response to the crisis have important implications for both the practice and theories of reform. In our assessment and discussion of financial stability in China, we take full account of China's specific conditions and constructed our own index system. The objective is to understand what China can and should do, against the backdrop of Western-dominated economic globalization, to safeguard our economic and financial stability. We consider the question from the points of view of macroprudential management, monetary policy, financial security network design, financial market structure, fluctuations in real estate prices, and government functions and behavior, and sovereign wealth fund (SWF).

We argue for the following eight theses. First, financial liberalization and inadequate financial regulation constituted an important trigger for the recent financial crisis in the United States. Improving the financial regulatory system is a key to minimizing systemic financial risks. Second, the failure of the USA financial regulatory system is mainly attributable to the lack of important elements, including a regulatory authority, coordination mechanisms, effective regulation of systemically important financial institutions, and sufficient understanding of their impact, and how it can be mitigated. Third, in order to strike a balance between preventing financial crisis and controlling moral hazards, regulatory authorities must not only have a good grasp of financial system stability and is prepared to make use of market-based instruments, in particular for the development and application of a financial security network, but also be willing to take precautions. Fourth, now that establishing a stable and effective financial system and the framework of a macroprudential management system in accordance with 12th Five-Year Plan has been put on the agenda, we must make sure it addressed to systemic risk response mechanisms, regulatory coordination, institutional compatibility, regulatory loopholes, financial infrastructures, and external financial risks. Fifth, improving the financial system is essential for preventing and dealing with financial crises. During a financial crisis, making adjustments to systemic deficiency as soon as possible can help reduce its negative impact. Sixth, government intervention is the most effective form of relief during a financial crisis. The government should, therefore, take timely, appropriate and effective measures during a crisis to tackle such problems as insufficient liquidity, troubled asset accumulation and the bankruptcy of financial institutions, and implement monetary, fiscal and regulatory policies and reforms to restore the functions of financial institutions and the market in terms of resource allocation. Seventh, dealing with financial crises calls for strengthening the banking system's resilience under contagion and improving regulatory policies for financial stability. "Proposed Amendments to the Basel II Framework" provides a useful guide for enhancing the management of CAR, increasing capital constraints over financial innovation, removing the incentives for regulatory capital arbitrage and for achieving unified regulatory and economic capital.

Eighth, the entire financial system has been subject to vulnerabilities and even systemic risks caused by such phenomena as the unreasonably high proportion of leverage in the shadow banking system, continual breach of the boundaries of the business of traditional commercial banks, bold, and complex financial innovations, deliberately incomplete information disclosure and circumvention of financial regulations, all of which requiring immediate and close attention.

Our study is innovative on a number of dimensions. First, it assumes a plurality of perspectives. We try, on the basis of a framework for systematic research on financial stability, to deconstruct the issue of financial stability. Second, methodologically, we integrated a diversity of research traditions, including those native to a variety of subjects, such as political economy, industrial and institutional economics, finance, law and economics, management science, game theory, incentive theory, and others. We draw on both theoretical analysis and empirical findings, and bring to bear other techniques such as econometric modeling, comparative analysis, case studies, market research, and other research methods. Third, we look at factors past studies of financial stability overlooked, including financial security network, financial structure, fluctuations in real estate prices, government action, and SWFs. This not only expands the scope of research on financial stability but also contributes especially toward better understanding of financial stability in relation to transition economies. Fourth, with China's political, economic, social, cultural, and financial developments in mind, we propose a systematic solution to the problem of financial instability in China, and principles, objectives, and strategies for building mechanism for ensuring China's long-term financial stability.

Throughout the research and in writing this book, we have been driven by a deep sense of social responsibility and yearning for a prosperous China. We are also deeply aware that there are many others making similar efforts to ours toward understanding this important issue. Building a mechanism for China's long-term financial stability requires joint efforts across the academia. We look forward to criticisms and suggestions from other experts and scholars.

He Dexu
March 2013

Author Biography

Dr He Dexu has a PhD in Economics. He is the Party Secretary and Deputy Director of Institute of Finance and Banking of Chinese Academy of Social Sciences (CASS). He is the Expert Reviewer of National Social Sciences Fund and Executive Member of China Society for Finance & Banking. He was a visiting scholar at the University of Colorado Boulder and University of Southern California. He was a postdoctoral researcher at Southwestern University of Finance and Economics and State Information Center. He specializes in Financial Institution, Monetary Policy, Financial Innovation, Financial Security, Financial Development, Capital Market, and Corporate Finance. He has presided over more than 10 Major Projects at State, Provincial, and Ministerial levels, such as National Social Sciences Fund Major Program, CASS Major Program, etc. He has published more than 10 monographs and more than 200 journal articles. Many of these have been honored with outstanding research achievements at Provincial and Ministerial levels.

Contents

Chapter 1

Financial Stability: Research Framework and Current Theories

In the process of economic theory development, the stability of the financial system has been the focus of the economists around the world. The studies on this topic can be broadly divided into two categories: the analysis of monetary economy instability from the Marxist perspective, on the one hand, and the various studies on financial stability by Western economists, on the other hand. The earlier studies in the second category were mainly the researches of financial stability from a macroscopic perspective. Marshall, one of the representative figures of the Neoclassical Economics and the founder of the Cambridge School, once studied the relationship between the financial markets and the volatility in industry and commerce. He deduced that unrealistic commercial and bank credit had contributed to the volatility of industry and commerce and had become one of the important causes of cyclical fluctuations in the economy. British economist John Maynard Keynes, while studying the economic cycle, was also very concerned with the influence of the financial market uncertainties on the marginal efficiency of capital (MEC) and further on the economic cyclical fluctuations. However, until the late 1970s, researches on the stability of the financial system were mostly closely related to the analysis of economic cyclical fluctuations, which failed to achieve independent status in the relevant scholarly field.

Moreover, most studies focused on whether and how financial activities would exert impact on the economic crisis, with little attention being paid to the actual causes of financial instability or financial crisis themselves. Later, the researches on financial system stability, by drawing upon the approaches in Modern Economics, such as Information Economics or Game Theory, gradually shifted their analysis from a macroscopic perspective to the microscopic, thus promoting the further study of financial stability.

1.1 DEFINITION AND EVALUATION

1.1.1 Definition of financial stability

Despite the fact that in recent years, the Swedish Central Bank and the European Central Bank have taken the lead in offering international financial stability and that more and more national monetary authorities made financial stability as one of their important operative objectives, to date there does not exist a consistent understanding and comprehension of financial stability. According to the summary of the International Monetary Fund (IMF) (Houben *et al.*, 2004), there had been more than 10 definitions of financial stability created by governments, central banks, and academia. Also, the Chinese scholars Zhang & Duan (2006) grouped the definitions of financial stability by international academia into five categories: Shock Resistance Hypothesis, Factor Description Hypothesis, Financial Functions Hypothesis, Systemic Risk Management Hypothesis, and Financial Instability Hypothesis. Roughly, the definitions of financial stability in contemporary studies can be divided into two categories: the studies in the first category refer to the definitions that directly describe the connotation of financial stability with its concrete performance and features, i.e., Duisenberg (2001), Wellink (2002), Padoa-Schioppa (2003), and Houben *et al.* (2004). The studies in the second category aim to indirectly describe their connotation with the performance and features that should not occur during stable financial periods, i.e., Crockett (1996), Mishkin (1999a, 1999b), Ferguson (2002), Chant (2003), etc.

(i) Direct description of the financial stability's features

The Swedish Central Bank, as the world's first central bank to set up a financial stability department and to publish the first financial stability report in 1998, defined financial stability as "the safe and effective operation of the whole payment system" and considered that the pillars to ensure the financial system's stability are: (i) a regulatory framework composed of regulations and decrees, complemented by the concrete actions of risk assessment and irregularities inspection of individual institutions; (ii) the timely monitoring of the central bank on systemic risk; (iii) crisis management measures. All these pillars require the division and cooperation of the central banks and the supervisory departments.

Since then, the central banks of many countries have made great efforts to define or discuss the connotation of financial stability. Duisenberg (2001), the first President of the European Central Bank, thought that although there was no consistent definition of financial stability, there does exist a certain common consensus: that under the condition of financial stability, each component of the financial system can perform its economic function freely. Wellink (2002), the then President of the Dutch Bank, believed that a stable financial system should be able to allocate resources in a proper way, withstand economic shocks, and prevent the negative impacts of shocks on the financial sector and the real economy. The Central Bank of Norway (2003) pointed out that financial stability means that the financial system could, without the interference of the real economic sectors, perform its various functions including intermediary financial transactions, payment and settlement, risk diversification, etc. Padoa-Schioppa (2003), the former member of the executive board of the European Central Bank, believed that financial stability means that the financial system is able to withstand economic shocks, to avoid the accumulation of contradictions, to continue to mobilize savings to invest in high-efficiency sectors and to accomplish the payment and settlements. The "financial system" in the aforementioned statement includes financial intermediaries, formal and informal financial markets, payment and settlement systems, technical support platforms, financial laws and regulations, and financial regulatory bodies. Hereby, the systematic study of financial system stability could be conducted through the studies of savings configuration, information disclosure and treatment, the risk transfer behaviors of brokers, as well as the methods of payment and settlement. The Deutsche Bank (2003) considered that financial stability refers to a stable and steady state, in which the financial system is able to fulfill its economic functions in a proper way, including resources allocation, risk diversification, convenient payment and settlement, etc. Even when the real economy is affected by external shocks and austerity, or large-scale restructure, the financial system should be able to maintain its stability and continue to operate normally. Burger (2007), a then Executive Board member of the Deutsche Bundesbank, noted that financial stability is the ability of the financial system to effectively carry out its main functions, namely the ability to allocate resources, perform risk diversification, payment and settlement, as well as the settlement of securities transactions. Even faced with market pressures or during a restructuring period, these functions could still be properly performed. Foot (2003), one of the initial managing directors of UK Financial Service Authority, stressed that financial stability needs to meet the following requirements: monetary stability; the unemployment level close to the natural employment level of the economy; the public have confidence in the major financial institutions and markets in the economy; the relative price changes of the physical assets or financial assets in the economy would not undermine the monetary stability and the natural level of employment.

Houben *et al.* (2004), researchers at the IMF, proposed that, regarding the state's financial stability, the financial system should be able to perform the following functions: the ability to realize effective resource allocation in various economic activities and in the allocation of intertemporal resources; the ability to effectively access and manage financial risk; and the ability to absorb the impact of the economic shocks. Schinasi (2004), an economist at the IMF International Capital Markets Department, pointed out that, in a broad sense, financial stability can be measured by the ability of the financial system; thus this concept is related not only to the disappearance of the real financial crisis, but also to the ability of the financial system in reducing, containing, and dealing with the unexpected events affecting the balance of the whole system. He believed that financial stability is usually defined and is based on the ability of the financial system, in terms of promotion and enhancement of economic operation, risk management, and the ability to absorb the impact of the economic shocks. When a financial system has the ability to promote economic performance and to address endogenous financial imbalances or the ones resulting from major adverse events, it is in a stable state. The financial stability needs to be measured by its ability to prevent the occurrence of financial imbalances, on the one hand, and the ability to remedy the imbalance when it has occurred, on the other hand.

In China, the People's Bank of China (PBOC), the first release of the "2005 China Financial Stability Report" defined "financial stability" as "financial stability refers to a state in which the financial system can effectively perform its key functions." This state has the following features: the macroeconomy operates in a healthy way; monetary and fiscal policies are prudent and effective; the financial ecological environment is continuously improved; financial institutions, financial markets, and financial infrastructures can play their key functions including resource allocation, risk management, payment and settlement, etc.; and, even when shocked by the impact of external factors, the overall financial system is still able to run smoothly.

Wu & Yun (2005), from the perspective of these characteristics, also gave their definition of what financial stability should include: currency stability due to money supply and demand balance; stable credit relations and order due to capital loan balance; the stability of financial institutions due to the ability of the financial enterprises to fulfill their contractual obligations without external assistance or intervention; the stability of the financial market due to stable financial assets price and its ability to reflect the economic fundamentals; the basic stability of the exchange rate due to the balance of international payments; the stability of the financial structure due to the coordination among different systems within the financial system, and its good adaptation to the economic and social development stage.

(ii) Description from the opposite of financial stability: Financial instability

The description of financial stability from the perspective of its opposite, i.e., financial instability, mainly emphasizes the impacts of financial instability and could contribute to a deeper and more comprehensive understanding of financial stability. Crockett (1996) proposed that financial stability is the absence of financial instability. Financial instability refers to the negative impact of the financial system on the real economic sectors, such as the negative impacts resulting from the sharp fluctuations of the financial assets price, or the collapse of financial institutions. This definition emphasizes the following four characteristics of financial instability: (i) the impact on the real economy; (ii) potential harm exceeds the actual hazards occurred; (iii) financial instability may arise both in the banking system, but also in the non-banking financial institutions, financial market, or other financial institutions; (iv) the bank is not the only institution to which close attention should be given — any organization, whether it is directly in payment and settlement system or not, should be given close attention, for as long as it is closely related to the other institutions of the payment and settlement system and could potentially jeopardize the entire payment system should it fall into payment trouble.

Mishkin (1999a, 1999b) believed that the financial instability resulted from the shock of information. As a result, the shocked financial system cannot properly fulfill its ability to allocate funds, and the funds cannot be put into the most productive investments. Ferguson (2002), the former chairman of the United States Federal Reserve Board, considered that to define financial instability seems more meaningful than to define financial stability. For central banks and other authorities, the most useful concept of financial instability is closely related to the market failures and externalities, which might potentially do harm to the real economic behavior. Financial instability has the following three characteristics: (i) the price of some important financial assets deviates from their actual value; (ii) the normal operation of the financial market and the amount of loanable funds are severely affected; (iii) the total expenditure significantly deviates (or will deviate) from the economic production capacity significantly.

Chant (2003) emphasized that financial instability refers to a state of the financial markets: the proper functioning of the financial market is impeded; as a result, the growth of the real sectors have been or would be threatened. There are two main ways in which financial instability could affect the real sectors: (i) financial instability has a negative impact on the non-financial institutions, such as families, businesses, and governments, and leads to the deterioration of their financial condition, which finally lose the ability to continue financing; (ii) financial instability has a negative impact on some financial institutions or a certain financial market, resulting in the loss of their ability to continue to provide and accommodate funds for businesses and individuals. There are different types of shocks resulting in financial instability, and the results of the shocks are different due to the differences in the time, location, the sector in which the shock originates, and the part of the financial system that is affected. The payment difficulties of a government in Africa on the date when the bond matures, the collapse of a small foreign exchange bank, the breakdown of a major bank's computer system in South America, or the crediting behavior of an SME bank in the Midwest of the United States — all and any of these could become the trigger to cause financial instability.

To sum up, financial stability should be a state, i.e., in the state of financial stability, in which the financial system can completely fulfill its function in resource allocation and risk diversification. To achieve and maintain this function, we must ensure the stability of the financial system elements. These include financial institutions (commercial banks, policy banks, securities companies, insurance agencies, financial asset management companies, trust, and investment companies, etc.), financial markets (stocks, bonds, notes, foreign exchange, and derivatives, etc.), the related financial infrastructures (laws, payment and settlement, accounting and auditing system, etc.), and the ability of the aforementioned elements to assess, prevent, and respond to the shocks of the financial risks, and, in particular, the systematic risks.

In addition, from the aforementioned definition, we can also find some inspiration: (i) the implication of financial stability is very broad and is related to the various components of the financial system — including finance infrastructures, financial institutions, and financial markets — and needs to be analyzed from a systematic perspective; (ii) financial stability is closely related to monetary stability and banking stability; (iii) financial stability not only requires that major financial crises do not occur, but also that the financial system itself can withstand and digest certain imbalances; (iv) the assessment of financial stability should be concerned about its impact on the real economy; (v) financial stability is a macro-, global, comprehensive, continuous, dynamic concept, instead of a micro-, local, discrete, static concept, and it does not require that every financial institution should maintain its optimal state at any time. We need to bear in mind that we are making the mistake of overgeneralization if we consider the state of the financial system to be instable when several financial institutions went bankrupt in the competition, or when there is a temporary financial difficulty at some point.

1.1.2 The framework of financial stability

A comparatively sound framework of financial stability can deepen people's understanding of the policies for financial stability and enhance the enforcement of financial regulations. Many international scholars and organizations have had discussions and analysis on the framework of financial stability without a consistent conclusion. Besides, most discussions are limited to academics and have not been applied to real policies. Many scholars adopt "the shock-reaction" model, a traditional method for analysis. They tend to analyze the policies of financial stability from the reaction of a financial system in the wake of an external shock and the related financial crisis (Krugman, 1979; Mishkin, 1999a, 1999b). According to the National Bank of Belgium, the external shocks, including international and domestic environment as well as the banking system, are transmitted through the interbanking risks and debts, ultimately resulting in financial instability.

Houben *et al.* (2004) have tried to conduct an overall assessment of the microeconomics, the currency, the financial market, and the cost on regulation and take financial stability as one system to analyze its potential risks and fragileness. They believe that the framework of financial stability should include analysis, assessment, and three feasible policies. The framework of instability posed by Large (2005) includes the analysis of the source of danger, the assessment of threats on financial stability, risk weakening, and the prevention and management of risks. Besides, some scholars and organizations believe that along with the information revolution, globalization, and financial innovation, an emergency response mechanism is also needed, while encouraging competition so as to maintain financial stability. A timely check and elimination of the time lag in the payment and clearing system is required so as to take advantage of the market forces constructively, in the prevention of the eruption and expansion of any financial crisis (Litan, 1997). In the Financial Sector Assessment Program (FSAP), published in May 1999 by the IMF and the World Bank, the systematic risks and fragility of the financial sections of the member countries are of serious concern. It aims to find out the advantages and disadvantages of the financial systems of the member countries through the assessment of their financial organizations, financial markets, payment systems, regulations, and legal systems, so as to control its major source of danger and come up with a responding method. In the prediction of financial stability, the FSAP points out that financial stability is evaluated from 28 aspects including interest rate risks, exchange rate risks, credit risks, liquidity risk, prices of the shares and houses, etc. However, the assessment tends to be subjective.

In conclusion, the framework of financial stability includes the prevention mechanism of financial stability, the assessment and precaution mechanism of financial stability, and emergency management, in the wake of a financial crisis. The specific elements are environmental analysis, target identification, risk management, responding method, and responsibility authorization. It aims to analyze the internal and external environment that triggers financial instability and the risks concerned, so as to establish certain prevention mechanism to reduce the incurrence of financial instability. Impacts from a financial system's internal elements and environment that affect financial stability include risks from financial organizations, from the financial market, as well as from the financial infrastructure. The external environments include the impacts from the real economy. Besides, in the context of globalization of the international currency system and economic globalization, the financial stability of one country might be influenced by the financial instability or instability of the real economy of other countries.

Financial stability aims to ensure the sound function of the financial system. At present, there are still debates about international financial stability. From the perspective of traditional economics, financial stability and currency stability share the same aim. High inflation might result in a fluctuant market, preventing the conversion of investment from deposit and causing financial instability (Schwartz, 1995a, 1995b). However, other scholars do not share the same opinion. They believe that the control of the formulation and organization of currency policies could influence people's expectation of economic development, thus affecting the stability of property prices and trigger financial instability (Borio *et al.*, 2002). From the perspective of real practices, financial stability and currency stability share the same aim in the long term, despite their conflicts and contradiction in certain periods. The assessment and precaution mechanism aims to monitor and give precaution to the financial system and the real economy, so as to timely respond with measures, minimizing the consequences of financial instability. The emergency mechanisms in place in the wake of financial crisis include responsibility authorization and measures taken by relevant departments. When the financial system is in crisis, phenomena such as squeeze among financial organizations, inflation, currency crisis, falling share market, and recession might happen, meaning the financial system cannot function regularly. At such times, government organizations including the central bank, regulators of the securities, banks, and insurances, Department of Finance, central government, as well as local governments need to have a clear understanding about their responsibilities and cooperate with one another, so as to effectively respond to the consequences of the crisis and reconstruct financial stability.

1.1.3 Assessment of financial stability

Over the last few years, countries throughout the world, along with some international economic organizations, have proposed many ways to assess the stability of the financial sector. Take the FSAP, for instance. Set up in May 1999 by the IMF and the World Bank, the program conducted comprehensive assessment and monitoring on the financial systems of member states and other economic entities. It mainly focused on the systematic risks and financial fragility; evaluated one specific country's macroeconomy via the three major analysis tools (namely financial soundness indicators, pressure test, and standard and criteria evaluation); appraised the efficiency of macroprudential regulation; made judgment on the fragility and risk-bearing capability, as well as the effectiveness of the financial infrastructure and financial sector supervision; and also controlled the major risks and root causes. At last, the program provided the priority of the policy measures needed to strengthen the soundness of the country's financial system. Another example is the Assessment Working Group for Financial Stability, established by the European Central Bank. The working group evaluated the country's financial situations by analyzing the banking system's health indicators, macroeconomic factors that affect the banking system, and contagion factors. In April 1997, the G10 Emerging Market Financial Stability Working Group disclosed a work report on the financial stability of emerging markets and classified the financial soundness indicators into several categories: legislation and judicial framework; accounting, disclosure, and transparency; interested parties' control and institutional administration; market structure; supervision and regulation on the authorities; and the establishment of a social safety net.

On November 7, 2005, the PBOC released China's first financial stability report — *China 2005 Financial Stability Report*. In this report, the PBOC initiated three major steps to maintain financial stability: (i) to monitor the financial risks by keeping a close eye on and analyzing the macroeconomic environment, financial market, financial institutions, financial infrastructure, and financial ecosystem; (ii) to evaluate the impact of macroeconomic environment, financial market, financial institutions, financial infrastructure, and financial ecosystem on financial stability with certain standards and methods; and (iii) to take corresponding measures based on the evaluation results. When the financial sector is stable, potential risks will be checked while preventive measures are taken. When the financial sector in on the verge of instability, bailout measures will be taken and liquidity support offered to financial institutions that have systematic effect and poor liquidity, with largely healthy financial condition and operation. Measures including restructuring, reform, and shifting mechanism will also be adopted to ensure the institutions' healthy operation. When the financial sector is unstable, risk–response measures will be taken immediately to liquidate, shut down, or restructure those institutions that are too insolvent to sustain their operation. Certain market constraints will be exerted to protect investors' interests and to maintain economic and social stability. Moreover, reforms in economic structure, financial institutions, financial market, financial infrastructure, and financial ecosystem will be promoted, to remove any weak links and enhance financial stability.

Specifically, the key methods for the financial stability assessment are as follows.

(i) Indicator description

Domestic academics usually start the evaluation of financial stability by setting up an indicator system. Feng & Guang (2001) conducted empirical research on the commercial banks' (single bank rather than the entire banking system) unsystematic risks and early warnings. By learning from Western countries' common experience and research findings in index selection, Wu (2002) initially measured the vulnerability of the banking system and empirically analyzed the causes from the perspective of the banking sector and real economy. Zhang & Sun (2003) believe that three parts constitute the financial alarm indicator system (which implies the likelihood of financial crisis in China): (i) indexes that reflect the macroeconomic development like GDP (gross domestic product) growth ratio, inflation ratio, and interest rate; (ii) indexes that reflect the asset quality, operating soundness, and credit growth ratio of China's financial institutions, such as credit growth ratio, credit growth/GDP, non-performing loan proportion to the total assets, capital adequacy ratio, and M2 growth ratio; (iii) indexes that reflect the utilization of foreign investment, foreign debt, utilization of foreign debt, solvency, and foreign exchange rate, including short-term foreign debt/foreign exchange reserves, short-term foreign debt/total foreign debt, recurring balance/GDP, total foreign debt/GDP, foreign direct investment (FDI) + recurring balance/GDP, foreign exchange reserves/total foreign debt, foreign exchange reserves/M2, and debt servicing ratio. Tang & Zhang (2002) argued that early warning indexes are the economic and financial indexes that can provide warnings before the actual occurrence of financial crisis, which are both qualitative and quantitative. Considering the different features and causes of monetary, stock market, and banking crises, the three early warning indexes should be adopted without interfering with one another.

A total of 18 early warning indexes were chosen for the monetary crisis: the deviation of the actual rate from temporal trend; export; stock price index; M2's proportion to international reserves; GDP; M1 excess supply; international reserves; M2 multiplier; domestic credit volume/GDP; actual interest rate; trade terms; domestic/overseas interest margin; recurring balance/GDP; M1/international reserves; foreign debt; total capital flow; short-term foreign debt; and control of capital account.

Meanwhile, 12 early warning indexes were chosen for the stock market crises: political environment at home and abroad; domestic major economic policies; economic growth trend; adjustment to the interest rate; stock price index; popularity psychology index; trade volume index; national industry policy; overall quality of listed companies; capital inflow; capital outflow; and financial crises abroad.

Then 16 early warning indexes were chosen for the banking crisis: actual growth ratio of GDP; consumption growth ratio; investment growth ratio; capital output ratio; change ratio of saving deposits; total loans of public sector; total loans of private sector; total foreign debt; inflation ratio; actual interest ratio; actual exchange rate; actual growth ratio of import; trade terms; capital adequacy ratio of the overall banking system; asset quality of overall banking system; and liberation level of interest rate. It is generally known that the level of financial crisis could be implied by the corresponding financial stability, or lack of it (see Table 1-1).

Some scholars proposed a three-level evaluation indicator system of financial stability based on the IMF's classification (see Table 1-2).

(ii) Subjective analysis: Pressure test

The FSAP released by the IMF and World Bank mainly evaluates the financial stability by the pressure test. By means of the subjective assumption that the risk factors will go thorough extreme changes and the test of the influence on financial stability caused by these changes, this method takes the risk of extreme events unable to be covered by historical data into consideration. In 2003, on behalf of the staff of the IMF and World Bank, a passage named *the Analytic Tool of FSAP* summarized the analytic techniques, scope, methods, and operating modes of the pressure test. By using the pressure test method, it evaluated the financial risks of 28 members in

Table 1-1. Financial stability and crisis.

Stability situation	Risk situation	Financial operation
Stable	No visible risks	Risk indicators are all within the safety margin, with stable financial market, orderly financial operation, effective financial supervision, and steady financial development.
Largely stable	Moderate risks	Financial signals are largely healthy, with certain indexes on the verge of pre-warning upper limit; low proportion of non-performing assets to the total assets; small portion of bankruptcy of operating financial institutions; currency depreciation pressures; financial operation largely in balance.
Unstable	Serious risks	The majority of the financial indexes start to deteriorate; non-performing assets exist in most financial institutions; high proportion of non-performing assets to the total assets; bankruptcy of many financial institutions, significant currency depreciation; financial turmoil and economic recession.
Financial crisis	Frequent crises	Lasting financial instability causes serious monetary crisis and banking crisis, along with serious currency depreciation and the bankruptcy of many financial institutions; financial collapse, economic regression, and social instability.

the following seven aspects: interest rate risk; exchange rate risk; credit risk; commodity price risk; liquidity risk; stock and real estate price risk; and other risk. Moreover, the passage pointed out that international standards should be established in financial sector supervision, the infrastructure of institutions, and market and policy transparency. However, such a method is over-subjective and fails to properly deal with the crucial problems related to risk measurement — the asset correlation is actually an extremely crucial factor for risk measurement. If the asset correlation is low in the asset portfolio, the portfolio risk will be low and vice versa. What the pressure test method considers is just the influence caused by a certain risk factor at a certain moment; therefore, it can only be regarded as a necessary supplement for the value at risk (VaR) method.

Table 1-2. Evaluation indicator system of financial stability.

First-grade indexes	Second-grade indexes	Third-grade indexes
Microprudential indexes	Indexes for economic growth	Economic growth ratio The proportion of fiscal deficits to GDP The proportion of bank loans to GDP
	Indexes for international balance of payment	The proportion of recurring account deficit to GDP Foreign debt indexes (foreign debt to GDP, debt servicing, debt ratio, share of each currency in the foreign debt) Foreign exchange reserve indexes (foreign exchange reserves to import payment, short-term foreign debt, and broad money) Proportion of short-term foreign debt to total foreign debt
	Inflation indexes	Inflation ratio Growth ratio of currency supply
	Indexes for interest rate and foreign exchange rate	International/domestic interest rate spread Actual interest rate Risk ratio of interest rate Deviation of actual exchange rate
	Political influence and others	Government and regulation risks Improper government intervention Supervision efficiency, financial orders, etc. Institutional factors (such as a deposit insurance system) Major emergencies
	Indexes for financial sector	Capital adequacy ratio (non-performing loan ratio, credit asset's concentration in some departments and debtors and credit scale) Asset and debt liquidity and symmetry indexes (asset liquidity ratio, share of loans borrowed from the central bank, deposit/loan ratio, borrowed funds ratio, deposit to total broad money, short-term debt ratio, and provisions ratio)

(*Continued*)

Table 1-2. (*Continued*)

First-grade indexes	Second-grade indexes	Third-grade indexes
		Profitability indexes (asset profit ratio, equity profit ratio, interest collection ratio, and non-interest asset ratio) Internal management quality indexes (payment structure, payment/income ratio, per capita earnings, and expense/income ratio) Financial institutions' sensitiveness to market risks (asset duration, debt duration, market cap sensitivity ratio, and foreign exchange exposure position ratio)
Microprudential indexes	Indexes for companies	Total debt to net assets The proportion of net asset income and revenue to interest rate and principle payment Growth of account receivable Growth ratio of total profit Growth ratio of sales revenue
	Indexes for households	The proportion of households' debt to GDP The proportion of repayment of the households' capital with interest to revenue
Market indexes	Monetary market indexes	Weighted average interest rate of interbank lending market Daily transaction volume of interbank lending market Weighted average interest rate of interbank bond market Daily interbank repo transaction in the bond market
	Bond market indexes	Bid-offer spread as percentage of middle rate Average daily transaction volume Average daily turnover rate
	Real estate market indexes	Real estate price index Residential real estate loans' share of total loans Commercial real estate loans' share of total loans

(iii) Quantitative analysis method

On the aspect of quantitative analysis of financial stability, in principle, people hope to measure the changes in the expected loss, which can be shown by the product of probability of financial crisis (PFC) and economic losses given stress (ELGS). However, the accurate calculation of these two indicators is faced with great challenges: the complexity related to entitative finance; the interaction between the entities and different participants of the financial market; the possible reaction adopted to face the impacts that may vary with the change of time; the nonlinearity between the consideration of bankruptcy, supervision, and constraint mechanism, and so on. What is more, it becomes harder to predict the expected loss, and PFC and ELGS may continuously change with the development of the structure, and even make constant changes with the controversial results (White, 2006). During the empirical study, researchers, usually focusing on the specific problems in the study, regard the vulnerability of the financial system, systematic bank crisis, major bank crisis, risk relevance, etc. as the proxy variables and measure the state of the financial stability on the opposite side.

Chinese academic Wu (2005) made inductive comparisons on the quantitative analysis method of financial stability with the Kaminsky, Lizondo, and Reinhart method (KLR method for short), a financial early warning method, Probit/Logit model, Markov-Switching Approach, Sachs, Tornell, and Velasco method ("STV method" for short), autoregressive risk model, binary recursive tree method, and the VaR method.

1.2 MACROTHEORETICAL ANALYSIS OF FINANCIAL STABILITY

1.2.1 The statement on currency and financial instability of Marxism

(i) Three levels of the analysis of currency and financial instability

The analysis on the currency and financial instability of Marxism can be divided into three levels. First, under the circumstance of the circulation of the simple commodity economy, the possibility of economic instability might purely stem from the social function of the currency. The argument of this aspect of Marx is consistent with his explanation of the monopoly of the direct exchange capability between the currency and other commodities. Therefore, the function of currency as a means of circulation inevitably means that. As long as there is no purchase, there will be no sale; but nobody will definitely and immediately go purchasing just because he has finished the sales (Marx, 1887). The original version of Say's Law asserted that the supply of commodities always produces an equal demand (implying the assumption of direct exchange of commodities), which, however, turns out to be totally wrong for monetary economy. Indeed, the opposition of sales and purchase itself "means the possibility of crisis" in the monetary economy. Its function as a means of payment of money in the process of simple circulation can also bring about the possibility of monetary crisis. As long as there is an appearance of a time when the chain reactions caused by the default on a certain special payment emerge and give rise to "a total disorder of the mechanism caused by whatever it is," then a series of interconnecting payment commitment and "the artificial institution in charge of clearing them" will break off. In this case, commodities must be sold at a price "of loss" to get money acting as a means of payment. For the owners of the commodities, this is a tough period: "the eagerness of his soul for money, the only fortune, is just like the thirst for fresh water of the deer." Therefore, the disaster of the commodity market will inevitably lead to "the sudden transformation of credit system to monetary system."

Second, in an economy that includes a well-developed exchange process supported by advanced credit and finance, the eruption of financial crises with a different range of influence and various orders of complexity is possible. The monetary crisis might be triggered by the complete break of the exchange chains of the ordinary industry and business of a specific country. The monetary crisis will be intensified due to the impact of the credit chains running through industry and trade.

Third, in a capitalistic economy, the real movements accumulated by capitalism will unavoidably result in financial crises. Marx raised several ideas about the inevitability of the crisis logic, the key of which was that in a monetary economy established on the basis of accumulation from industrial capitalism, from the abstract perspective, the inner possibility of the monetary crisis becomes inevitability, which will be verified especially in the periodic crises — the characteristics of accumulation of capitalism.

Marx has distinguished two monetary crises: the monetary crisis that occurs in a special period of when the total crisis of industry and business (the first type) is forming; and the other monetary crisis that is independent of the total crisis of industry and business (the second type). He pointed out that the matter of whether the monetary instability stems from the social function of money, or the second type of monetary crisis, is not the characteristic of capitalistic economy. The chain of the payment commitment of currency exchange and interconnection has long existed before the establishment of capitalism. However, as long as the market process has not reached the depth of the kernel of social economic reproduction, it is still an external phenomenon and the social influence of the monetary instability is comparatively limited. However, the social meaning of the impact of monetary mechanism and the meaning of the impact of the bad weather, disease and war, are different.

(ii) Fictitious economy and financial stability

The earliest systematic discussion of fictitious capital is found in Karl Marx's *Capital*. Reliant upon the financial system, fictitious capital comes in the form of stocks, bonds, real estate mortgages, etc. It gives momentum to real economy and makes the use of capital more efficient by making its way into the production, distribution, exchange and consumption of material goods, and other economic activities. As Marx observed, abstract labor is the only source of value, which is defined as homogenous human labor embodied in commodities. Therefore, fictitious capital does not create any value in its own right, and its existence depends on that of real economy. Once detached from real economy, fictitious economy would become rootless and spawn economic bubbles. Obviously, the United

States's recent financial crisis of the mid to late noughties is nothing but the typical result of an overly fictitious and liberal economy. Jonathan Tennenbaum, a German economist, echoed this argument, contending that real economic and financial security have been adversely affected by the excessive expansion of fictitious economy. In his treatise "Financial Cancer: a General Crisis of the Global Financial and Economic Order," he proposed an inverted pyramid model for the economy, with four layers from bottom to top: material production; commodity exchange and service trade; financial assets (such as bonds and stocks); and then pure fictitious capital (such as derivatives and futures). Generally speaking, under the current economic conditions, this model represents a monstrously unbalanced way of economic development, where the growth of the upper layers far outpaces that of the lower ones. The resulting distortion will wreak havoc on a sound and solid macroeconomic basis that is much needed by the financial system, and will eventually cause the collapse of the "pyramid" (Xiang, 2005).

1.2.2 Western macrotheory analysis of financial stability

(i) Financial stability in the business cycle theory

In Western traditional macroeconomic theories, the analyses of bank crises are often supported by business cycle theory, as can be seen in the hypothesis about the insecurity inherent in the banking system (proposed by Thorstein Veblen in *The Theory of Business Enterprise* and *Absentee Ownership: Business Enterprise in Recent Times*), and the cumulative expansion caused by a market interest rate lower than the natural interest rate (proposed by Wicksell in 1898). Keynes (1936) emphasis on anticipation and uncertainty represents a major contribution to the discussion of financial insecurity in economic cyclicality. He attributes the cyclical fluctuation of the economy to that of the MEC. According to him, a crisis is triggered not only by overinvesting as a practice, but also by an investment environment that fails to fulfill the investors' expectations. In other words, typically, it is a falling MEC rather than a rising interest rate that is to blame. A widespread optimism about investment returns in times of prosperity leads to the proliferation of capital goods, and the returns on new investments are unlikely to drop drastically as long as the economic boom continues; however, a reversal of the market trend can cast doubt on the profits — such speculation will circulate rapidly, causing a dramatic plunge in MEC and then a recession. Borio & Lowe (2001) explained the inherent cyclicality of the financial system, pointing out that both the perception of risks and the will to take risks change with economic fluctuations. Deposit/loan surplus, asset prices, bank risk ratings, and the accounting measurement of expected losses (such as loan loss reserves) are all pro-cyclical, which means that the interaction of these factors with real economy can magnify the effects of economic fluctuations.

(ii) Financial instability hypothesis

Minsky (1972, 1985, 1991) put forward the "financial instability hypothesis" — a theory fairly influential in the history of financial crises. He held that the features of lenders (as represented by commercial banks) and borrowers endow the financial system with inherent insecurity. In real economy, there exist three categories of finance: "hedge finance"; "speculative finance,"; and "Ponzi finance." The process of economic cyclical changes will witness the replacement of "hedge finance" by "speculative finance," and then "speculative finance" by "Ponzi finance." Widespread "replacement" will hike up the asset prices for the assumed beneficiaries, and then cause overheating and overinvesting, which will be soon followed by intensified speculations and bubbles in the entire economy. It is in this phase that the worry about the future takes hold, which will develop into panic prior to a market meltdown once the bank loan payments are not kept up. This shows that the financial fragility is decided by the behavioral traits of lenders and borrowers.

In effort to shed light on the recurrence of financial crises, Minsky named the following two culprits besides the "long waves" of capitalist development: (i) "generational ignorance," namely the fact that the pain of past financial crises no longer preys on the minds of the lenders today, when cyclical bonanzas present a new rosy picture, keep the expected asset prices going up and fuel credit expansion; and (ii) "rivalry pressure," namely the fact that the lenders fear that the fierce competition will deprive them of customers and market shares predisposes them to unwise lending decisions.

(iii) Monetarist viewpoints on financial stability

Monetarist academics represented by Friedman & Schwartz (1963) highlighted the stabilizing effects of currency on the financial system. They held that demand for currency is a steady function, money quantity is a determinant of prices and output, and that its growth and changes are a decisive factor to the emergence of financial crises. In *Monetary Trends in the United States and the United Kingdom*, their research on the six bouts of the United States's financial tailspin and economic recession occurring from 1867 to 1960 led them to the discovery that banking or currency was somehow responsible for four of the six.

Brulmer and Meltzer, American monetarist academics, found the causality between (volatile) money stock growth rate and bank crises (Zhang, 2004). According to them, the growth rate of money stock contributes greatly to the emergence of financial crises. Even in times of economic equilibrium, drastic deflation — caused by the central bank's mismanagement of money supply — will push banks to sell their assets in order to retain the reserve currency they need. It follows that the resulting drop in asset prices will cause a rise in the interest rate, which will undermine banks' solvency and depositors' confidence. Insolvency and illiquidity spell bankruptcy for banks. And this, in turn, will further lessen money supply, causing problems for banks, and eventually trigger a financial crisis.

(iv) Relations among financial stability, economic development, and economic growth

Generally speaking, Western researchers consider the relation between financial security, economic development, and economic growth to be both mutually restrictive and beneficial at the same time. On the one hand, sound financial intermediaries and a stable financial market serve well for economic development and hence economic growth; on the other hand, financial instability or even crisis is devastating to economic development and growth, and even brings about regression (Goldsmith, 1969; King & Levine, 1993). In addition, the economic growth rate, quality, and structure can also affect financial stability (Mishkin, 1999a, 1999b).

Financial development can be underdeveloped, overdeveloped, or well suited in relation to economic growth. But in each of these three cases, financial instability can cast shadow on economic development and growth. At present, we see an outpouring of financial innovation, continuous update of technology, and a growing number and variety of financial institutions, goods and service. As a result, financial institutions have overlapping business operations, higher efficiency and greater scale advantage, while this also means that financial regulation has to widen its control in order to tackle more looming financial instability.

Empirical research has revealed that the synchronicity of credit cycle, asset price cycle, and financial regulation cycle is a hotbed for most economic crises. Normally, economic upward trend means sufficient capital and less credit risks for banks and other financial institutions, hence their tendency toward credit expansion; while in times of downward trend, the reverse applies — banks' tendency toward a credit squeeze leads to less liquidity and economic contraction. And credit expansion/squeeze often goes together with skyrocketing/plummeting asset prices, and spawns economic bubbles that will eventually trigger an economic crisis.

The way economic growth rate influences financial security can be described as follows: if the economy develops so fast as to outpace the growth of demand for production factors, the financial world will also rush along on a fast lane that carries too many risks for an unsound system to bear. On the other hand, a sluggish economy or even stagnation harms businesses, and leads to higher credit risks, and hence makes it harder for financial enterprises to keep afloat. The influence of the quality of economic development on financial stability is embodied in the fact that the continuous and stable development of real economy provides an indispensable sound basis for financial security, and hence ensures the sound development of a financial system well suited to the economy. The economic structure also affects financial stability, given that an ill-structured economy threatens to throw the financial system into disorder, especially when undue reliance upon investment or exportation puts economic development on shaky ground by making the real economy more vulnerable to external financial risks.

1.3 MICROTHEORY ANALYSIS OF FINANCIAL STABILITY

Since the 1980s, many economists have started to explore financial stability and crises, a macroeconomic phenomenon, in a micro perspective. They have been making major strides in such research by developing doctrines, theories, and analytical models, such as information economics, principal–agent theory, and game theory.

1.3.1 Diamond & Dybvig (1983): The bank-run model

The bank-run model came from the sunspot theory proposed by Kindleberger, who ascribed banking instability to the uncertainty about depositors' liquidity requirements, and a lower liquidity of bank assets in relation to bank liabilities. With the use of game theory and the argument about information asymmetry, Diamond & Dybvig (1983) profoundly explained the roots and repercussions of bank runs. They held that bank runs stem from confidence problems, and come at high price. Bank bankruptcy has a two-fold negative impact — the suspension of productive investment and the destruction of optimal risk sharing among depositors. Bank runs can lead to the collapse of the monetary system and other economic problems. Governmental deposit insurance can be used as a hedge against and an antidote to bank runs, but on condition that the government must collect optimal tax, otherwise the tax distortion and cost problems caused by the use of this remedy can cut into social welfare.

Then, Wallace (1988) supplemented and refined the bank-run model. Gorton (1985, 1988) designed an information-based model, where depositors' lack of information about banks leads to their misjudgment about their future deposit returns and banks' solvency. In other words, due to the existence of banks' private information, depositors tend to make a worse decision according to "investment noise" than they do in a full information environment. It follows that the problem of stability is not inherent in the banking system, but can be totally under the control of banks themselves. Chari & Jagannathan (1988) categorized depositors into those with more information and those with less information, the latter of whom act according to what others do. In this sense, bank runs are the irrational consequence of rational actions on the part of some individuals. Jacklin & Bhattacharya (1988) discussed the effect on the banking system caused by uncertainty about the rate of return on production, and identified several contributors to bank runs, considering bank runs to be "systematic" incidents triggered by changes in relevant economic indicators. Dowd (1992) furthered the research and concluded that if banks have sufficient capital, there will be no public fear of capital loss, and hence no bank runs. However, until now there is no corroborating research evidence as to how to define such "sufficiency," in terms of how much capital a bank has to possess.

1.3.2 Information asymmetry — "adverse selection" and "moral hazard": Weakening of the financial system's key functions

In the financial market, widespread and ineradicable information asymmetry greatly discounts the market effectiveness, and can cause *ex ante* "adverse selection" and *ex post* "moral hazard."

As for the theoretical analysis of "adverse selection," the most prominent is Stiglitz & Weiss (1981) argument that adverse selection and improper incentives are always present in the credit market. They pointed out that the factor most liable to cause financial predicament are the investment projects (e.g., real estate and stocks), which are handsomely profitable in times of prosperity but highly problematic in times of economic downturn. The investors in these projects are often ready to pay higher interest in the credit market. In addition, from the perspective of the internal control system of financial institutions, the managers are more inclined to those highly risky but more lucrative projects, due to the mechanism where they are more rewarded for performance success than they are punished for failure. On the other hand, lenders are likely to cut loans because they are unable to identify high-risk borrowers, hence the supply of loans will drop in a high interest rate environment. Rising interest rates can lead to the contraction of the credit market, and fewer loans can endanger the solvency of families and enterprises, which has no benefit for the operation of banks and financial institutions. Furthermore, rising interest rates can have a ripple effect on both the stock market and foreign exchange market, thus destabilizing the financial system. Briefly, the accumulation of risk factors caused by "adverse selection" can eventually realize the worst case scenario — a financial crisis.

As for "moral hazard," Mishkin (1999a, 1999b) directly connected banking crisis to moral hazard, attributing banking crises to the fact that the sharpening of the asymmetric information problem in "adverse selection" and "moral hazard" makes the financial market unable to direct capital to those individuals or institutions with the best opportunities for productive investment. He pointed out that when there is a lack of proper credit terms, the "moral hazard" caused by lenders of last resort could severely destabilize the banking system. Liu (2002) said that the Asian financial crisis is a convincing proof of the fragility of financial system, and this nature is rooted in "moral hazard." In addition, some academics thought that the central banks' role as lenders of last resort could cause this "moral hazard." On the one hand, bank managers and shareholders will be bold enough to engage in excessive risk-taking behaviors (Freixas & Rochet, 1997); on the other hand, with the bailout of near-bankrupt financial institutions by central banks, those depositors without deposit insurance will become less motivated to supervise their depository institutions (Kaufman, 1991; Tirole, 1996).

1.4 RISK SOURCES AND CASUAL FACTORS: THEORETICAL AND EMPIRICAL RESEARCH FINDINGS

Risk sources of financial stability can be grouped into two types: the first one is exogenous risk source resulting from macroeconomic fluctuation and emergency shock; the second one is endogenous, mostly caused by risk accumulation in financial institutions, turbulence in the financial market, imperfect financial infrastructure and improper monetary policy measures (Schinasi, 2007). In additional, on the basis of Chinese reality, some domestic academics probed into some specific causes of financial instability in the period of a transition economy.

1.4.1 Exogenous risk sources and causal factors

(i) Macroeconomic fluctuation

Macroeconomic fluctuation may cause severe shock to financial stability. An unreasonable national economic structure will lead to international payment imbalance, which if not relieved by efficient macroeconomic policy, may trigger monetary and bank crises, particularly in the case of impact from hot money. Traditionally, academics pay more attention to the relations between financial crisis and factors of real GDP growth (negative correlation, Frankel & Rose, 1998; Kaminsky & Reinhart, 1999), external real interest rates (positive correlation, Eichengreen & Rose, 1998; Goldfajn & Valdes, 1995; Kaminsky & Reinhart, 1999), domestic real interest rates (positive correlation, Demirgü-Kunt & Detragiache, 1998; Mishkin, 1998), large capital inflows (positive correlation, McKinnon & Pill, 1997), capital outflows (positive correlation, Demirgü-Kunt & Detragiache, 1998; Kaminsky & Reinhart, 1999), inflation (positive correlation, Bordo & Murshid, 2000; Demirgü-Kunt & Detragiache, 1998; Hardy & Pazarbasioglu, 1999), fixed exchange rate system (positive correlation if it is external shock, and negative correlation if threat to internal stability, Eichengreen, 1998; Eichengreen & Arteta, 2000; high cost is needed when there is crisis, Domaç & Martínez Peria, 2000). However, the following factors attracted more attention from academics after the breakout of the subprime crisis.

(a) *International balance of payment*

First, let us consider international trade. Qiang (2007) held a view that, in the meantime, foreign trade flow has resulted in a corresponding financial flow, thus forming a channel to mutually influence and affect each other through trade and finance. The matter of which influential connections and interrelations there are between China's continued high ratio of dependence on foreign trade, as well as trade surplus and the stability of China's financial system, is an important topic that deserves our attention.

Second, foreign exchange reserve. Concerning the relation between foreign exchange reserve and financial stability, Yuan (2006) believed that excessive foreign exchange reserve increases the hedge operation cost of the central bank and weakens the independence of the monetary policy, as well as the effectiveness of the monetary policy control of the central bank.

Third, international capital flow. There is no final conclusion of the relationship between the international capital flow and financial stability. Some studies suggest that international capital flow can promote financial stability. Its main representative is Markowitz (1952) who, on the basis of assets portfolio theory, suggests that international capital flow accelerates financial integration, thus benefiting financial stability. However, more academics hold the idea that international capital flow, especially a short-term one, goes against the financial stability. For example, Radelet & Sachs (1998) regarded the large amount of capital flow drawn to Asia in the 1990s as the root cause of the Asian financial crisis. E (2000) pointed out that while the continuous flow of various capitals into the Asian market promotes financial deepening, enlarges financial market scale and improves the financial market efficiency, it also leads to problems of volatility rise in the financial system and frequent financial market turbulence, and thus the capital flow results in instability of financial system. Combining relevant experience of developing countries since 1970s, Zhang (2004) has made empirical study on the relation between the capital account and the financial instability, illustrating the negative impact of excessive capital inflow on macro and microeconomy and financial sector, and discussed the prerequisite, order and relevant policy arrangement of market liberalization under the "incremental model." Through analyzing the lessons of the negative effect and its action mechanism from the FDI to the Malaysian international balance of payment and financial stability in the middle and later periods of the 1990s, Wang & Pan (2006) proposed the idea that FDI is not always beneficial to international balance of payment and financial stability in developing countries. They also found it may also be one of the important factors causing financial crisis. Chen (2007) pointed out that, from 2002, China's non-foreign direct investment capital inflow and "errors and omissions" accounts have been updated from the former operational mode in the previous decades to a positive figure, indicating the secret inflow of mass speculative capital under the expectation of appreciation of the renminbi (RMB), posing a negative impact on China's financial stability.

(b) *Financial liberalization*

Diaz-Alejandro (1985) is among experts who were the earliest to be aware of the financial risk brought by financial liberalization. In "Good-bye Financial Repression, Hello Financial Crash," he studied the early financial liberalization experience of Chile in the middle and late 1970s and found that it caused the financial crisis. Caprio & Klingebiel (1996) discovered that since 1970s, the banking crisis has been an increasingly common phenomenon in all countries, with the major reasons of macro-economic instability brought by financial liberalization, especially the instability of export and price. Among 29 examples of banking crisis studied, 20 are resulting from the deterioration of trade conditions. In addition, in the process of promoting financial liberalization, there is a high hazard proportion of 26 out of 29, resulting from delayed financial regulation measures. Demirgü-Kunt & Detragiache (1997) are among the earliest scholars to have systematically studied the correlation between financial liberalization and financial fragility. They chose the years in the period from 1980 to 1994 as the sample range to estimate the macroeconomic and financial variables, and in particular the impact of real interest rate variable, which represents the financial liberalization on the probability of bank crisis. They found out that some factors have prominent correlation with financial crisis, including changes in real interest rate, sudden outflow of capital, inadequate bank liquidity, and excessive lending ratio to private sector, as well as overquick credit growth. Caprio *et al.* (1999) stated in their research report that financial liberalization influences the financial sector and overall economic operation profoundly. They had investigated the effect of some financial liberalization measures of interest rate control cancellation, financial institution privatization, as well as entry condition easement of the financial institution market, and pointed out that these measures will produce a new financial crisis due to their different starting conditions and results. By analyzing the economic statistics of 27 emerging market economy countries from 1973 to 1998, Weller (2001) discovered that if an emerging market economy country has realized financial liberalization, it is more prone to suffer from shocks of monetary crisis and bank crisis. Dooley (1996) and Rossi (1999) both indicated that the negative effect of financial liberalization appears in countries with unsound system, with the problems of lacking an appropriate bank regulation system, universal corruption, and poor enforcement of "law and order." Their research also revealed that financial liberalization does not always increase the possibility of financial crisis. However, if reform of financial liberalization is combined with poor policy and institutional environment, it will cause great financial risk. The negative impact of these policies is inconspicuous against the environment of financial repression, but the inadaption of institutions and policies will become particularly obvious in the situation of liberalization.

(c) *International financial regulation and cooperation*

Along with the integration of the financial market, consensus and cooperation among the financial regulation institutions of various countries is increasingly improved, while the differences in national interests and responsibilities of these countries have been the main barrier in further cooperation, especially in terms of their voice and influence within the entire international financial system. White (2006) suggested that the present essential issue is that a unified system is lacking, which may force countries to change their relative domestic consumption level and relative exchange rate to some extent, and reduce orderly resolution of external imbalance.

(ii) Shock of incidents

Various high-level political incidents (including terrorist attack and war), natural disasters, bankruptcy of large enterprises, etc. will possibly inflict heavy losses on market confidence and influence the normal operation of the entire financial system. For example, Ba *et al.* (2007) noted that one important thing to maintain financial stability in the future is to take precautions of the interactive influence of unexpected disturbance factor on global asset investment. The IMF points out that the bird flu virus may give rise to a destructive effect on the international financial system and world economy, as its spread will impact on normal economic operation, as well as being expensive to eradicate. If it happens, the regulator should give emergency instruction on a business sustainable development plan, test the basic functions of the financial system, guarantee the operation of financial system in the situation of workforce shortage and increased demand of liquidity and cash, as well as promote strategic communication to help minimize any overreaction in the market. Measures of pressure test and response to the sensibility of the financial system, infectious disease, geopolitics, and local conflict as well as the increase of liquidity, need sufficient attention for the financial stability and regulation of all countries.

1.4.2 Endogenous risk source

(i) Risk accumulation of a financial institution

The risk accumulation of a financial institution is mainly acquired from the various financial risks faced by the financial institution itself, such as credit risk, market risk, liquidity risk, as well as foreign exchange risk. Risk accumulation may trigger the failure of a single financial institution, afterwards leading to a domino effect, which causes the bankruptcy of large numbers of banks and the breakdown of the entire financial system. As pointed out by Wu (2002), the most important financial institution is the bank: "... the stability of the bank system is the core of financial stability, which is a basic conclusion drawn from the study of the financial industry in the 20th century." Wu (2005) did an analysis of the relation between the quality of bank credit and financial stability. He came up with an idea that a basic element of financial stability is the fitness of a financial asset as a form of value and the physical asset operating in the real economy; the separation of the substance and form of value will incur the possibility of value deviation of the aforementioned financial asset and physical asset; once the bank credit becomes the main method to raise capital, the possibility may be realized; and the resulting so-called "bubble economy" will influence the financial stability. Conclusive research by Gavin & Hausman (1996), Sachs *et al.* (1999), Kaminsky & Reinhart (1999), and Eichengreen & Arteta (2000) all suggested that overquick growth of bank credit to the private sector will induce bank crisis.

The risk accumulation of a financial institution is rooted in its own internal instability to a great extent, and regarding this, academics have the following explanation: (i) information asymmetry brings about adverse selection. Smith (1987) borrowed the conclusion of insurance contract analysis from Rothschild & Stiglitz (1976), who analyzed relevant issues by the method of adverse selection and put forward that the internal instability of a bank resulting from competition is derived from the nature of deposit contracts. (ii) Substitution of competition risk and asset risk. Coggins (1998) indicated that the security constraint of a bank consists of competition risk and asset risk, which check and balances each other, trade off and takes turns. The bank supervisor is more willing to replace asset risk with competition risk, as there is a period of time lag in the appearance of the former. (iii) Internal instability of the credit mechanism. Mill (1848) suggested that business upturn easily generates credit expansion, price rises, burst economic bubbles, and financial crises.

(ii) Financial market turbulence

The major side effects of financial market turbulence are counterparty risk, asset price bubble, market run, and infection. Of these factors, the counterparty risk is the danger that one party fails to carry out a contractual obligation, the subprime crisis involvement of which will trap the entire financial system into a miserable situation. Asset price bubble means that there is prone to be excessive expansion in market confidence during the continuous rise in a "boom" period, resulting in irrational behavior of enterprises, residents and financial institutions, fostering asset price bubble, and increasing the risk of future market adjustment. Once the market expectation is reversed, the burst of the asset price bubble may even trigger the breakdown of the financial system. Market squeeze refers to the loss of market confidence due to the outburst of various financial risk events, including the bankruptcy of large financial institutions and sharp decrease of asset price, which gives rise to the shortage or even exhaustion of market liquidity and further systematic risk, endangering the entire financial system. Major causes of financial market turbulence comprise financial structural imbalance, improper shifting of financial innovation risk, and excessive range of asset price fluctuation.

(a) *Financial structural imbalance*

Financial structure means the proportional relationship of quantities, or the composing state of financial intermediaries and financial instruments during the financial process. The existence, nature, and relative scale of different types of financial instruments and financial institutions embody the financial structure of a country, which could be divided into a financial super structure, financial instrument structure, and financial intermediary structure (Goldsmith, 1969). Stiglitz (1985) held the idea that the imbalance of financial structure often results in economic recession, thus it is not surprising that improper control will lead to the outburst of financial crisis. Demirgü-Kunt & Levine (1998) described how 155 countries took advantage of relevant information, in order to verify the relationship between financial structure and economic development set forth by Goldsmith. Their study showed that as wealth increases, countries with larger scale banks, non-banking financial institutions and stock markets have stronger financial effect and higher efficiency. In countries of differing income levels, there is no clear change rule presented in the scale of financial structure and increase of income, but the stock market effect is stronger and more efficient in countries with high income. Through a comparative study of the bank and financial market, Levine & Zervos (1993, 1998) found that the contribution function of the stock market and banks on economic development is relatively independent. Guo (2005) carried out empirical research on the evolutionary trend of financial tilt in advancing countries such as the United States, Japan, and Germany for the first time, and put forward the viewpoint that the financial tilt trend is the natural, historical, and gradual development, and evolutionary process of the financial structure. She stressed that the artificial, subjective, too fast and too early "poor transition" to reverse financial tilt is unrealistic and counterproductive, providing a new perspective for financial stability. Ying & Liu (2006) studied the effect of financial structure function on financial stability and came up with an idea that the interaction between the financial structure and the real economy affect financial stability; the reaction of financial structure on the economy impact upon financial stability; and that the cooperation of the financial structure and the real economy influence financial stability.

First, let us consider financial consolidation. In the analysis at the level of financial intermediary structure, the financial consolidation receives much concern due to significantly increasing market concentration. However, regarding the impact of financial consolidation on risks, there are two different views: a class of academics believes that financial consolidation would reduce the financial system risk and help financial stability. For example, Beck *et al.* (2006a, 2006b) stated that large banks have better risk diversification effect; the banking system with higher degree of concentration could increase profits; and the system of a few large banks is relatively easy to regulate. Through the three aforementioned effects, financial consolidation can reduce overall risk. Carlson & Mitchener (2005) suggested that financial consolidation would strengthen competition in the entire market, forcing the banks of poor quality to leave the market, thus reducing overall risk. Another class of academics believes that the increased concentration after the financial consolidation may add risk to the financial system as a whole. For example, De Nicoló & Kwast (2002) indicated that the risk of individual institution could be dispersed through financial consolidation but the financial interrelation is also increased, thus raising the combined risk; and the overall risk may be lifted due to the concentration increase of financial activities. Boyd & De Nicoló (2006) indicated that when the concentration increases, the market control power of a few large financial institutions would be strengthened, decreasing the market competition, raising the opportunity to engage in risky behavior, which will escalate the overall risk.

Second, consider the level of competition. The economic circle defines the level of competition on the basis of market power, which refers to the discussion about whether the manufacturer could influence the market price. The level of competition is different from its concentration, the influencing factors of which include market structure, contestability, intra-industry competition, as well as economic development (Claessens & Laeven, 2004).

There are three different views concerning the level of competition and the stability of a banking system: (i) a "franchise value" paradigm means that there is a negative correlation between the level of competition and stability, and a more concentrated market structure could improve profitability and in turn increase the franchise value of banks, as the high franchise value would reduce the incentives making banks shoulder excessive risks and ultimately reduce the vulnerability (Schaeck *et al.*, 2006); (ii) a "risk shifting" paradigm means that the level of competition and stability are positively correlated, as a low level of competition gives rise to the increase of loan interest rates and further lead to credit risk arising from moral hazard (Stiglitz & Weiss, 1981). The increase in the risk of business failure will cause the increase of problem loans by banks and boost the banking industry's instability; the fierce competition is forcing banks to intervene in riskier business to compensate for the eroded marginal profit, and then lead to risk increase in bank portfolio, rise in vulnerability, and even bank failures (Amable *et al.*, 1998; Boyd & De Nicoló, 2006; Boyd *et al.*, 2004; Carletti and Hartmann, 2002; Canoy *et al.*, 2001; De Nicoló & Loukoianova, 2007); (iii) there is a "U" shaped form between the level of competition and stability — Martínez-Miera & Repullo (2007) took the incomplete correlation of the failure possibility of individual enterprise into consideration, and put forward the theory that in an environment of low competition level, when the interest rate rises, the risk shifting effect will cause more bank failures; at the same time, there is a marginal effect sourcing from that, and the borrowers who have not failed pay higher interest rates and increase banking revenues. Therefore, as the level of competition grows, the possibility of bank failures declines at first and then rises after a certain point.

(b) *Inappropriate shifting of financial innovation risk*

With regard to the relation between financial innovation and financial stability, there are still different views. Some academics believe that financial innovation can optimize the financial structure, improving financial efficiency, so that the stability of the financial system will be more stable. For example, Merton (1992) believed that financial innovation is the motivational force to improve the efficiency of the financial system and promote financial structure optimization. Some other academics hold the idea that financial innovation may impact on financial stability and lead to financial fragility. Carter (1989) stated that financial innovation actually covers growing financial fragility, which is financially a policy of containment, and ultimately inspires speculative financing based on the future income stream and asset price expectation, which is difficult to realize. The impact of the increasingly growing global derivatives market on financial stability cannot be ignored. Financial trading derivatives could stabilize market conditions as well as generate unexpected shocks, and the rise of emerging market derivatives may become an important factor to focus on in the future regulation of financial stability, due to the lack of stability of the real economy and the stock market. Greenspan (1996) suggested that financial derivatives are of great permeability with more systematic risks; meanwhile, as the nature of financial derivatives is cross-border, systemic risk will present more globalization characteristics. It shows that the development of the financial derivative market breaks the traditional boundaries between the banking industry and financial market, derivatives and native products, as well as between national financial systems, thus spreading the risk internationally, while still increasing the instability of the global financial system.

(c) *Excessive range of asset prices fluctuation*

There are two main distinctly different ideas in the existing literature: the traditional theory and the "new environment hypothesis." The traditional theory insists that maintaining price stability is conducive to a stable financial system. After observing and analyzing the 18th and early 20th century phenomena of systematic and non-systematic financial crises and inflation that occurred in the three countries of United States, Britain, and Canada, Bordo *et al.* (2000) drew a conclusion: from the historical perspective, ignoring the price fluctuation caused by monetary or non-monetary factors, the financial crisis usually occurs after sustained inflation.

Bergman & Hansen (2002) carried out modeling analysis from the data of the monetary and banking crises that occurred in Sweden in the 1990s, and formed a idea that since the effects of price shock are stronger and more persistent compared with other shocks, price stability, and financial stability are objectives of mutual consistency, instead of mutual competition within the range of monetary policy. The theoretical and empirical analyses conducted by Demirgü-Kunt & Detragiehe (1997), Hardy & Pazarbasioglu (1999) supported this view to certain extent. However, the "new environment hypothesis" theorists proposed a view totally opposite to the traditional view. They argued that since the 1990s, the low inflation that appeared in developed Western countries created a "new environment," which required a re-examination and even an overturn to the previous ideas concerning the relation between price stability and financial stability. In the view of the "new environment hypothesis" theorists, a low and a stable inflation rate makes people over optimistic for the future economic prospect expectation, fuel asset price bubbles, and increases the vulnerability of the financial system. They conducted further analysis that suggested that the monetary policy aiming at maintaining price stability has triggered the turmoil of the financial system and amplified the latent risks in the financial system, which is not conducive to its overall stability. Along with the emergence of low inflation and financial stability conflict in various countries, such as Japan in the 1980s, the "new environment hypothesis" theorists tried to employ correlation analysis, namely in the situation that the pricing power of an enterprise is lower, or there is positive shock on the supply side in the macroeconomy, or there is an expectation of low inflation, inflationary pressure does not always appear as inflation itself. Therefore, even if there is no significant price fluctuation, financial instability is still possible to emerge.

Chinese academics Duan & Zeng (2007) commented on the relation between asset price fluctuation and financial stability, and they believed that the wide-range fluctuation of asset price and rapid expansion of credit interact with each other, being an important cause of financial instability. At present, theoretical research on the relation between asset price fluctuation and financial stability focuses on: studying the interaction between asset price fluctuation and credit expansion further affecting financial stability; studying the interaction between asset prices fluctuation and bank liquidity further affecting financial stability; emphasizing the effect of information asymmetry in the situation of asset price fluctuation affecting the financial economy; studying the transmission of future disequilibrium information by asset price fluctuation further affecting financial stability. Most empirical studies support that there is a significant correlation between the wide-range fluctuation in asset price, credit expansion, and financial stability. From the perspective of conditions triggering financial instability, the factors of fluctuation facing asset price, a good financial and economic environment, institutional environment and policy environment, each play an important role in maintaining the stability of the financial system. In the literature on the relation between price fluctuation and financial stability, the real estate price has attracted attention due to the subprime crisis. Zhang & Sun (2006) pointed out that the impact of the real-estate cycle on financial stability is mainly in real-estate credit risk exposure, government guarantee risk, and the mismatch risk in the period of long-term deposit and short-term loan. They proposed appropriate policy recommendations based on the following: vigorously solve the problems in the banking industry itself; regulate the behavior of local governments; and effectively supervise the foreign investment entering China's industry of real estate.

(iii) Incomplete financial infrastructure

Any incomplete clearing and payment system, financial legal system, accounting standards, credit environment, and other incomplete financial infrastructure will trigger risks. Each of these vulnerabilities could likely directly affect the functioning of most financial sectors. Moreover, because the carrier of the financial infrastructure is a single financial institution, the vulnerability of this infrastructure may also be affected by the risk attached to an individual financial institution. Among all infrastructures, the payment system is the core one of the financial system: once there is a break off in the payment and settlement chain, it is likely to create problems in the whole payment system, giving rise to systemic financial risk.

(a) *Legal system*

La Porta *et al.* (1998) believed that the legal system is the main source of investor rights, and the key to financial regulation is to attain effective legal protection of the rights of small and medium investors. Since the legal framework under transition economic conditions needs to improve, enterprises engage in a wide range of opportunism and illegal practice (Nee, 1992; Peng & Heath, 1996), which are sometimes even connived and inspired by local governments.

(b) *Accounting standards*

The fair value measurement principle in accounting standards has been heavily criticized and blamed in the subprime crisis. Plantin *et al.* (2005) argued that the fluctuation in the assets value sometimes caused by fair value accounting would distort the true price information it has stored. They analyzed the motivation of banks when given the choices of selling or holding loans. As a bank knows the most about its borrowers, it has the best understanding of the value of the loan. Its managers will be rewarded because of the bank's accounting profit. In the situation where loans are measured at historical cost and the market price is increasing, although the market may underestimate the value, loans are still likely to be sold, when selling is the only way to make profit. While holding loans is most favorable to shareholders, the bank's managers will continue to sell loans to make profit and get paid accordingly. Fair value accounting can avoid this problem of agency. Loans will not be sold at the point when the value is rising, and marking the assets as market value has the same beneficial effect for profit and managers' payment. However, in the case of an error, the fair value may lead to the uneconomical sale of long-term non-current loans. In the account book and market, the value of a loan is the price at which the seller is willing to sell. But if there are only a handful of potential buyers, the price will be very low, but managers want to sell at a higher price. Because all banks with the same assets have the same motives, therefore the selling of assets leads to lower prices. In fact, it is most advantageous for the bank's shareholders to hold loans to maturity date. In terms of long-term assets, it is more attractive to sell out. In this way, the fair value itself would distort the real price, reflecting the actual value of assets. And the expectation of lower price will promote its sale at an even lower price. Information derived from the market price will become defective, resulting in an increasing deviation from the reported net value to the actual value.

(c) *Credit disclosure*

From the existing literature, there emerge two kinds of viewpoint: the "disclosure-stable" viewpoint and the "disclosure–fragile" viewpoint. The former believes that full information disclosure and high market transparency could give full play to the rule of "survival of the fittest" in the market, and that supervisory departments can detect any crisis caused by weak banks early on (Tadesse, 2005). The latter holds the idea that information disclosure is likely to mislead the public, who then mistake certain bank financial information as a common problem running throughout the entire banking system, thus inducing bank runs or a stock market crash (Calomiris & Mason, 1997; Gilbert & Vaughan, 1998; Kaufman, 1994).

(d) *Deposit insurance system*

Currently, in the international academic circle, there are two types of views derived from numerous literature sources on the relation between the deposit insurance system and financial stability: the pros and the skeptics. People in favor of the deposit insurance system suggested that, as an institutional arrangement to prevent bank run, it could effectively promote financial stability and development. They believe that it is an essential institutional arrangement that avoids bank run and reduces the enormous social cost caused by its occurrence, and is the optimal policy for this purpose (Diamond & Dybvig, 1983). Moreover, the pros indicated that in terms of the effect of maintaining financial stability, compared with the method of suspending cashing, the deposit insurance system can completely prevent and eliminate the appearance of a run on the bank's balance, and will not reduce the its function of providing liquidity (Bhattacharya *et al.*, 2004; Chari & Jagannathan, 1988). Compared with the lender of the last resort system, the deposit insurance system has the advantages of strong credibility and reducing the occurrence of adverse selection (Diamond & Dybvig, 1983).

However, the skeptics adopted a distrusting and negative attitude to the idea that the deposit insurance system can contribute to stable financial order. Starting from problems arising from the implementation of the system, they suggested that the implementation of the system would result in adverse selection, further confusing the financial order, and increasing the PFC. As for the effect of maintaining financial stability, the skeptics considered that deposit insurance is not significantly better than the lender of last resort means, and with it providing liquidity as the main measure, cannot effectively address the problems of the banking panic and information asymmetry in a financial crisis. In addition, if a country adopts a deposit insurance system its expense is relatively high, especially a fully covered insurance after a financial crash, thus deepening the crisis and delaying the recovery (Honohan & Klingebiel, 2000). The skeptics have also effectively backed up their viewpoint by virtue of a lot of empirical results. For example, Saunders *et al.* (1990) analyzed the situation of the United States, Japan, Korea, and other countries to confirm that the deposit insurance system has undermined financial stability and increased the possibility of the outbreak of financial crisis through prompting banks to expand venture capital, governments to increase spending, etc.

(e) *Financial safety net*

A broad financial safety net consists of three types: prudential regulation of financial regulation authorities; the lender of last resort system; and the deposit insurance system of the central bank. A narrow financial safety net generally covers the latter two only. The underpinning theory is that prudential regulation can prevent problems, while the lender of last resort system can help a bank to maintain its liquidity, and the deposit insurance system can eliminate the run. All three have their own advantages and disadvantages and are difficult to place alongside each other, so that they could jointly achieve and maintain financial stability. But a financial safety net has its pros and cons. Its advantages are the aspects of risk prevention, risk compensation, and crisis relief processing; while the disadvantages are that it may induce moral hazard, adverse selection, leading to misallocation of resources and cost burden (Lin, 1999). For example, Nier *et al.* (2008) believed that the weakening aggregate of the banking system's overall net assets may cause low-aggregate capitalization, which may also be the result of the individual bank's own incentives to maintain a sufficient capital buffer caused by an excessive financial safety net. Therefore, the incentive effect of the financial safety net may largely increase the possibility of a system crash.

(iv) Improper monetary policy measures and financial regulation system design

In existing research literature, monetary policy is interwoven with financial stability policy. From the perspective of monetary policy's impact on financial instability, there are three types of conclusions in relevant research. Firstly, if the monetary policy measure is improper and the fluctuation range of inflation is large and extremely unstable, it will give rise to a reassignment of real wealth between the depositor and the borrower, thereby further generating changes in the financial and risk conditions of financial institutions. Secondly, inflation to a low level or below zero and pushed by a continuously constrictive monetary policy will cause risk; as in the case of lower inflation rate, the attraction of cash holding is greater than that of bank deposit. Run off in bank deposit may reduce bank profit, meaning that the bank may go bankrupt. Thirdly, in terms of setting the interest rate level, temporary sharp change in nominal short-term interest rate will increase the uncertainty of the financial market as well as variable-ratio of business failure, and especially in the situation of excessive monetary policy, pose great negative impact on the bank balance sheet in a credit crunch period. Therefore, adopting timely and proper interest rate reaction against the inflation shock is beneficial to long-term financial stability. William took positive asymmetric monetary policy as an example to indicate that the expansive monetary policy signifies that the existing unbalance remains unsolved in the process of strengthening constraint, on the contrary expanding the initial balance (foreign trade balance or internal debt balance) or increase the asset price.

(a) *Monetary and financial stability*

With regard to the study of the relationship between monetary stability and financial stability, primarily there are two different views consisting of traditional theory and "new environment hypothesis." Traditional theory, with "Schwartz (1988) Hypothesis" as the representative, insists that financial instability is usually caused or worsened by a general price fluctuation, thereby monetary policies maintaining price stability may promote financial stability. Monetary stability is a sufficient condition to achieve financial stability; policies aiming at maintaining price (currency) stability can also be employed to achieve financial stability (Bordo & Wheelock, 1998). Other academics in favor of the traditional theory adopt a very cautious attitude for the consistent relation between the monetary stability and financial stability. They believe that there is a certain consistency between financial stability and monetary stability, and simply agree that monetary stability can promote financial stability, or monetary stability is beneficial for financial stability (Issing, 2003), instead of being a sufficient condition to financial stability (Bordo & Wheelock, 1998). The "new environment hypothesis" theory believes that the stability-oriented monetary policy strategy is likely to cause the formation of higher interest rates, and the negative effects it produces will affect financial stability. Mishkin (1996) analyzed that the use of high interest rate policies to control inflation will deteriorate the balance sheet of banks and the net worth of enterprises, especially when they attract capital inflows and generate excessive debt and high credit risk. Currency mismatches may also result because foreign capital inflows are transformed into domestic currency in the name of credit or loan. Cukierman (1992) held the idea that the low inflation policy requires rapid and substantial rise in interest rates; therefore, if banks cannot quickly convert assets and liabilities, the interest rate mismatches will be increased, leading to greater market risk. Issing (2003) accordingly pointed out that monetary policy should not only be targeted at price stability, but also pay direct attention to financial imbalances itself. This direct attention consists of two parts: the first is trying to take measures to avoid or reduce the accumulation of financial imbalances; and the second is, in the case of the aforementioned situation of measures shortage, trying to decrease the hazards and cost caused by financial instability to the lowest level.

(b) *Financial regulation system design*

A government's implementation of financial regulation is to correct the fragility, externalities and monopoly of the financial market for the public interest. Merton (1992) suggested that the functions of the financial system are more stable compared with those of financial institutions, and provide a functional perspective for managing and supervising financial institutions.

However, the flaws of regulation system design may worsen financial stability. For example, Barth *et al.* (2004) took 152 countries (regions) as samples to test the impact of bank regulation measures on bank development, efficiency and vulnerability, and it turned out that the government's measures to strengthen the regulation were not able to stabilize the banking system and in fact, had the opposite effect. Barth *et al.* (2000) selected the level of economic development and the quality of government as control variables, using a variety of econometric methods, to study the countries with the occurrence of banking crises. The empirical results showed that the greater the extent a country restricts its commercial banks' involvement in security and non-banking commercial activities, the more likely the country is to have a fragile financial system, and is prone to financial (banking) crises. Quintyn & Taylor (2003) indicated that the independence of regulations is of equal significance to financial stability as that of monetary policy. Herrero & Pedro del Rio (2003) made empirical analysis on 1,492 imbalance observation reports concerning 79 countries (27 industrial countries, 32 emerging countries, and 20 transitional countries) covering a time span of 30 years (1970–1999) by virtue of the binary model and assessed the impact of monetary policy-making on the possibility of banking crisis. The research findings suggested that the target selection of the central bank influences the possibility of bank crisis. In particular, if the central bank has a limited and rigorous target and pays close attention to price stability, the likelihood of bank crisis will be cut.

As a department shouldering the heavy responsibility of financial stability, the high regulation quality of the central bank is the key to financial stability. Schinasi (2003) believed that there are several reasons making the central bank destined to play a role in ensuring financial stability. First, the central bank is the sole provider of means of payment and emergency liquidity. Second, the central bank can ensure the normal operation of the entire national payment system. Any single bank issue is likely to spread through the payment system, which may trigger dysfunctional operation of the entire payment system, and even create a domino effect on a larger scale. Third, banks are the key link in the transmission mechanism of the monetary policy, which affects the economy. Once the commercial banking system is in trouble, it will be more difficult for the central bank to take any necessary measures so as to achieve its monetary policy objectives. Thus, the central bank can naturally benefit from sound financial institutions and a stable financial market. At last, there is a clear link between monetary stability and financial stability. Once there is financial instability, any credit would have been destroyed and people often rush to get the legal tender with strongest liquidity, which means that the bank will begin to tighten its credit and money supply. If the situation continues and develops, the monetary aggregates may have a sharp contraction and eventually lead to a recession in economic activity.

Then how to improve the regulation quality of the central bank? The independence and policy transparency of the central bank are two topics under the spotlight. Concerning the independence of the central bank, Kydland & Prescott (1977) initiated the study of dynamic inconsistency related to rules and discretion, and pointed out that the independence of the central bank should be strengthened. In fact, generally people believe that the independence of the central bank would promote price stability (Alesina & Summers, 1993; Lybek, 1999), which should also help to promote financial stability. Policy transparency can be divided into target transparency, instrument transparency, and awareness transparency (Hahn, 2002). Transparency has four properties: openness; clarity; honesty; and common understanding (Winkler, 2000). In their study, Howells & Mariscal (2002) pointed out that enhancing the transparency of the central bank's monetary policy operation can not only make monetary policy more effective, but also ensure a low cost to achieve the policy objectives of the central bank. Through establishing an econometric model, Chortareas *et al.* (2003) made empirical research on whether the increase in the monetary policy transparency can reduce the cost of the central bank to suppress inflation. The results of econometric testing on the 21 OECD countries showed that the higher the monetary policy transparency is, the lower the cost to suppress inflation by policies.

1.4.3 Specific influencing factors in China's transition economy

Through analyzing the objective function of enterprises, banks, local governments and central government and demonstrating a corresponding game model, Yu & Sun (2007) concluded that there is severe information asymmetry in the quantity index (such as GDP) oriented political performance evaluation system, as well as between the central and local governments, which acts as the primary cause to put the central government in a dilemma of "economic growth and macro control." For this reason, the central government should urgently reform the political performance evaluation system, establish a bank credit monitoring system, promote the availability of the central bank to local economic information, and guide the behavior of local governments effectively, to enhance financial stability and scientific management institutionally. Huang & He (2007) established a microcosmic model of the central bank and financial institutions, and analyzed the theoretical model and current situation. From the perspective of property right, they suggested that against the framework of China's stable financial policies, the independence of the central bank has been damaged and its functions of stabilizing currency and finance have been restricted to micro financial institutions, due to its *de facto* property relation with micro financial institutions. To maintain the independence of the central bank, the government must sever the property relation between the central bank and the micro financial institutions.

1.5 FINANCIAL RISK CONTAGION AND FINANCIAL STABILITY: INVESTIGATION OF THE FINANCIAL NETWORK

Under economic globalization, standardization of financial innovative productions facilitates the spread of information, while intensifying information asymmetry. Tight connections among the global financial information network further enhance the possibility of financial risk contagion, and enable it to show the unique qualities of complicated network activities. As Gai & Kapadia (2008) point out, the financial network is robust to random failure, yet fragile to calculated attack, as expected for a complex network ("Robust yet Fragile"): its increasing linkage and risk sharing will reduce the possibility of contagion, but a large number of financial connections may raise the potential for extensive risk contagion.

1.5.1 Risk contagion and financial stability from the perspective of network

Generally, there are two ways to study the relation between financial risk contagion and financial stability from the perspective of financial network. The first way is to explore the contagious effect through direct connection. The groundbreaking work in this field is *Financial Contagion,* by Allen & Gale (2000a, 2000b), which studies how banking systems, under different network structures, cope with contagion. Consumers are assumed to have the liquidity preference of Diamond & Dybvig (1983), and the bank deals with liquidity shock perfectly via the interbank deposit. The connection created by deposit exchange exposes the financial network to the risk of contagion. The study takes incomplete network as an example and assumes that the failure of one bank would trigger the collapse of the whole banking system, demonstrating that the financial system will be more flexible to the contagious effect if all the banks are put in a complete net structure under the same parametric condition. Therefore, an incomplete network is more susceptible to contagion, while the comparatively complete network is more flexible in that the damage of the bank portfolio can be transferred to more banks by interbank contract.

Freixas *et al.* (2000) bring forward a model to discuss what the network negative externality caused by the risk of a single bank means to the whole financial system. When liquidity demand is created by the uncertain consumption of consumers, the connection among banks will be realized through interbank credit lines, which can ensure that banks can hedge the regional liquidity risk. As Allen & Gale (2000a, 2000b) put it, interbank connections enhance the resilience of the whole system to react to single bank solvency, but the drawback lies in the incentive to close inefficient banks being decreased. Leitner (2005) constructs a model, pointing out that the success of agent project's investment relies on the other connected agents' investment. The reason for that is because resources endowment is randomly allocated among agents, and one single agent may not have enough funds to make the necessary investment. As a result, to prevent the collapse of the whole network, the agent might help others. The principle of Leitner's research lies in how to upgrade the network design and seek a compromise between minimization of risk sharing and total collapse.

Vivier-Lirimont (2004) raises the question of optimal networks from a different angle. He holds that interbank risk transfer increases the deposit utility under the optimal network system. He finds that only a very dense network is compatible to Pareto optimal allocation. Dasgupta (2004) also believes that interbank connection of holding common deposit is a source of contagious collapse. When a depositor receives information about a bank's fundamentals and believes that others might draw his deposit, he will want to draw his deposit from the bank before that may occur, and that is where the fragility comes from. Actually, contagion not only happens in banks. Cummins *et al.* (2002) make an analysis on how the catastrophe risk market structure causes contagion, and describe what the network structure should do to limit the insurance industry's reaction to major disaster.

Similar to these works, some papers study contagion through network techniques in mathematics and theoretic physics. For instance, Eisenberg & Noe (2001) study the default of companies in a single clearing mechanism with such techniques and methods. They first demonstrate that a clearing payment vector determines the connection level among companies. Then an algorithm is developed to evaluate the impact on the clearing payment system by small-scale attack. The algorithm gets the natural metric of a system's risk based on how many waves of defaults are needed to fail a specific company in the system. Similarly, Minguez-Afonso (2007) research the liquidity and system risk of a high-value payment system, such as the accounts receivable and accounts payable liquidation of companies, and interbank payment systems. Gai & Kapadia (2008) put forward the model of the financial network's contagion, in a way that is similar to detecting the spread of disease in a network in epidemiology. They evaluate the fragility of a financial system based on the banks' capital buffer and connectivity degree, and the market liquidity of non-performing bank assets. They find that comparatively high connectivity reduces the possibility of the widespread of default, but the influence of attack on the financial system is stronger and more significant. In addition, the resilience of the financial system to large-scale attack depends on specific impact weakness related to structural fragility.

The second method is focused on the connectivity of indirect liability table. Lagunoff & Schreft (2001) construct a model to connect the agent with his feel of return on portfolio. In this model, agents susceptible to shock rearrange their portfolio, which makes some connections fail and exerts an influence on two related financial crises — one of them happens gradually with increasing costs and more failing connections; the other happens instantly with insightful agents, taking pre-emptive actions and turning to more secure portfolio to avoid future costs caused by contagion.

Cifuentes *et al.* (2005) put forward a model and believe that financial institutions connect through holding portfolios. If everyone holds the same amount of portfolio, then the network is complete. Although direct connections are incorporated through common credit exposure in the model, the contagion is mainly driven by the change of capital price. The shared view held by the aforementioned works is that the financial system is with internal fragility. The fragility is not only embodied in the macro risk factors facing the financial institution externally, but also generated by the pressure imposed on other institutions by the decreasing prices caused by some banks' compulsory sale of their assets.

Babus (2007) makes further complement to the works on network effect and establishes a model to connect banks to reduce the contagious risk and construct an insurance mechanism inside the network. Based on the process of forming connectivity posed by Allen & Gale (2000a, 2000b), he points out that network with better connectivity is more resilient to contagion. The model predicts a threshold that will obstruct the occurrence of contagion, suggesting that banks should connect with each other and reach the requirement of such a threshold. However, the hidden costs of integrating into the connection hinder banks from reaching that level. Castiglionesi & Navarro (2007) also research whether banks should try to decentralize the network structure to optimize it. They assume that banks invest on behalf of depositors and positive externality will be generated on returns of the investment. When the banks' capital cannot be served to make investment by deposits, fragility comes. If the chance of bankruptcy is low, then the decentralized solution is near to optimal.

In addition to theory discussion, a considerable number of researchers try to find the evidence of the contagious failure due to financial institutions' claims to each other. Most of these works estimate different bank systems' bilateral credit relations via information on the capital credit tables, and then test the stability of interbank market by simulating a single bank collapse. For example, Upper & Worms (2004), Sheldon & Maurer (1998) respectively analyze the banking system in Germany and Switzerland; Cocco *et al.* (2005) provide experimental evidence to the loan relations in the Portugal interbank market; Furfine (2003) and Wells (2004), respectively, study the interconnectivity of American and British banks; Boss *et al.* (2004) make empirical analysis on the network structure of the Australian interbank market and discuss the impact on the network stability caused by the disappearance of a certain point. Degryse & Nguyen (2007) evaluate the risk caused by banks' failing chain reaction in the Belgian interbank market. They find that the banking system is highly resilient even when it faces massive shock. The worst case of simulation shows that the contagion costs of banks is lower than 5% of the capital of the total balance sheet in the Belgian interbank market, while the costs of Germany's banking system is as high as 15%. The size of costs is to a great extent decided by the way banks connect (evaluated by the credit exposure of interbank market). To most countries, the data are derived from a bank's balance sheet, because the information of total exposure of the reported institution compared with other banks can be provided. To predict the bank-to-bank exposures, we usually presume that banks expand credit evenly. In fact, this assumption requires banks to be connected in a complete network. In this way, the assumption may deviate from results in view of theory research holding that a network with better connectivity is more resilient to the spread of shock. Different from simulations, Iyer & Peydro-Alcalde (2007) test the financial contagion with the data from the interbank exposure when a big Indian bank fails; he finds that banks having high interbank exposure with the failing bank will suffer from higher deposit extraction risk, and that the risk of bank deposit runs with unsatisfactory fundamentals is higher.

Overall, the basic conclusion of the aforementioned works is that higher connectivity of financial network reduces the possibility of the widespread of default. In other words, the more complete the financial network structure is, the more resilient its reaction to contagion will be. But it will also result in the impact on the financial system caused by shock becoming more significant.

1.5.2 Characteristics of financial network and financial stability

Since robustness to random failures and fragility to the calculated attacks of financial network have an influence on financial risk contagion and financial stability, then how does the financial network structure affect risk contagion? In other words, what associations does a financial organizational system's structure have with the instability of financial system? Comparatively speaking, are concentrated financial systems, such as those of the Netherlands and Switzerland, more likely to make risks contagious and then lead to financial instability than the decentralized financial systems of Italy and Germany? Meanwhile, are financial systems composed of less large banks and less small fringe banks more sensitive to financial risks? Furthermore, how does interbank exposure interact with a financial system's capital and its control? Is setting capital adequacy ratio to financial institutions enough to constrain the systemic risk in network? Nier *et al.* (2008) establish a financial network consisting of 25 banks (25 network nodes) with a range of fluctuation being 10–25, and set the external capital scale to be 10,000 units with the Erdös–Rényi probability benchmark between two nodes being 0.2 and the fluctuation range being 0–1, to make simulation analysis on the relations between network structure and financial stability. From the perspective of the central bank's supervision, the key parameters deciding the financial network systemic structure include: (i) capitalization level; (ii) exposure scale; (iii) connectivity level of banks; (iv) concentration level of financial system. These parameters determine the resilience of the financial network to risk contagion.

Firstly, we will focus on capitalization level. Nier *et al.* (2008) simulate the relations between banks' net capital and the resilience of banks' system to study the connections of the capitalization level of banks and contagion. The result of the research is that the higher a financial institution's capital soundness is, the more resilient the financial institution will be to contagious effect, and the two factors have relatively weak monotonic negative correlation. But contagion does not reduce linearly with the bank capitalization level. When the first bank defaults, higher net capital absorbs the most impact. When net capital decreases to a certain level, the second round of default will happen, because the first one cannot resist the external impact any more. More damages will transfer to lenders and raise the possibility of a second round of default happening. When a bank's net capital continues to decrease but does not go down to the level that can cause a new round of default contagion, we observe that at within 1–4% net asset range, the number of defaults is nearly at a constant, since the net capital of market participants is still enough to take risks. However, once the level of net capital is lower at 1%, more defaults will be triggered, which will lead to the drastic rise of defaults. The analysis shows that polymerization blow makes the range of contagion or default chain effect increase substantially.

Secondly, exposure scale will be studied. The increase of the industry assets ratio exerts two distinctively different effects, which are potentially opposites, on banking systems. First of all, it means the transmissions of shock among trade creditors' rise and the impact effect created by deposits decreases, which is to say, the spread of the shock is more serious. Next, contagious effect might be intensified, because the overall net capital will increase due to the set bank holding the capital to buffer exposure, and the growth of interbank market scale. Actually, when interbank capital is at a lower level, the first round of default will not cause contagion. This is because customers' deposits cover most costs and the damages transferred to the creditor bank are small enough for the bank's net capital to digest them. When the ratio of interbank capital surpasses the threshold, then a second wave of default will come. The reason is that more shock transmits to the creditor bank, whose net capital is not enough to compensate the costs. Nier *et al.* (2008) believe that when interbank capital rises, the first bank's net capital and the default external capital of the creditor bank will also increase. More damages will be taken by the first bank and the creditor bank's net capital, and transferred to relative banks in the third round of defaults. Overall, the increase of interbank debt scale will raise the threat of contagion, even if the bank has prepared its capital buffer to such risks.

Thirdly, we will analyze the level of connectivity. Interbank connectivity has two opposite effects: on the one hand, as the channel to spread the shock to the whole financial system, it plays a role of shock-transmitter; on the other hand, it is the shock-absorber, sharing these impacts (Nier *et al.*, 2008). First, when connectivity is at a very low level, the increase of connectivity will reduce the resilience of system, because the possibility of shock transmission is raised by connectivity. When connectivity is at a high level, the increase of connectivity may reduce or raise the system resilience. But when the level of connectivity is high enough, the further increase of connectivity no doubt reduces contagion and the shock-absorber effect will play its part to make more and more banks resist the shock. The connectivity level effect is also associated with the contagious net assets. In an incomplete financial system with bank capital, only the net asset absorbs a small proportion of shock, and the other part of it will be transmitted to other banks. At the time, when connectivity level is increased, interbank connectivity will act as the shock-transmitter instead of shock-absorber, due to the low level of net capital and the rise of bank failure. So we can make such conclusions that a banking system with incomplete capital is very vulnerable and can be more fragile with higher level of connectivity. However, the effect is just the opposite for banks with complete capitals. Although interbank connectivity still transmits shock from one bank to the other, higher net capital serves as a buffer and enhances the load capacity of interbank connectivity, which will play the role of shock-absorber and increases the resilience of the financial system. On such a basis, banking systems with complete capital are more resilient to shock, and particularly so with higher level of connectivity. So the basic conclusion of the research is that the effect of connectivity level is with non-monotonic character; that is, the small increase of initial connectivity will raise contagious effect, but when a certain threshold is reached, the connectivity level will enhance the financial system's ability to absorb shock.

Fourthly, the concentration level of the financial system will be studied. The more concentrated the financial system is, the more it is prone to be subject to similar or bigger systemic risks. The shock scale related to the impacted banks' external capital increases with the rising number of defaults. Moreover, the banking system under the same shock ratio is more concentrated with a larger number of defaults; the contagious risk will be higher.

Overall, financial risk contagion is the focus of financial instability. Under globalization, the world's financial information network is tightly connected, which promotes the contagion of financial risk and the unique qualities of complicated network activities. Analysis of the model of risk contagion in the financial network shows that it is robust to random failure and vulnerable to calculated attacks, which are to say, the possibility of contagion will be reduced by the financial network's increasing connectivity and risk sharing, but large amounts of financial connectivity will raise the potential of widespread contagion. The risk contagion of financial innovation is influenced by the structural character of financial network: (i) the more complete the financial institution's capital is, the more resilient the financial system's reaction to contagious effect will be; (ii) the increase of interbank debt scale will raise the threat of contagion; (iii) interbank connectivity plays the role of both shock-transmitter and shock-absorber, so the small increase of initial connectivity level will enhance the contagious effect, but when a certain threshold is reached, connectivity will promote the financial system's capacity to absorb shock; (iv) the more concentrated the financial system is, the more it is prone to subject similar, or even bigger, systemic risks.

1.6 MEASURES TO MAINTAIN FINANCIAL STABILITY

Financial stability has the character of quasi-public products, including non-competitiveness of consumption, non-exclusiveness of supply, and strong externality. Financial stability is an important behavior of macroeconomic stability and plays a significant role in social stability. The social economic aspects can only interact with stable finance to realize the scientific development of economic society. However, the government needs to take steps to uphold financial stability, due to market failure and the high risks of the financial system. The vice president of Sweden's central bank, Kristina brought forward the three pillars of financial system stability: (i) the financial supervision framework composed of regulations and laws; (ii) risk evaluation, daily supervision, and crisis management of the institutional risk system, the daily supervision of which includes oversight of single banking institutions, system stability, and financial basic infrastructures; (iii) crisis management measures. The IMF have regularly published the *Report on Global Financial Stability* since 2002, focusing on the "systemic and structural" deficiency of the world's financial market and the transmission channel of risks among financial institutions and countries; it mainly offers suggestions regarding how to maintain financial stability from the aspect of structural reform. As the first central bank in the world to set up a financial stability policy and publish a report on this, Sweden's concern for banking focuses principally on the importance of the security and efficiency of payment systems for financial stability.

Generally speaking, apart from the financial supervision concept, the principles and methods embodied in laws and regulations and the financial supervisory institutions' function positioning and division of responsibilities, and the measures needed to maintain financial stability, can divided into three parts: a financial institution's self-management of risks; microprudential supervision; and macroprudential supervision.

In terms of the financial supervisory institutions' function positioning and division of responsibilities, there are three main forms in the world. The first one is the supervisory institution that divides boundaries and responsibility in different fields, according to the business of financial departments, such as those in America, China, France, Greece, and Spain. The second regroups different financial departments' supervision responsibility into one single institution, like the Federal Financial Supervision Bureau in Germany, the Financial Service Bureau in Briton, and the Financial Supervision Bureau in Sweden. The third mode is between the first two modes, which allocate the supervision responsibility to two institutions — one responsible for maintaining the financial stability, and the other focusing on supervising the financial business. Separate supervision is usually subjected to the limitation of information communication and supervision authority division, so the establishment of a single supervisory institution, or strengthening the cooperation among different supervisory institutions, becomes the direction of financial supervision's development. For example, Belgium and Portugal established the Financial Supervision Committee, composed of the central bank and financial supervisory departments, which is responsible for coordinating and managing affairs related to the financial market and institutions. Germany and France set up the Financial Stability Committee with the Ministry of Treasure, the central bank, and supervisory institutions, in charge of the business concerning financial stability. When it comes to the practice of our own country (China), the responsibility for maintaining financial stability is mainly held by one bank, three committees, and the Treasury Ministry. However, with the development of financial innovation and financial markers, there are problems such as how to strengthen the coordination of supervision, establish the information share mechanism and promote communication during work, and the combination of financial regulation, prudent supervision, and management.

1.6.1 The central bank's performance of its function to maintain financial stability

As the main power for maintaining financial stability, the central bank's financial stability function is under development from being a lender of last resort, to create a deposit insurance system, establish a financial security network, and construct an all-round financial stability framework. From the view of the central bank, its function to maintain financial stability is primarily embodied in macroprudential management. Oosterloo & Haan (2004) point out that there are two means adopted by the central bank — the previous prevention policy tool included the macroprudential tool (prudential supervision framework, efficient implementation of bank supervision measures, and early warning system), and the microprudential tool (a regular comparative analysis of the position and capital adequacy of financial institutions, monitoring of liquidity status and risk and inspection of internal control system) — whereby the possibility of harmful financial instability will be reduced. There is also the post response tool, which is to provide urgent and mobile support to financial institutions, and the liquidation and reorganization of banks.

Previous prevention measures include evaluation and warning systems, monetary policy, moral advice, and a deposit insurance system, and so on. The steps needed to maintain financial stability is first to establish the evaluation and warning system, and then conduct real-time monitoring and assessment analysis over the financial system. Currently, the representative financial warning systems are the index frame of the financial warning system established by Evans *et al.* (2000), the IMF core index set (2003), and the IMF incentive index set (2003). To realize the stability of the financial system efficiently, the central bank must be able to master the information of all sorts of macroeconomic situation, financial market and institution, and basic financial infrastructure, so that it can find the factors that may lead to financial instability as early as possible. Moreover, a single financial institution's financial soundness can be ensured by a deposit insurance system and the possibility of a financial institution's bankruptcy can also be reduced. Meanwhile, moral advice is also an efficient — but often ignored — method to prevent financial instability. Through moral advice, the central bank can transmit risk information to financial markets and institutions and make instructions accordingly, so the behavior of the major participants will be influenced. *China's Financial Stability Report in 2005* has listed it as one of the policies adopted by the central bank.

When financial instability happens, the institution responsible for financial stability must provide short-term urgent mobile support for the troubled financial institution or the whole financial market. According to the research by Frydl & Quintyn (2000), the support of the central bank to the troubled financial institution should be offered, before the systemic character of the bank crisis can be identified. When a bank — or several banks — begin to retreat from depositors and creditors home and abroad, those people cannot borrow directly or can only get money from the interbank market with higher interest rates, and then the central bank becomes the lender of last resort. In principle, the central bank should only help those banks with insufficient liquidity but solvency. However, in the early stage of the crisis, it is hard to distinguish between liquidity and insolvency. Goodhart (1999) also stresses that in the case of crisis, it is impossible to distinguish between liquidity and insolvency. Therefore, the central bank interferes with most of the high-risk loans as the lender of last resort, but these risks and costs might be imposed on taxpayers.

Short-term mobile support can be provided to the whole market as well as a single financial institution. According to the Economic and Financial Committee (2001), offering the market urgent mobile support can distinguish loose monetary policy (such as providing preventive liquidity). It is a way to alleviate market pressure brought by temporary external adverse shock, such as terrorist attack. However, the aim of changing monetary policy is to maintain long-term price stability.

In practice, the first reactive measure taken by each country's central bank is to use the balance sheet to provide short-term liquidity to the financial system. It offers the agency still with solvency the liquidity it needs through discount loan, and makes claims that the needed liquidity will be released in a timely manner by the discount window, or provides liquidity to the whole market through temporally loosening the monetary policy. Most central banks will make it clear that these short-term mobile supports need sufficient collateral as their condition. As one central bank put it, "We do not think the central bank has the obligation to provide security to institutions with insolvency."

Once the nature of the crisis is identified, the bank's insolvency is widely known, and then measures like deposit insurance fund are required to stabilize the financial system (Frydl & Quintyn, 2000). Although the original intention of setting a deposit insurance fund is to prevent risk contagion among banks and a corresponding liquidity problem, many countries use that to reorganize the trouble banks and they may also use the mobile support to achieve this goal (Economic and Financial Committee, 2001).

Most countries establish some form of deposit insurance, but the way they set up the deposit insurance fund is quite different. For instance, the deposit insurance system is methodically elaborated in the Credit System Supervision Act issued in 1992 in Holland, to facilitate its central bank to implement deposit insurance. In Turkey, bank supervision and the administration institution manage the deposit insurance fund. Moreover, in the United States, an independent federal government institution — the Federal Deposit Insurance Company — runs the deposit insurance fund.

When the failure of one single financial institution may result in systemic problems, the government will decide to pay the bill for the institution's debt. In the beginning, nationalized capital might be high, but the government may resale the capital it has got at a reasonable price (Economic and Financial Committee, 2001).

The management of systemic crisis is related to the specific role of government. In the United States, the Federal Deposit Insurance Company usually has to deploy the least deposit insurance fund to solve the problem of bank failure. However, there is a systemic exception, which is that once the project of least fund exerts an adverse impact on the economic situation or financial stability, while the non-least fund way could avoid or alleviate the consequence, then the treasurer has the right to give up handling this project. According to another central bank: "If a bank's failure affects systemic stability, then it's up to the government to decide whether tax revenue would be used to prevent systemic crisis. But it can only be referred to when single agency fails in using an active settling project." The aim of systematic bank reconstruction is to restore its liquidity and profitability, improve its capacity as depositors and borrowers, and regain the public trust (Dziobek & Pazarbasioglu, 1997), but not the anti-measures taken by the central bank within its responsibility. This is because the intervention of reinvesting capital for financial institution comes at high cost, and it is a challenge for the government and the central bank to cooperate with the supervisor.

1.6.2 Financial institutions' internal control

Wu (2004) holds that the first thing we need to do is to improve the self-restraint mechanism of financial institutions — the internal control mechanism to uphold financial stability. This is consistent with the supervision and management theory written in Basel Accord, to shift the focus from the external supervision to the internal control. Financial internal control belongs to the modern management of financial institution and the self-discipline of the financial institution. It is a generic term applied to the internal financial institution's methods, measures, and procedures to implement risk control, system management, and mutual control methods over the business activities of the functional departments and their staff members in order to accomplish established working objectives and prevent risk. For financial business, the establishment and improvement of internal control mechanism is not just a method, but also the essence for it to survive. The investigation of the Basel Committee on Banking Supervision shows that the problem of internal control mechanism leads to a financial business' failure in the world at large.

These facts prove that it is necessary for a financial institution to have a good and strict internal control mechanism to make external financial supervision effective. No matter the central bank and other official regulatory authorities, or industry associations and other self-discipline organizations, or social supervision, all they can do is to exercise off-site inspection and the occasional on-site inspection to financial institutions. None of these can replace the self-constraint of a financial institution in its daily business. Hence, it is necessary for the internal control of the financial institution to ensure the accuracy of its financial report and enhance the reliability of the inspection's result. With the rapid development and continuous application of high-tech to the financial industry, financial business becomes and much more complicated and the importance of internal control is more necessary in financial supervision. Because a financial institution is the main body of financial innovation, new financial products and tools are emerging to pursue profits and evade financial supervision. But the methods and measures taken by financial supervision departments are usually relatively backward. To avoid financial risk caused by the financial institution's self-innovation, strengthening its own internal control is the premise and foundation of carrying out effective financial supervision. The practices of international financial supervision prove that no matter how strong the external financial supervision's power is and how meticulous the supervision is conducted, its effects would be compromised if there is a lack of cooperation from the internal control of the institution.

According to the Basel Committee on Banking Supervision (1998), strategic planning, establishment of internal control environment factors and the target of business activities, risk identification activity, risk management, implementation of control activity, information identification and communication, and supervision assessment and corrective action, should all be included within a financial institution's internal control.

1.6.3 Coordination and cooperation of the central bank, supervisory institutions, and Department of Finance

Most Western researchers believe that different institutions should hold their own respective responsibility for upholding financial stability, rather than it being held by the central bank only. Goodhart (1995) put forward that: "The central bank does not have necessary capital foundation and resources to shoulder the responsibility of bigger rescue action, so it will turn to the support of the private bank system and other sources in crisis management. But now it becomes harder even impossible for the central bank to seek help from private banks with the participating of more competitive multinational financial institutions. The central bank is forced to turn to the Department of Finance to deal with even the smallest crisis within the bank system." Under the circumstances of modern market economy, crisis management has been beyond the capacity of the central bank, which has to intensify the coordination and cooperation with other relative institutions to maintain financial stability. Meanwhile, support from the central bank only cannot ensure the grasp of timely and comprehensive information to uphold financial stability. Macro finance relies on the good support of micro finance; the establishment and exercise of the central bank's financial stability policies requires a powerful information platform. Although the central bank has its own independent database, a lack of the first-hand materials from supervisory institutions will result in the failure of policies. Therefore, it is necessary for the central bank to establish the coordination mechanism for information communication in order to maintain financial stability. Lastly, when the central bank takes post-responsive actions as lender of last resort, it also needs the close coordination of the supervisory institution. If not, it may lead to the central bank's system as lender of last resort not being put into place properly, which might cause financial instability. Hence, it is necessary for the central bank, supervisory institutions, and Department of Finance to coordinate with each other on the basis of specifying their duties to maintain financial stability.

We have already discussed that as the first central bank in the world to set up a financial stability department and publish a report on financial stability, Sweden's banking concern is principally on the security and efficiency of payment system in financial stability. Its payment system covers all of the financial market, different financial institutions, all payment tools, and their technical and management support systems. Large (2005) also points out that the cooperation of the central bank, Department of Finance, and supervisory institution should be a part of maintaining financial stability and crisis management. He makes clear there should be three necessary functions involved in upholding financial stability: supervision and management over financial institutions and market; exercise of oversight over the whole financial system; and financial support, which is especially important in the case of financial collapse. Generally, the "roles" of supervisory institution, the central bank, and Department of Finance are corresponding to the aforementioned functions. Therefore, the cooperation, evaluation and protocol of the central bank, Department of Finance, and supervisory institution should be a part of maintaining financial stability and crisis management. But so far there is a lack of research on how to construct such a coordination mechanism. What is noteworthy is that William stresses that we should prevent the occurrence of the "synthetic fallacy" problem, which is to say that we assume that all the other institutions take the same action, but it may not be suitable for one single institution to use the seemingly correct method, and the problem of the whole system may be worsened because of that.

He (2007a, 2007b) also points out that we should not only rely on some short-term or temporary emergency measures to realize financial stability, but should establish a long-term mechanism. This requires us to pay close attention to the state of financial operations under the financial opening conditions, and take measures like prevention, rescue and crisis management accordingly. More importantly, we should also deepen financial reform, facilitate financial innovation, and improve the legal system to promote the steady and sound development of financial industry to strengthen the overall capacity and competitiveness of financial system. William says that a new macro financial stability framework should be established to resist systematic imbalance on both domestic and international levels.

1.7 OVERALL ASSESSMENT OF DOMESTIC AND FOREIGN RESEARCH

With a comprehensive review of various research documents, although there is a large number of works and theoretic discussions over financial stability in domestic and foreign academia, many of the theories and pragmatic problems are not well understood. What is financial stability? How do we measure the financial stability of a country. So far no particular conclusion has been reached. What impacts might be exerted on the country by intensifying financial internalization? What experiences have the developed and developing countries gained in the process of financial internalization? There is a shortage of systematic study. In terms of how to strengthen the prevention of financial risk effectively for a country, the current research needs to be further deepened. The relation between financial openness and financial stability is not as simple as what we imagined. Generally speaking, the competition will be fiercer if the financial industry is more open, and the shock on the financial system will be bigger. In the cases of Singapore and Hong Kong SAR, the increased openness of their banking industry will not necessarily lead to more financial instability and higher risk, which need further research. Currently, the concentration of international financial capital increases the liquidity and speculativeness of international capital, while at the same time the integration of physical and virtual economy is strengthened, which is mainly reflected by the increasing convergence of international commodity futures and options market with the international financial market and intensifying volatility. This phenomenon also needs highly attention and further study.

Presently at the micro level, there are more in-depth studies concerning financial risk, while at the macro level such researches are few and without deep discussion in many areas. For instance: (i) the recognition and measurement of financial openness and security need to be further studied; (ii) the evaluation of macro financial fragility and stability requires further exploration; (iii) with the extension of the channels and means of international capital flow, the flow rate and velocity grow continuously and the effects of spillover and contagion from the communication and interaction between the international and domestic markets are more prominent — the method and mechanism of communication together with effective prevention measures all need deeper research; (iv) questions such as whether there is a causal relationship between the sophistication of a country's financial basic infrastructure and its financial security, and what the quantitative relation between financial stability and economic development is, and how to choose and upgrade the financial supervision and financial stability and efficiency, should all be further studied; (v) under internal and external equilibrium conditions, what quantitative relation should be maintained between exchange rate, interest rate, foreign debt, capital account balance, foreign reserve, and financial stability? This also needs in-depth analysis; (vi) cross-border financial acquisition's control over a country's financial service sector and the monopoly and anti-monopoly are all significant areas that require further and deeper discussion.

Chapter 2

Monetary Policy and Financial Stability: From the Perspective of Financial Accelerator

The foundation of the China Banking Regulatory Commission (CBRC) on April 28, 2003 marked the end of the era when the People's Bank of China (PBOC) acted as monetary policy, financial supervision, and commercial bank at the same time. Instead, the PBOC can give more attention to monetary policymaking and policy implementation. Meanwhile, it still attaches great importance to financial stability, which is one of the key objectives of monetary policy in China. Years of studying the financial practices in countries all over the world have revealed that financial and monetary stability, as dual goals of monetary policy, have common ground although are sometimes at odds with each other. Thus to address discrepancies and deal with the relation of the two goals in a graceful manner are crucial for the central bank to perform its obligatory duties.

2.1 CONSISTENCY BETWEEN MONETARY POLICY AND FINANCIAL STABILITY

2.1.1 Effect of monetary policy on financial stability

Monetary policy is of great importance to financial stability. Its effect on the latter is recognizable in two ways: commodity price and the rate of interest.

(i) Stability of commodity price

A stable commodity price is a necessity to ensure a sound financial situation, for the reason that inflation distorts price signal, undermines effective dislocation of resources, and accelerates the production of asset bubble.[1] Proper measures should be included in a country's monetary policy to keep a steady currency value of the country. Otherwise, inflation will develop into hyperinflation at a blistering speed. Once the inflation becomes out of control, commodity price rises sharply, depreciating currency, and making nominal interest rate lower than the inflation rate. There will be a big bank run when the actual rate of interest ends up being negative. In the meantime, financing activities in monetary markets pushes the nominal rate of interest up due to inflation, resulting in decrease in security prices and erratic state of stock markets. In the later phase of hyperinflation, the public loses confidence in the country's currency, starts to rely on paper money, and even resorts to exchange of goods. Under such circumstances, the country's currency system will collapse, triggering chaos and instability of its financial system (He, 2007). In addition, inflation will be driven downward to a low or even a negative level if a country adopts a continuously tight monetary policy, putting banks at the risk of bankruptcy as their deposits decrease when people start to prefer cash instead of bankbooks.

(ii) Stability of interest rate

A stable interest rate is also crucial to guarantee financial stability. Large fluctuation of the interest rate is likely to create additional risks for the management of financial organizations and therefore to disrupt steady conditions of financial markets. Take a sharp increase in interest rate as an example. The rise will cause immense capital loss to long-term bonds and

[1] For instance, the banking crisis that Nordic countries were faced with in the late 1880s and early 1890s occurred because of the then loose monetary policy and delayed policy adjustment.

mortgage loans, making organizations owning the lost assets suffer. Secondly, it discourages consumption but attracts deposit for banks; enterprises have low demands for loans, leading to inactive investment and overall economic activities. Moreover, the increase drags down stock prices and thus disturbs capital markets. That is why global financial crises in historical records are, in most cases, attributed to the rocketing rate of increase. Therefore, measures should be taken by a country in its monetary policy to stabilize the rate of home currency. Meanwhile, an imposed control over the rate of interest is also unfavorable to the stability of the financial system. If the interest rate is unable to adjust itself according to changes of economic conditions, it becomes unresponsive to the economic environment and disharmonious with the rules of economic development. Consequently, a sudden adjustment measure will see an overreaction of financial markets.

2.1.2 The role of financial stability in monetary policy

(i) Financial stability assists the realization of monetary policy goals

With regard to the concept of financial stability, we can find that monetary policy and the policy of financial stability overlap each other. For instance, currency steadiness is one of the ultimate goals for both policies. As a public function, financial stability aims at a series of objectives such as stability of price, rate of interest, and financial markets. Meanwhile, it is widely acknowledged that reducing the inflation rate and realizing price stability are basic and standing goals of monetary policy (He, 2007). Thus theoretically speaking, the policy of financial stability covers the monetary objectives too.

(ii) Financial stability promotes the implementation of monetary policy

Approaches taken for financial stability by a country contribute to efficient implementation of relevant monetary policy. During economic crisis, for example, a government takes such steps as providing liquidity, government guarantee, and nationalization to ensure a stable financial situation, which facilitates an easy monetary policy. In the period of business expansion, measures such as bridging government expenses, enforcing macro control, and raising tax burden level in order to prevent bubbles from expanding give support to a tight monetary policy. Thus, the policies of financial stability and of monetary concerns are interdependent and interwoven, playing an important role in guiding the development of a nation's economy and society.

2.2 CONFLICTS BETWEEN MONETARY POLICY AND FINANCIAL STABILITY

Apart from being on the positive side of influence, financial stability can sometimes hinder the enforcement of a monetary policy due to its difficulty in qualification and complicated operating mechanism.

2.2.1 Liquidity added during financial crisis deviates from monetary policy goals

The financial accelerator effect works in between the financial markets and the real economy.[2] For this reason, in order to break the vicious circle of the financial accelerator effect, it is essential to add liquidity to financial organizations to address a financial crisis. The resurgence of the New Keynesianism has brought government intervention to the forefront of economics since the financial crisis in 2007. Governments across the world gave generous help to the financial markets that were lacking

---

[2]Instable status of finance leads to the lack of mobility within the system, affecting capital supply for the real economy, and decelerates the increase in investment, which further decreases the net value of enterprises. Given that funds offered to an enterprise by financial organizations are virtually based on the guarantee or equity of the enterprise, the lowered net value of the enterprise means it will get less fund supply than before. Investment will shrink and impede normal economic development if the cycle continues, thus forming the financial accelerator effect.

liquidity. China also launched an investment plan worth 4,000 billion RMB to stimulate the national economy. However, as an expansive economic policy works continuously, the rise in prices will exert pressure on social economy. Under such circumstances, the expansive monetary policy will lead up to deviation of money supply and deterioration of inflation expectation if liquidity assistance continues. Therefore, it seems that monetary authorities are in a dilemma when it comes to aiding financial organizations in the hot water of a financial crisis. On the one hand, they should offer liquidity to the organizations in order to get them out of trouble; on the other hand, they have to adopt a tight monetary policy, withdraw liquidity, and raise the rate of increase so that a low inflation can be assured (Wang, 2005). Thus, any improper move in dealing with liquidity or canceling quantitative easing policy at the wrong time can activate the positive feedback mechanism in a monetary policy, and generate a situation where economic stagnation and inflation coexist, posing worse harm to the social economy.

2.2.2 Monetary policy for low inflation disfavors financial stability

The monetary policy for maintaining currency stability and low inflation is likely to put the financial system into danger of liquidity shortage and block the management of financial organizations. Many countries are deploying a monetary policy aimed at keeping commodity price stable and to constrain inflation. As a result, it is necessary to establish a tight monetary policy by, for example, raising the discount rate and the reserve requirement ratio, and to invite sale on the open market. The tight policy results in the reduction of liquidity and of the ability to respond to risks concerning financial organizations. The working fund will not be able to deal with a bank run, if there is any. As to the open market advocated by currency authorities, the consequence would be an increase in market interest rate, the ensuing lift of the cost of debt, and insufficient capacity to replenish liquidity (Wang, 2005). Briefly, an anti-inflation monetary policy weakens financial organizations to the degree of being too impotent to withstand risks or unfavorable elements and therefore being likely to go bankrupt. Nevertheless, the monetary policy aiming at low inflation, although exerts an influence on financial stability, is never the root cause of instable financial situation. Only when there is an excessive credit expansion, will the fragile financial organs and system become weaker in the face of external shocks, such as changes in economic fundamentals or macro policies, or other emergencies, triggering financial crisis.

2.3 STRENGTHENING CENTRAL BANK COORDINATION BETWEEN MONETARY POLICY AND FINANCIAL STABILITY

Since monetary policy and financial stability have something in common, but in the meantime go against the other, central banks need to be careful about coordinating the two when enforcing monetary policy if they want to achieve optimal allocation of funds and resources, and to maintain financial stability.

2.3.1 Create stable and loose monetary conditions

Theoretically speaking, there are two dominant and opposite opinions regarding the relations between currency and financial stability, namely the traditional theory and the new environment hypothesis. Most academics believe that financial instability is usually caused or worsened by overall price fluctuation and therefore that a monetary policy targeted at stable prices facilitates financial stability. It is easy to find that the severe economic or financial crises that have occurred since the 1930s all ended in instable currency value. For example, the inflated consumption and investment in China in the 1980s was virtually inflation; the financial crisis in Asia and the break of the real estate bubbles in Japan in the 1990s were presented by the sharp depreciation of home currencies. Moreover, money movement demonstrates a nature of imbalance in both space and structure under the background of credit economy. This property can be adjusted by commercial banks, although more often than not the adjustment ends up with skewed interests as the banks are profit-oriented, which worsens the imbalanced condition of currency structure and makes the banks' economic activities present pro-cyclicality. Taking into account, the limited ability of commercial banks in adjusting monetary environment, the central bank needs to readjust by proceeding from the overall social interests on behalf of the country. This time, the adjustment represents the interests of a whole country rather than those of individual economies, in which way the monetary policy can be more rational and efficient in guiding the circulation and structural adjustments of currency in social economy, and in realizing monetary stability.

2.3.2 Rational control over total money supply

Macroscopically speaking, both inflation and deflation are indicators of a nation's insecure financial conditions. Inflation brings about constant growth of market prices due to excessive money supply, while deflation arouses continuous drop of market prices because of insufficient money supply. There is no exception for a country's economic development, be it economic or financial operating, to be affected and harmed by immoderate inflation or unremitting deflation. As for China, its history shows no record about the outbreak of financial crises, although this does not mean that its monetary market can be free from systemic risks, which usually show up in some special periods when the inflation data stays high, money depreciates at a fast speed, and domestic commodity prices appear to be uncertain. So in order to prevent inflation, currency authorities should maintain a neutral money supply, which refers to a money supply that fits natural economic growth rate and a normal financial deepening coefficient. Research of China's financial practices over the years reveals the fundamental factors needed to maintain the country's financial stability. These factors are economic stability and managing the relations between preventing financial risks and facilitating economic growth in a proper fashion; to keep a steady increase in money supply under the condition of raising the quality of loans; and to implement prudent monetary policy for the sake of a continuously fast and healthy development of national economy (Meng, 2005).

2.3.3 Stabilize the interest rate of RMB

As the financial market becomes increasingly open, the marketization of interest rate turns out to be the main factor of financial market reform in China. It includes the marketization of determination, transmission, structure, and management of interest rate. By marketization of interest rate, it means that the level of interest rate offered by financial organizations when the operating lease in monetary market is decided by market demand and supply. In other words, the rights to decide and change interest rates are handed over to financial organizations, which would adjust their interest rates based on their own financial conditions and their prediction of market movement. As a result, an interest rate system is formed, where various interest rates are in a harmonious state of allocating interests and are capable of achieving effective layered transmission with the benchmark rate of the central bank as the guide. The marketization of interest rate is one of the crucial steps required for China to push its financial industry into market, as well as one of the indicators of national economic operation's shift to the mode of market economy. With regard to the price of funds, the short-term interest rate is one of the most important economic variables — it is mainly influenced by community prices in markets, and the relation of supply and demand of funds. Therefore, it will certainly play a prominent role in promoting financial stability if it remains stable in a certain period, as the rise and fall of interest rates are bound to reflect financial instability such as inflation and deflation. It is possible for the central bank to stabilize interest rates by making full use of monetary policy instruments. For example, the open market operation, like the open transactions of securities, can directly exert an influence on the level and structure of interest rates and stimulate or discourage economic growth. At the meantime, given that China is still exercising regulation on interest rates, to adopt a prompt and gradually advancing policy of interest rate adjustment might be the best approach for China in its course of marketization of interest rates.

2.3.4 Establish an effective communication and coordination mechanism between financial stability and monetary policy

Since there are conflicts and contradictions between financial stability and monetary policy, it is necessary for the currency authorities to strengthen the coordination of the two when enforcing monetary policy. A central bank, for example, needs to coordinate from two aspects. On the one hand, it should communicate with the market. As a micro market entity, a financial organization is often faced with the problem of asymmetric information during its decision-making process, leading to the deviation of asset prices from fundamentals, and generating asset bubbles that arouse financial crises. Being a sector that makes macroscopic decisions, the central bank can guide the direction of market expectation by communicating with main market players. On the other hand, there should be communication between macro decision-making sectors. The coordination in terms of financial stability and currency policy involves a wide range of fields and sometimes requires resources from several sectors. Thus, the power of only one ministry or financial supervisory department is not enough. To ensure the authority and efficiency of an organization's coordination, we should establish a high-level organization of such a kind to be in charge of nationwide work to coordinate for financial stability. For instance, a joint working team formed by "One Bank and Three Commissions," the PBOC, CBRC, China Securities Regulatory Commission (CSRC), China Insurance Regulatory Commission (CIRC), and staff in the Ministry of Finance of China, has been established to exchange ideas regularly, take prompt measures whenever there is any problem, and to prevent the spread of risk. At the same time, it should be clarified that the PBOC is of dominant position in the organization. A mechanism is set up led by the PBOC, for example, a coordination group, which is responsible for making data collection and exchanges routine work and building a system for information search and notification. Briefly, this coordination mechanism will help solve a series of complicated problems that a single sector cannot tackle.

2.4 THE EFFECT OF MONETARY POLICY AS A FINANCIAL ACCELERATION

Monetary policy has long been deemed a scientific subject. Academic endeavor has witnessed the involvement from monetary neutrality to demand management, to supply shock by the schools of rational expectation and real business cycle, and to new Keynesianism. However, in tackling the latest global financial crisis, governments across the world carried out a flexible, fluctuant, and unconventional monetary policy, which, different from gradualist one in normal times, is much closer to art rather than science. As the world economy is slowly recovering, it is the time for academia to think over the advantages and disadvantages of the monetary policies during the crisis. Nowadays, the economic cycle presents the features of financial business cycle. By introducing his core concept of counter-crisis into the crisis analysis, Ben Bernanke, the Chairman of the Federal Reserve System (FRB), proposed the theory of the financial accelerator model, which allows us an innovative perspective of observation.

Bernanke and others (Bernanke & Gertler 1989; Bernanke *et al.*, 1996, 1999) coined the financial accelerator theory based on their study of the Great Depression. It introduced financial market friction into the analytical framework of economic fluctuation, and expounded the mechanism of initial reverse impact being worsened and transmitted through state changes of credit markets due to imperfection of the markets. As to monetary policy, the financial accelerator effect results in the cyclic endogenous nonlinear character of monetary policy efficiency and poses a direct impact on the effectiveness of expansive monetary policy of counter-crisis nature. In the meantime, the financial accelerator theory reveals the pattern of "financial crisis — increasing credit cost — constant drop in real output" and the micromechanism of feedback cycling between financial turbulence and economic downturn during the crisis. This is the internal mechanism of operating monetary policy during crisis. Thanks to the research of large crises by taking the theory as its theoretical support, the FRB can provide prompt and effective response to the financial crisis this time around, saving the American economy from the danger of recession and avoiding another Great Depression.

To put it simply, the financial accelerator theory refers to the effect that enlarges and fortifies initial economic impact by changing the conditions of credit markets (Bernanke *et al.*, 1996). In reality, one of the characteristics of the financial system is the common presence of asymmetric information, which is likely to lead to adverse selection and moral hazard, giving rise to the "entrust agency" problem between borrowers, to lift the cost of funds for external financing, or say form external finance premium (Bernanke & Gertler, 1989). Let us suppose that there are contradictions in credit markets, or that cost and total financing demands do not change, or there is asymmetric information. In this case, we find a negative correlation between extra cost in external financing and net asset value of borrowers (Bernanke, 1996). Moreover, the negative relation between external finance premium and the net asset value of borrowers is the key to the transmission mechanism of the financial accelerator. Apparently, the asset net value such as profits of an enterprise or asset prices will change positively with economic cycle, forcing external finance premium to alter negatively. Consequently, the corporate financing was affected, followed by fluctuation of investment, expenditure, and production of the enterprise (Bernanke, 1996). Thus, negative shock or the natural ending of economic expansion could make financial conditions worse and affect the access to credit for enterprises and families. At the same time, the demands for external financing, for example, involuntary inventory financing, bring about the fall of expenses or yield, aggravating economic downturn. In short, the mechanism where changes in credit markets expand and transmit the effect of initial monetary shock is called the financial accelerator (Bernanke & Gertler, 1989).

Thanks to the financial accelerator effect, the transmission mechanism displays not only the direct traditional effect of fund cost, but also indirect effect through asset price and credit. We can give an explanation for this based on the theories of Bernanke & Gertler (1989). Suppose that there are phrases 0 and 1, and an entrepreneur invests in phrase 0 and receives output in phrase 1. There are also two ways of investment, which is fixed capital K and variable input x_1. At the end of phrase 1, the entrepreneur can sell fixed capital at a price q_1 and the variable input (raw materials in this case) is completely depreciated when it was used. The output of phrase 1 is $a_1 f(x_1)$. $f(\cdot)$ means added concave function. Moreover, the entrepreneur is likely to own money flow and liabilities inherited in previous time. Therefore, the expression of variable input is

$$x_1 = a_0 f(x_0) + b_1 - r_0 b_0. \quad (2\text{-}1)$$

b_1 refers to liability. New liability will be paid off in phase 1 with an interest rate of r_1. The entrepreneur chooses x_1 and b_1, to maximize the net output of phase 1. The transfer of fixed asset ownership will be costless if s/he breaches a contract. In other words, fixed asset can be used as a pledge.

Thus, we find that the funds provided by borrowers are constrained by the net present value of fixed asset, i.e.,

$$b_1 \leq \left(\frac{q_1}{r_1}\right)K. \tag{2-2}$$

Combining equations (2-1) and (2-2), we get

$$x_1 \leq a_0 f(x_0) + \left(\frac{q_1}{r_1}\right)K - r_0 b_0. \tag{2-3}$$

We can discuss the generational approach of the financial accelerator effect on a monetary policy based on the framework acquired here. If the enterprise net present value (q_1/r_1) K is less than the optimal investment x_1* [x_1* satisfies the equation $a_1f'(x_1) = r_1$], the external finance premium is equal to the difference between $a_1f'(x_1)$, the shadow value of internal funds and r_1, the credit cost in markets [i.e., $a_1f'(x_1)$-r_1]. The reduction in net present value of the enterprise assets lifts up external finance premium $a_1f'(x_1)$-r_1 and cuts down the expenditure and output.[3] The direct and indirect effects of monetary policy can be seen clearly from the aforementioned. Direct effect shows as the traditional approach of capital cost, or the increase in r_0, the interest rates on debt, dragging down expenditure of a company, for it cuts down the net cash flow, $a_1f(x_1)$-r_0b_0, with present interest payment removed, showing the influence of changes in internal financing sources on investment of the company. Indirect effect refers to the rise of interest rates, and reduces the investment of a company due to the decrease in the net asset value (q_1/r_1), meaning a drop in the net present value of borrowers. This effect demonstrates the influence of changes in the external finance premium of a company's net value on the company's expenditure on investment. Therefore, by resorting to the two effects, a tight monetary policy lowers the asset-value-based financial position of

[3]This is under the circumstances of the tightening constraint of equation (2-3) and as the net present value (q_1/r_1) K decreases, the variable input x_1 decreases as well. According to the general settings regarding production function, marginal productivity $f'(x_1)$ climbs and so does $a_1f'(x_1)$, the shadow value of internal assets.

borrowers, lifts up external finance premium, and cuts down the possibilities of financing, compelling enterprises to tighten constraint on financing and to draw back expenditure and investment.

Figure 2-1 demonstrates the relationship between monetary policy and financial accelerator effect. The core of the financial accelerator's operating mechanism is the change of real financing cost caused by external finance premium. The real financing cost of families and enterprises can be acquired by adding a risk-free interest rate and an external finance premium. The monetary policy has a direct influence upon risk-free interest rates, which is considered as the traditional approach of interest rate or of capital cost, as is shown in I in Figure 2-1. Meanwhile, the monetary policy generates the financial accelerator effect by exerting influence on the balance sheet of an enterprise, or a family and bank credits, which is the indirect effect that acts on the economy through affecting external finance premium and then real financing cost, as is displayed in II. Moreover, III shows that prominent changes in asset price severely affect enterprises, families, and banks' balance sheets during financial turbulence, further fortifying the impact of financial accelerator on entity economies. Briefly, a monetary policy exercises effect on the net wealth of an enterprise or a family through assets and liabilities and on banks through credits, and enhances the financial accelerator mechanism by

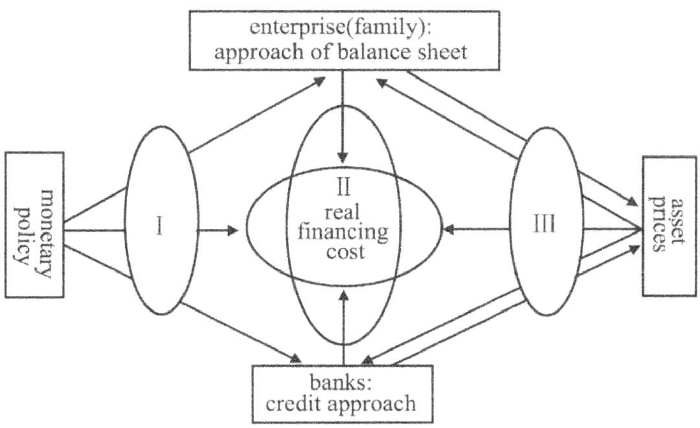

Figure 2-1. Financial accelerator effect of monetary policy.

influencing asset prices. Consequently, a monetary policy will become a driver for the financial accelerator and enlarge the cyclical fluctuation of the economy if it is low in flexibility, effectiveness, and prospectiveness.

2.5 EFFICACY OF COUNTER-CRISIS MONETARY POLICY: A STUDY OF FINANCIAL ACCELERATOR THEORY

During the latest financial crisis, the relaxation of monetary policies by major economies is reflected from two aspects. On the one hand, the rate of interest was reduced by a large margin after the crisis and the world entered into an unprecedented era of ultra low interest rates. On the other hand, the central banks of major economies adopted a quantitative easing monetary policy and added a large quantity of liquidity to markets through diversified non-conventional currency channels, to mitigate financial tension and to guarantee a sound operation of credit markets. At the same time, they made efforts to ensure financial stability, in particular to prevent financial organizations from going out of business (Bernanke, 2008a, 2008b).

2.5.1 Expansionary monetary policy and its effect

The FRB has slashed interest rates ten times since September 2007 to December 2008, three times of which were a decrease by 75 basis points. During that period, the federal funds rate (FFR) decreased from 5.25% to 0–0.25%. The Bank of England has lowered benchmark rate by 350 basis points to 1% in five consecutive times. On October 31, 2008, the Bank of Japan decided to reduce the interbank unsecured overnight interest from 0.5% to 0.3%, which was unprecedented. Despite that, the FFR and the interest rate of American government bonds were cut by a large margin in the initial period of interest rate reduction, while loan interest rates for both individuals and enterprises increased. Commercial banks and other financial agencies pulled back on loans and the tight credit market remained unchanged. These events made people pay attention to the effectiveness of low-interest-rate monetary policy.

In fact, the rise of actual loan interest rate at the initial stage of implementing such monetary policy can be interpreted by the financial accelerator theory. The scale of the financial accelerator mechanism is closely related to the primary economic state and financial conditions of economies, accounting for the business-cycle-based, dynamic, endogenous, and nonlinear features of the mechanism. Since the fine financial state of economy and economies require less finance premium for external financing of an enterprise of a family, the negative shock from current economy, if rich in funds internally, will exercise little impact on investment. On the contrary, bad financial conditions are likely to cause terrible deterioration of information issues and ascend external financing costs, highlighting the function of the financial accelerator on economic recession. The cycle-based endogenous nonlinearity of the monetary policy means that the adjustment of risk-free interest rates dominates the overall financing rate, if both the economy and the financial market are experiencing little fluctuation. Since the effect of the financial accelerator is not prominent, there will not be great changes in external finance premium. Meanwhile, when the economy and finance fluctuate greatly, external finance premium will change severely to make the dual effects, directly and indirectly, of the monetary policy possible. What is more, under the circumstance of extreme financial turbulence, there is a possibility that external finance premium leads to the variation of financing rates and weakens the function of risk-free rates. As a result, at the beginning of the crisis, the risk premium rose higher and the actual financing rates ascended, regardless of the down-regulation of the FFR. Financial markets suffering crises usually present such phenomena as exorbitant risk pricing and high credit spreads. However, reducing the interest rate is the most direct and most effective way to deal with the growing degree of asymmetric information caused by financial restriction, to block the transfer of the crisis to the macroeconomy and the interactive feedback system in between, and to keep the macroeconomy away from turbulence as much as possible (Bernanke, 2008a,b; Mishkin, 2008a).

2.5.2 Reasons for carrying out non-conventional quantitative easing monetary policy

The financial accelerator theory was concluded from the study of the Great Depression. It reveals the inner mechanism that the cyclical feedback system of financial disturbances and the economic-activity contraction leads to profound and lasting economic turbulence. Fisher (1933), the prestigious academic who analyzed the Great Depression, pointed out that the wide-range deterioration of balance sheet for borrowers and simultaneous free-fall drop of output and of prices from 1929 to 1933 caused a self-accelerating vicious cycle of debt deflation in the American economy. The worsening of credit market conditions turned out to be not only a passive response to the decline in actual business activities, but also a major inducement to economic recession and depression.

Let us have a look at the dynamic evolvement stage of the financial accelerator (Figure 2-2). During economic expansion, the main performance of the financial accelerator is the spiral cycle of "net asset value and security value increase — external finance premium decrease — credit expansion — output augments — asset net value ascends." The extraordinary increase in credits leads to the problem debt of economic sectors; the level of leverage rises, and the economy becomes highly fragile. The

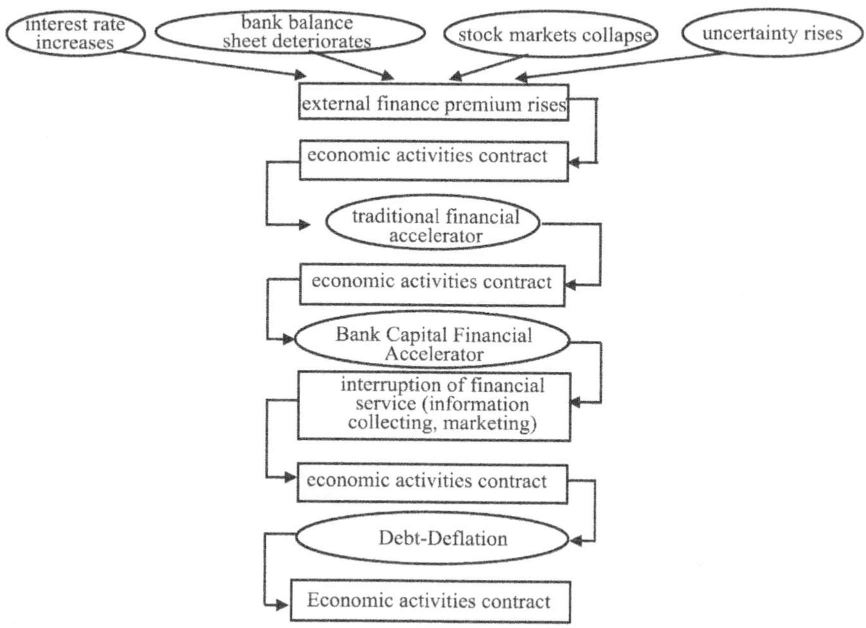

Figure 2-2. Dynamic evolvement of the financial accelerator.

increase in interest rate and changeable prices in the stock markets result in reduced profits of enterprises, cash flow, and asset net value. In the meantime, the information issues worsen to the degree of external finance premium rising, banks pulling back loans, and economic activities contracting. At this time, the financial accelerator begins to function but with light influence, which is demonstrated by credit reluctance and more severe credit rationing. The constant deterioration of fundamentals pushes up loan-default rates, which results in the augmentation of loan losses and provision, along with the decline of profit and capital. Moreover, the asset price fall leads to liquidity shortage; the collective irrational selling of risk capital by financial organizations is prone to cause sharp decline of asset price and deterioration of balance sheets. Under the supervision requirements like capital adequacy ratio, the bank capital accelerator exerts contractive force on credits. During the period when the crisis was in full swing, the financial accelerator effect mainly works through the bank capital financial accelerator.[4] When a crisis comes to its most serious level, the circulation turns out to be faster and fiercer. Driven by deep panic, financial organizations will rush to sell their risk capital, causing irrational price fall, bankruptcy of banks, termination of intermediary service, systemic crisis in banks, and even collapse of the complete finance system.

One of the grave consequences if the financial system collapses is the overall paralysis of the role as information intermediary that financial organizations once played. As Fisher (1933) remarked, the deterioration of conditions in financial markets not only simply means a passive response to the decline of actual economic activities, but also shows itself as a major force that triggers economic recession and depression. All activities regarding investment and financing in the market are done with the assistance of financial organizations, by market creating and information collecting. Once the financial system collapses, such services will not be offered as efficiently as before. In addition, the blocking of information will lead to adverse selection, moral risks, and more severe credit crunch, thus the

[4]A bank's balance sheet is pro-cyclical. Under the regulation of capital, an endogenous change will happen to loaning behaviors. In this way, the fortification and transmission of the economic cycle is possible. Therefore, the bank capital financial accelerator comes into being.

contraction issue of economic activities becomes more critical. By analyzing the significance of currency and total finance volume during the Great Depression in America, Bernanke (1983) emphasized that the collapse of the financial system was the key factor that decided the depth and duration of the Great Depression. Besides, there are two major reasons for the credit flow being interrupted in banks. The first reason is the breakdown of banking system, and the second is the rapid reduction of net wealth of borrowers. The credit crunch resulting from these turned economic slowdown into the Great Depression from 1930 to 1933. Moreover, the second top consequence of the financial system's collapse is the negative impact on money supply. The remarkable decrease in money supply and rocketing of interest rates are inevitable if banks go bankrupt and bank run happens. This further gives rise to debt deflation as Fisher (1933) described and drags the economy downward into a widely spread and lasting recession.

In the whole process, the key to enlarge and transmit shocks by the financial accelerator lies in information issues and the central position financial organizations have in producing information and creating markets. Therefore, it is necessary to guarantee that the financial system works well in crises or turbulences. As one of the most important aspects embodied in the counter-crisis monetary policy, the quantitative easing policy introduces a large quantity of liquidity into markets through all kinds of non-conventional channels. This is a key step that aims at ensuring financial stability, retaining a normal operation in credit markets, and restarting the functions of financial markets. In confronting this crisis, all governments and currency authorities joined hands to rescue the financial organizations on the verge of bankruptcy in order to avoid a banking crisis and the collapse of the financial system. In this way, the economy recovered quickly, unlike the situation with the Great Depression.

2.6 MONETARY POLICIES THAT IMPROVE FINANCIAL STABILITY: FOCUSING ON ASSET BUBBLE AND INFLATION RISK

In the recent financial crisis of 2007, central banks added a large amount of liquidity to markets in time, which restarted the functions of the financial system and successfully prevented economy from going into recession.

However, what is worth mentioning is that the expanded liquidity did not necessarily bring about economic rejuvenation. On the contrary, it transferred quickly to assets. Thus, the globally practiced quantitative easing monetary policy is prone to generate another round of asset bubble or runaway inflation expectation. If currency authorities can no longer control overinflation expectation, it is probable that severe inflation issues are to occur in the future (Mishkin, 2009). From the perspective of the financial accelerator theory, the monetary policy for the post-crisis era should attach intense attention to asset bubble and inflation risk.

Firstly, set monetary stability (or stability of currency value) as the primary target of monetary policy. When the currency value is unstable and debt contracts tend to be short term, the balance sheets of non-financial enterprises are likely to suffer due to difficulties of cash flow or liquidity if the interest rate is increased. In this case, financial and economic systems become more fragile. When inflation occurs, the lowered actual debt value encourages financing; inflation, asset prices and debt guarantee effect are interwoven because of the financial accelerator, promoting the expansion of total demand and lifting the general level of market price. Conversely, the "debt deflation" cycle will come into being, along with inflation for the reason that the actual debt value augments. It is shown clearly in the financial accelerator theory that inflation is the main cause of debt crisis and extended economic recession, like the Great Depression. Therefore, maintaining monetary stability should be given top priority under the flexible framework of inflation targeting.

Secondly, stick to a flexible asset-price-based monetary policy as a responding rule. With the assistance of the financial accelerator, asset price rises to stimulate the total demand and cut down the demand if it lowers. The currency authorities should carry out a regulatory policy that leans against the wind, aiming at stabilizing total economy. Taking that into account, a monetary policy is supposed to pay close attention to the ups and downs of asset price and its influence on the economy. This requires the currency authorities to keep an eye on the total demand inflation that might happen when asset price changes, and on credit growth that is related to the variation of asset price, total demand, and commodity price. Specifically speaking, the central bank should not respond to the change of asset price if the price fluctuation does not break away from the fundamentals and further trigger growth in credit, total demand, and pressure of inflation. When inflation pressure is formed due to the changes in asset price, the central bank should actively adjust monetary policy so that the pressure can be resolved at primary stage. Otherwise, if the monetary policy fails to respond to the pressure or enhances the pressure, the regulatory power of the policy will be an unremitting harm to economy.

Moreover, improve the flexibility and foresight of monetary policy. The existence of the financial accelerator effect accounts for the increasing growth of currency, growing complicity in regulating monetary policy, the asymmetry and nonlinearity of the policy, and low-policy effectiveness. Thus, the implementation of monetary policy should make efforts to increase its flexibility and foresight, and to counteract the amplified action of the financial accelerator on economic turbulence. To constrain the working of the financial accelerator through monetary policy, we should have an efficient control over inflation by inflation targeting, for inflation remains at a certain level, the expectation of microeconomic units is stable, and the nominal variable viscosity poses minor force to push forward the financial accelerator. In the meantime, the existence of the financial accelerator should be taken into account when establishing and implementing monetary policy. During this process, the central bank should decide on the proper policy instrument, and the scale and timing of adjustment for responding to policy operation by predicting and judging the credit market, in which way the uncertainty caused by the financial accelerator is to be erased, and the rationality, steadiness, and foreseeability of macro control fortified. Besides, we should take into consideration the influence of asymmetric and nonlinearity by the financial accelerator during the implementation of monetary policy, as well as the difficulties in financing faced by small and medium sized enterprises when carrying out tight monetary policy. When it comes to economic recession, the more powerful and aggressive policy and other supporting policies are preferred. To realize price stability, currency authorities should pay attention to the impact of capital adequacy supervision on the economic cycle. As with a bank system of inadequate capital, more prompt and quicker response from currency authorities is demanded, only by which can the monetary policy constrain the effect of bank capital financial accelerator under the capital adequacy supervision.

Lastly, take economic growth, currency stability, and financial stability into a unified target framework. These three elements, as demonstrated by the financial accelerator, are of logical consistence internally, so they should be taken into consideration instead of simply pursuing counter inflation, which is dangerous and not advisable. For example, there is an overall inflation occurring to economies during a period of economic expansion, but the results might not be satisfactory if only certain measures to constrain inflation, like rising interest rates, are taken. That is because enterprises are pushed to the verge of problem debt by the financial accelerator at the same time. The rise in interest rate will disfavor the cash flow in enterprises or families, cut down the expected rate of return of the financial organizations, break the asset price bubble to unsettle financial markets, and produce backward effects from the financial accelerator to give rise to drastic economic fluctuation or even recession. Therefore, currency authorities must take into account the financial conditions and financial position of economies. Moreover, as the financial accelerator effect tells us, monetary and financial stability are two policy targets that are woven together and mutually intensified, requiring that the efforts taken in pursuit of either of them should give consideration to the other. Therefore, it is necessary for a currency authority to be scrupulous on regulatory policy concerning counter inflation. To be specific, monetary policy addressing inflation and asset price variation should give full consideration to debt accumulation and the level of leverage, as considerable changes in asset price are likely to cause credit expansion or shrinkage, which affect business cycle fluctuation. Thus, it is suggested that central banks aiming for monetary stability in the short term should consider the negative influence that the asset price fluctuation may exert on credit alteration, finance, and the economy in the end.

To conclude, given that easy liquidity may bring about asset bubble and inflation risk in a post-crisis era, monetary policy should take reverse operation and draw back overused liquidity as soon as inflation is about to rise when the financial market starts to revive. At the same time, the policy should coordinate the relationships among economic, financial, and monetary stability as much as possible under the framework of flexible inflation targets.

Chapter 3

Government's Function and Financial Stability

Essentially, the relationship between governments and financial stability, or the relationship between governments and market, is an old topic. With the development of financial globalization and economic integration, the explosion of regional and worldwide financial crisis situations is happening more and more, causing countless losses of financial assets and social wealth, and bringing great damage or even disaster to the development of economy and society worldwide. Nowadays, every country is attaching increasingly importance on financial stability, in the study of which academia is making fruitful achievement. Viewing from the perspective of financial stability, this chapter will discuss government position and behavior, and studies government regulation in financial stability, theoretically, and practically.

3.1 THE GOVERNMENT IS NECESSARY FOR MAINTAINING FINANCIAL STABILITY

3.1.1 Financial stability is a special quasi-public production

Based on the non-competitive and non-exclusive principle in public economics, articles can be classified into three categories: personal articles, competitive, and exclusive; public production, non-competitive, and non-exclusive; quasi-public production, including exclusive but non-competitive "club production," competitive in consumption but non-exclusive public resource production, and public production not sufficiently exclusive and competitive in consumption with positive externality. These productions vary in the way of resource allocation. Normally, the supply of personal articles can be effectively solved within the market mechanism; governments directly provide public production; quasi-public production is supplied by governments, or by governments and markets both.

In a sense, financial stability can be seen as a non-exclusive quasi-public production with positive externality. Financial stability is a sign of the stability of macroeconomy, as well as a stable society. Enterprises and residents, as participants of market economy, can only make transfer, delivery, loan, and other financial activities in the context of a stable financial system. Financial stability is a public production needed for every economic actor, with which the economy and society can develop steadily. Therefore, governments, together with markets, should provide this quasi-public production to economic actors.

3.1.2 The failure of markets requires governments' appropriate intervention in financial markets

The history of the development of finance indicates that market failure is commonly the trouble source, according to which governments can intervene in financial markets. Stiglitz (1989) pointed out that governments should be involved with maintaining the stability of depositing, financial system, and the development of banks and capital markets in the context of markets' failure. Because of such factors as imperfect competition, information asymmetry, economic externality and scale economy, the financial market with little or no regulation will further aggravate the instability of finance, for which governments should take such measures as macro control and timely intervention. Firstly, the scale economy and imperfect competition possess instable financial factors. Owing to the great influence of scale economy on financial markets, many financial institutions have to expand and set up new business networks, which could possibly lower the competitive tension and then raise the price of financial services. Consequently, the chances of optimal allocation of resources are slim, harming financial stability. Secondly, the adverse selections and moral risks caused by information asymmetry will hazard financial stability. Many economists have proven the universal existence of markets' failure and then make the conclusion that it is essential for governments to regulate the market (Stiglitz, 1982). For instance, the most active capital hunters, who are the most likely to gain the acceptance of the lenders, are always the borrowers who most likely trigger bad consequences. Therefore, the adverse selection inevitably increases the financial instability. Governments' intervention is natural in that information is largely public production. Thirdly, the negative externality of financial markets calls for governments' intervention. A typical case is that the bankruptcy of a bank may produce a chain reaction, bringing down depositors' trust in the banking system, which then leads to a banking crisis or causing serious financial panic. In light of the huge destructive power of negative externality, it is essential that governments intervene in the financial market.

3.1.3 High-risk finance requires governments' regulation

The financial industry is full of high risk itself. However, many risks will be amplified indefinitely if financial leverage plays its role, which is a direct threat to the stability of the financial sector. Financial investment is high yield and high risk, different from investment in other industries, in that it is based on the low interest rate and interest-free financing of financial institutions. For instance, the price of such financial products as stock, futures, and foreign exchange fluctuates every day, for which the investment of some will soar in a short time, while others vanish into nothing. This is nothing but common in financial futures market, as has been the case in the past and will be in future. The high risk that accompanies financial sectors will put those sectors in danger at any time, threatening social and economic stability. Therefore, it is natural that governments control the risk and maintain the stability of financial markets.

3.1.4 Governments' intervention is a traditional system

Western scholarships came up with the *Laissez-faire* policy, in which they assume that finance will maintain stable by itself. However, it is obvious that this policy is an exceptional case, while governments' intervention is a traditional system (Dowd, 2004). The Laissez-faire policy system only runs in complete information symmetry and perfect competition, which the actual world is far from having. Therefore, the world of Laissez-faire policy is far from being workable. Contrary to Laissez-faire policy, governments' intervention doctrine has such advantages as the macro control of the central bank and its accompanying rules and laws, with which the inflation and financial instability can be solved. This indicates that governments' intervention is needed from the very beginning. In other words, it is historically true that governments intervene in financial system.

3.2 THE FUNCTION AND THE ROLE OF THE GOVERNMENT IN MAINTAINING FINANCIAL STABILITY

3.2.1 Definition of government

Normally, there are governments in both the broad and the narrow sense. Governments in the broad sense include state legislature, administrative law enforcement departments and judicial organs; governments in the narrow sense only include the state administrative organs, including the central government and local governments. The government of each country has specific functions, within which the economic condition, structure of social class, and principal contradiction will change in several aspects. These aspects include: the adjustment of the range and depth of function; the transfer of the center and focus of its system; the optimization of its active structure, procedure and mechanism; and its integrity and capability of function. The organizational structure of a government is its core; the transfer and adjustment of its function will require structural change accordingly, which will contribute to the transformation of its role and capabilities.

This chapter discusses the relationship between governments' behavior and financial stability on the premise of the changing structure of finance, and the concept of government is further defined in width and in functional structure. The central bank, the China Banking Regulatory Commission (CBRC), the China Securities Regulatory Commission (CSRC), and the China Insurance Regulatory Commission (CIRC) are all included in this chapter too. Under the law of China, the People's Bank of China (PBOC) is a functional department of the State Council, while the CBRC, CSRC, and CIRC are public institutions affiliated to the State Council. Since the State Council grants their power and function, they make the concerted effort to maintain financial stability as the State Council does. However, the State Council can never place them.

3.2.2 The role governments play in maintaining financial stability

It is essential for governments to intervene in the financial market: moderately regulated, the financial market will tend to be stable; immoderately regulated, the financial market will be endangered. Therefore, governments have to find their positions in intervening in the financial market. The absence and overage of regulation are inadvisable.

Firstly, governments' intervention is intended to eliminate imperfect competition and negative externality of financial markets. The markets are commonly recognized as the best choice for optimizing the allocation of resources, however, they are not omnipotent in that they run into failure; governments are supposed to intervene in financial markets in time. Therefore, governments should not only give full play to the market in its allocation of resources, but also strengthen the monitoring on financial monopoly and unhealthy financial behaviors, and provide financial markets a platform for information disclosure.

Secondly, the role of governments is one of rule maker and night watchman. The development of the financial markets is based on rational system and operation environment provided by governments. As rule makers, governments are responsible for making and providing an open, fair, and just law system, known as "fair game rule." In addition, governments have to ensure that these "game rules" are fully observed. As night watchman, governments must regulate financial markets, which can be interpreted in both a broad and a narrow sense. In a broad sense, financial regulation includes regulation on financial institutions, financial markets, financial operation, and financial policies. In a narrow sense, financial regulation covers internal supervisory and auditing systems, regulation on self-disciplinary organizations, and other quasi-intermediaries.

3.3 THE USA GOVERNMENT'S RELIEF EFFORTS IN TWO FINANCIAL CRISES AND ITS LESSONS

Financial resource,[1] which is fundamental and vital, has direct influence on sustainable development. Therefore, when financial institutions fall into trouble, particularly the larger ones, governments will inject capital into those institutions in order to save them. Since the 1900s, capital injection by governments has been a common method employed to help those institutions. The objective is very clear — that is, to prevent these financial institutions going broke, which may cause financial turbulence, panic, and even huge crisis. The USA government is one of them. Their methods, especially improving relative economic systems, have set a good example for our government.

3.3.1 The USA government's capital injection plan in the Great Depression

In the Great Depression, many financial institutions went broke. To prevent the spread of financial crisis, the USA government adopted some measures. In 1932, the Reconstruction Finance Corporation (RFC) was set up to help bankrupt financial institutions. In the beginning, the RFC's terms of credit were as demanding as those of commercial banks. As a result, only a few banks got assistance and financial risks were still spreading. In March 1933, American Congress issued the Emergency Banking Act, which accredited RFC with more rights and more flexibility.

---

[1]According to the description of Bai *et al.* (2001), financial resource can be divided into three levels. The first and the most basic level is the core financial resource, or money capital or funds in a broad sense, the lack of which will result in the severe constraint of social and economic development. The second level refers to entity-based medium resources, including the financial organization system and instruments, acting as the basis upon which the functions of finance play their roles. The third level is the whole-function-based high-level resource that involves the entire functions of the financial system and the institutional environment favorable to the system. This level is the result of interaction between the flow of money capital and the financial system, and between constitutive parts of the financial system.

Table 3-1. The USA government's relief efforts in the Great Depression.

Measures	Contents
Terms of loan	Applicants should accept scrutiny by the RFC and their value should be assessed as well as their possibility to get rid of crisis and operate again. If their possibility were zero, RFC would reject them for funding.
Actively participated in banks' management as prior stockholder	(i) Realized capital injection by purchasing preferred stocks. (ii) Controlled the dividends of common stock strictly. (iii) Intensified supervision over banks, including stock rights. Incompetent bank officials were dismissed. (iv) Strengthened control and management over risks. Made sure banks were still to be regulated by the market, instead of shifting risks by capital injection.
Guaranteed the independence of decision-making to prevent interest groups or RFC from controlling banks	(i) Limited budget. The Congress had supervision and regulation over the RFC's budget to make ends meet. (ii) Strict decision-making and accountability mechanism. Every capital injection decision should pass through collective vote. If an official placed a vote independently, he would take all responsibility. Officials would be held accountable for any loss caused by taking the wrong decisions.

Then, the RFC bought problematic banks preferred stocks as the main form of capital injection to help them out of the trouble, and at the same time, make some economic gains. The RFC played an important role in helping the United States get out of financial crisis. In reality, the achievements were very much related to the economic regimes. At that time, there were strict rules on capital target, process supervision, decision-making, and so on, which constituted the original principles of capital injection (Table 3-1).

After the RFC, Federal Deposit Insurance Company (FDIC) became the new institution to maintain financial stability and help problematic financial institutions. Since the 1950s, the FDIC has been improving the practice of assistance systems. The American government put forward a "necessity" principle that the banks that could get assistance from the FDIC must be a necessity in a community. In the 1980s, the Garn–St. Germaine Depository Institutions Act was issued, which gave the FDIC more rights and powers. The Competitive Equality Banking Act accredited the FDIC with the creation of bridge banks, so the FDIC had more time to find solutions that were more permanent. In 1990s, in order to prevent loan crisis because of overflow injection capital, the American government issued the FDIC Reform Act, which required the FDIC to follow lowest cost and earliest disposal when dealing with broke banks and deposit institutions. To be clear, those measures carried out by the USA government played an important role in maintaining financial stability and achieved great success.

3.3.2 The USA government relief efforts in the noughties crisis

To whether the noughties (2007) financial crisis caused by subprime crisis, the USA government made relief efforts by taking the measures as depicted in Table 3-2. This time, the financial crisis struck the United States as badly as the Great Depression and it had negative influence on other countries too. However, one thing was for sure — the American financial mechanism maintained stability because of the active relief efforts made by the government to avoid it breaking out systematically.

3.3.3 Lessons from the USA Government's crisis relief efforts

The USA government, aiming for financial stability, designed and implemented its capital injection relief efforts to mitigate the risks and bad results caused by the financial crisis. At the same time, the government regarded the prevention of over-interference, mechanism abuse, and ethical risks as a core element, and improved and regulated terms of capital injection, decision-making processes, and supervision after capital injection. The USA government worked hard to achieve two goals: to maintain financial stability and to reduce the cost. Lessons we learn from these aforementioned measures are as follows.

Firstly, it is a government's responsibility to cope with financial crisis and maintain financial stability. Whether at the time of the Great

Table 3-2. The USA government relief efforts in the noughties crisis.

Time	Contents
March 2008	In order to rescue Bear Stearns, which was in liquidity crisis, Federal Reserve approved a special deal between JPMorgan Chase and Bear Stearns. JPMorgan Chase offered a great deal of capital to Bear Stearns.
July 2008	Relief efforts for Fannie Mae and Freddie Mac: (i) the Ministry of Treasury raised loans for them. (ii) The Ministry of Treasury had the right to purchase any of them when necessary. (iii) This allowed them to get loans directly from Federal Reserve.
July 2008	The House of Representatives released the amount of 300 billion dollars with the Housing Assistance Act, which accredited rights to offer help for mortgaged households in trouble.
September 2008	The USA government declared four steps of relief efforts for Fannie Mae and Freddie Mac. (i) The Federal Housing Finance Agency took control of them. (ii) The Ministry of Treasury signed a purchase plan of senior preferred stocks. (iii) The USA federal housing credit bank created a new, bonded lending facility. (iv) A temporary plan of purchasing mortgage-backed security of government sponsored enterprises was implemented.
September and October, 2008	Federal Reserve declared a high rate loan of 85 billion dollars as long as the USA government got 79.9% stocks and got the veto right to other shareholders. In October 2008, Federal Reserve allowed the American International Group (AIG) to mortgage their investment-grade, fixed-yield security. In return, AIC got 37.8 billion reliefs.
December 2007, March, September and October 2008	Federal Reserve made concerted efforts together with the European Central Bank, the Bank of England, and the Bank of Japan. (i) It injected capital to the domestic currency market through open market operation. (ii) It set temporary currency exchange rules and adjusted exchange time and scale according to the changing situation. (iii) Since October 2008, Federal Reserve, the European Central Bank, the Bank of England, the Canadian Central Bank, the Swedish Central Bank, and the Swiss National Bank declared a reduction of interest on many occasions.

Data resources: collated from public reports.

Depression or present day, and no matter what kinds of economic theories argued, the USA government played a leading role in resolving the crisis, which precisely indicates that even in the most developed capitalist country, market economy has some fatal weakness. Therefore, governmental interference is necessary for market economy. To conclude, it is the government's natural duty to maintain financial stability, both in developed and in developing countries.

Secondly, the government must make appropriate institutional arrangements and prevent, interfere, as well as cope with a crisis immediately. From the perspective of relief efforts, many measures were carried out systematically. They were rational in response to the new challenges. However, in essence, the relief efforts belonged to remedial measures, in the same way as doctors take stopgap measures for patients. Even though the United States upholds Neo-liberalism, it still interferes in the economy frequently. Is it sarcastic for the USA government to exaggerate Neo-liberalism? Kunt and Detragiache argued that it was easier for a crisis to break out in a liberalized financial system, except in those countries with sound mechanism and environment.[2] Its paradoxical behavior tells us that market economy needs government's interference and macro control measures. Only effective mechanism and institutions can ensure safe and well-organized economy operations.

3.4 FINANCIAL CRISIS AND GOVERNMENT RESPONSE

Financial crisis breaks out due to both market operation and inappropriate government policies. The rise of Keynesianism government's interference and market self-regulation have been intertwined since the Great Depression, and especially when crisis occurs, it is necessary for government to act as last stabilizer. Their major tasks are to recover market functions, improve the mechanism of resources allocation, as well as maintain stability of the macroeconomy.

---

[2]Quoted from Cao (2004). This is what Kunt and Detragiache have concluded after their quantitative analysis on cases of over 50 countries from 1980 to 1995.

3.4.1 Government's role in financial crisis

Government played an important part in financial crisis. Friedman & Schwartz (1963) studied government's role during the Great Depression. They thought Federal Reserve would lead from the first bank crisis to the second and even worse one. However, Roosevelt's New Deal rescued the American economy. In general, government policy is a major inducement of financial crisis. However, government is also the only "lender of last resort." Bordo *et al.* (2001) have studied the history of financial crisis for over 120 years. They found that crisis would last for 2 or 3 years and cause 5–10% gross domestic product (GDP) loss. What is more, financial crisis was closely related to economic recession. It is worth noting that since the collapse of the Bretton Woods system, the frequency of crisis has increased — bank crisis and currency crisis in particular — which brought much pressure on economy and government. They argued that appropriate government interference would reduce the impact of financial crisis. Government played a fundamental role.

To some degree, government is not only a "lender of last resort," but also a crisis stabilizer and absorber. Fischer (1999), quoting Bagehot Methods, argued that a market punishment mechanism was the most effective way to prevent ethical risks, and it was the key to government's success.

"Lender of last resort" loan activities should follow three principles: limitless mobility to borrowers with repayment ability; rate of punishment; and attached conditions such as assurance. Bagehot thought that in some special situations, there might be exceptions. This particular term became Federal Reserve's expedient. Furthermore, government should take relative financial policies and industrial policies, as well as others to reduce the negative impact of the crisis, because the specific departments and free market could not raise the capital involved.

In the relationship between government and market, government's interference did not obey market rules. Allen & Gale (1999) reached a conclusion by the analysis of Norway and Japan that government should come into play before and after the crisis. At that time, market could not obtain self-adjustment. Only government could flow enough capital to the financial institutions and bring them back to the market again. Claessens,

Klingebiel, and Laeven thought that when the systematic financial crisis broke out, government's interference was the key to solving the problem. Government's interference with financial reconstruction was not contradictory to market adjustment — it was a simulative factor. Financial reconstruction needed a series of timely reform policies made by the government, accompanied by some supporting measures according to different problems and industries.

3.4.2 Basic principles of the government in response to financial crisis

Obviously, the government plays an irreplaceable role in response to financial crisis and its intervention is a necessary method to reduce the financial market's lack of liquidity, recover its ability to accommodate market funds, and promote economic recovery. However, many researches that stress the importance of the government's role in response to risks argue that there is a complex art involved for the government to deal with financial crisis and intervene in the market, rather than simply the more, the better. With the increase of frequency and diversification of the financial crisis, different coping mechanisms have emerged, such as post-crisis treatment, the establishment of safety nets (stressing on the overall process) and preventative measures. Nevertheless, more researches have put forward the requirement for government intervention.

The principle given top priority is timing. According to Bernanke (1993), the time that a financial crisis lasts depends on the recovery of the credit channels and repayment capability of the debtor. If the government intervention takes place in time, the time needed for the market to recover would be shorter and its effectiveness would be higher. From the perspective of the impact of crisis, earlier financial rescue would largely reduce the financial burden and slow down the sharp drop of output. People like Bordo *et al.* (2000) emphasize that the initial stage of financial crisis is the most effective time for risk management, the assertive interventions of government would keep the loss in a smaller scale, and the financial loss would be smaller. The South Korean Foreign Ministry (1999), when summing up the experience of South Korea and other East Asia countries on the response to financial crisis, pointed out that due to the severe conditions of the IMF, Korea lost the optimal rescue time. It would have been a better choice of policy to inject liquidity into the country of crisis in the initial stage of the crisis, rather than to take the tight macro measure. If this had been the case, the integration cost of economy would have been smaller.

At the same time, the principle of pertinence is also very important. In the early stage of financial crisis, liquidity would be largely expanded. At this moment, the key point of government intervention should be preventing credit overexpansion and ensuring the ordering of credit flow (Freixas *et al.*, 2000). At the time when financial crisis erupts, the prices of financial assets fall sharply, and the liquidity of financial agencies is in severe shortage, injecting liquidity and providing certain government guarantee would be a better choice of policy. When the crisis has been deepened by the bankruptcy of financial agencies and the surge of distressed assets, the government should place emphasis on clearing these distressed assets, market confidence, and function recovery.

In the timely and effective rescue process of financial crisis, the government should properly handle the relationship with market. Before great financial crisis, there exists a clear boundary between government and market, for it is generally believed that the best way to improve economic effectiveness is free market. However, Chang & Velasco (2000), Radelet & Sachs (1998) argue that multiple equilibria exist in the evolution of market, among which there is an undesirable equilibrium — namely financial crisis. If the government adheres to the policy of Laissez-faire, then the final voidance might be further crisis. For example, in the American financial crisis, if the market behavior of short selling were not restricted, the prices of financial assets would experience a sharper fall in the free market and under the accounting principle of mark to market. Of course, the government should obey the principle of moderation in the rescue process. That is to say, government intervention and the power of market should be combined properly to ease the impact of crisis, or government intervention might cause the inducement of moral risks (Furceri & Mourougane 2009).

Moreover, in the rescue process of financial crisis, financial sustainability should be given great attention. Financial rescue is a process that costs a lot of time and money and financial crisis itself has great negative impact on financial revenue. In addition, the clearing of distressed assets, rescue of financial agencies, and the restructuring of the financial market would also cost a great sum of money. For example, in the Latin American debt crisis of the 1980s and the 1990s Asian financial crisis, Argentina and Indonesia experienced a financial loss of over 50% of GDP. The average time that a crisis lasts is 2–3 years, during which time the government would be confronted with gigantic deficit. Without specially arranged rescue funds, the financial situation of the government would be unsustainable. The experience of Latin American countries indicates that it is unsustainable to pay the stale debt that financial crisis brings with new debt. Rather, it might cause an even larger crisis.

3.4.3 The government's policy choice in response to financial crisis

On a background of financial crisis when capital flow and resource allocation is caught in a disordered situation, government intervention is an effective way to reduce the impact of crisis. Apart from handling the principles of timing, moderation, and sustainability, the government also needs to use targeted policies and measures. The governmental strategy should include policies for both the short and long term. Generally, the policy for government to intervene in financial crisis can be divided into several stages, such as pre-crisis intervention, crisis intervention, and post-crisis intervention. There are different key points for policy in different stages.

(i) Policy response in financial crisis

In the process of dealing with financial crisis, the policy measure in the development of crisis is the most important. Proper policy measure can limit the crisis in time as well as reduce its damage, while failed policy might lead the crisis into another abyss. In the stage of the eruption and deepening of financial crisis, government policy should pay attention mainly to liquidity, distressed assets, bankruptcy of financial agencies, and monetary policy.

First, timely injection of liquidity is the most effective method to ease the financial market's liquidity deflation and the fund shortage of financial agencies. This situation is usually improved by massive cash injection to the financial system, provided or guaranteed by the government. In the 1934 Great Depression, the government provided 500 million dollars to establish the RFC and inject capital into banks and a large number of financial agencies (Cambridge Economic History of the United States, 2008). In 1998 and 1999, the Japanese government started to inject capital to banks with a total amount of 120 billion dollars. In 1998, the Financial Regeneration Act was passed and the later capital injection reached a total amount of 520 billion dollars, which became the biggest rescue activity in the world's financial history at that time (Liu, 2004).

Second, the management of distressed assets is directly related to the regular function performance of financial agencies and market. In financial crisis, government usually establishes a capital management corporation or other similar agency to deal with a large sum of distressed assets and separates these distressed assets from the financial system. In the Great Depression, one of the most important activities was the establishment of the RFC, which promoted investment through assets management and loan origination, and laid the important foundation for the recovery of American financial system after the Great Depression. Two-thirds of the loan issued by the RFC in 1932 flowed to financial agencies. In 1993, Sweden also established the Bank Support Authority and Special Asset Management Corporation to save the financial market. In 1992, the Swedish government also approved a reconstruction fund of 14 billion dollars and to a take over the biggest bank — Nordbanken. Even after the stock price upswing of the bank, the scale of Sweden's government rescue to the bank was still over 9 billion dollars, accounting for 3.6% of its GDP in 1993 (Drees and Pazarbasioglu, 1995). Similarly, in April 1999, Japan established the Resolution and Collection Corporation. On the one hand, it took over the non-performing loans (NPLs) of real estate financial companies and bankrupt banks; on the other hand, it purchased NPL from other financial agencies.

Third, the management of bankruptcy of financial agencies always puts the government in a dilemma. When dealing with this problem, the government usually separates big financial agencies from middle or small-sized ones. If a medium-sized bank rescue were optimal, then rescuing any bigger bank would also be optimal. Moreover, the large-scale financial agencies have the "too big to fail" effect owing to a diverse range of business and large number of clients. When there are some problems in large-scale financial agencies, it is usually necessary for the government to take measures and save them, or their huge destructive power would further endanger the financial system (IMF, 2008a, 2008b). However, under the policy orientation of "too big to fail," relatively clear pertinence usually exists between scale and risk. This "too big to fail" rescue policy influences the choice of bank scale and asset risk, which may result in the bank's pursuit of larger risks or bigger moral risk. However, in terms of middle and small-sized financial agencies, the supervision authority usually takes action on a market principle and only makes proper arrangement for the debt of these agencies. In general case, financial agencies with severe problems must be dealt with as early as possible. The agencies that are to go bankrupt shall accept their destiny; otherwise, the accumulation of problems would further influence overall financial stability. At the same time, agencies with problems must be pushed to rectify and reform as early as possible, the eradication of NPL must be accelerated, bankruptcy of financial agencies must be reduced, and the social cost must be decreased. Goldstein (2008) emphasized that for systematically important financial agencies, especially non-bank financial agencies, prompt corrective policy and well-organized bankruptcy and closure rules should be applied to strengthen the sustainability of rescue activities and decrease the level of moral risks.

Fourth, the effectiveness of monetary policy to economic depression is usually worse than fiscal policy, but in the stage of financial crisis, appropriate monetary easing policy is also a necessary tool (Chailloux *et al.*, 2008). Taking the Great Depression as an example, after the Great Depression, monetary easing policy was reflected in the sharp depreciation of USD. On April 18, 1933, Roosevelt's government effectively carried out the depreciation of USD by passing the Emergency Agricultural Mortgage Law, which allows the president to decide the price of gold and prohibits the non-official export of gold through administration orders. As a result, USD started to separate from the official price and dropped. Until July 1933, the price of USD had fallen about 40% in comparison with the Great British Pound (GBP). Monetary depreciation not only has the capacity of improving trade conditions, but also effectively promotes economy expansion (Bernanke, 1983).

Fifth, in and after the crisis, stability of market emotion and the recovery of market confidence are of key importance. The United States is always the defender of classical market economy rules and promoter of government intervention in the international market. However, after the eruption of subprime crisis, American officials including the American President, Chairman of the Federal Reserve and Finance Minister have all given "guarantee to the market with credit of the country" on various occasions. They constantly emphasized government's ability to ease the impact of subprime crisis and stabilize the financial system (Bernanke, 2009). Moreover, more notably, the United States carried out a united rescue through the European Central Bank, the Bank of England, and other monetary authorities of major economic entities, which further strengthened the stability of market emotion. Although the subprime crisis was continuously upgrading, the "mind games" of the government authority were still active and effective in the crisis rescue and the stabilization of market emotion.

(ii) Policy response after financial crisis

As the end of financial crisis is uncertain, the policies and measures after financial crisis, in fact, do not have very clear directions. They are usually connected with the policies in the eruption and deepening stage of financial crisis, and are formed by the expansion of policies in the financial crisis. At the same time, the government is creating new policies and measures in the process of crisis rescue, system reflections, and structural reform, to form a complete systematic response policy after the financial crisis.

Fiscal stimulus policy is, in fact, a combination of policies, which is usually issued in the deepening stage of financial crisis, and mainly implemented in the later stages and after the end of the crisis. After the Great Depression, with Japan's banking crisis and the financial crisis in Asia, and with other major crises, many governments chose to ease their monetary policies first, and then issue major economic stimulus plans and expand fiscal expenditures to promote the economic recovery. After solving the problems of distressed assets, financial agencies and liquidity, the priority of government policy is usually to recover the function of the financial market and promote the economic recovery. In this process, increasing investment is a key point, therefore to expand fiscal expenditures after the crisis is very important and necessary. In the Great Depression, the ease of government policy is more importantly reflected on fiscal policy. Roosevelt's government launched three crucial reforms: reform of the banking system, increasing the management of government on production and establishing a social "safety net," among which the first two reforms started in the famous 1933 "New Deal." In the second quarter of 1933, Roosevelt proposed many acts to the Congress, which led the way for the economic recovery and restructured American economy. The establishment of a social "safety net" was started in the second tenure of Roosevelt and the "Second New Deal" was devoted to expanding the benefit of economic recovery to the whole social public (Cambridge Economic History of the United States, 2008).

In addition, after major financial crisis, corresponding financial reform or system adjustment would be conducted. The eruption of a financial crisis usually has a certain historical background, policy orientation, system elements, and flawed financial system. For instance, unpractical reconstruction of the gold standard was a crucial cause of the Great Depression, as this made the monetary policy too tight. After the Great Depression, American government issued the Emergency Agricultural Mortgage Law, which set USD free from the restriction of the gold standard. The Glass–Steagall Act was also issued, which established the system structure of separate operation and separated supervision. This act influenced the American financial system for nearly 70 years.

(iii) Policy choice before financial crisis

In fact, the policies and measures in use before a financial crisis are all aspects of system reflection and correction after the crisis. The main point of pre-crisis policy is to pay attention to the management of financial risks, prevention and early warning of financial crisis, timely financial system reform, and so on.

In the management of financial risks, information disclosure and the principle of transparency are the key points. The introduction of transparency is to solve the problem of publicity of game rules and other information that need to be disclosed. All kinds of financial agencies that play an essential role in financial activities should report truthful data to the supervision authority according to the International Accounting Standards (IAS). In the financial crisis in Asia, an important experience of South Korea, Japan, and other countries is that there is not enough transparency in financial operation. Many financial agencies concealed substantial NPL, and it was not until they were caught into payment crisis and finally bankruptcy did the supervision authority start to know the truth. Without enough supervision and owing to the information opacity and insufficiency of information disclosure, systematic financial risks remain deeply concealed. Therefore, placing emphasis on information transparency is an effective method to strengthen the management of financial risks.

Prevention and early warning of financial crisis requires the financial supervision authority to establish a relatively complete system of supervision, warning, and prevention. From Asia's experience of financial crisis, it has been noted that the supervision of financial risks is unfulfilled and the prevention mechanism for financial crisis is incomplete, no matter in terms of a single country or the international community. Therefore, some researchers argue that apart from the suggestion that financial supervision authorities and the IMF should strengthen the supervision of capital flow (especially short-term capital flow and hedge funds, international balance of payment and foreign debt of its member countries), that they should also provide advice and policy suggestions to related member countries in case of unusual occurrence, so as to fully perform their function of early warning and effectively prevent the occurrence of financial crisis. However, the reality that subprime crisis can generally evolve and upgrade to worldwide financial crisis makes it more important to establish the crisis warning and prevention mechanism (especially the establishment of an index system).

To strengthen the information transparency of financial agencies and establish an index system, financial supervision and the reform of its system might be a basic requirement. The Great Depression pushed the American financial system into the mode of separate operation and supervision, while this latest financial crisis might transfer the financial supervision to mixed supervision, and the supervision structure might be changed from umbrella supervision to functional supervision. In 1933, the Glass–Steagall Act was approved after Roosevelt's New Deal. Moreover, in the most recent round of American financial crisis, the American government has realized the ineffectiveness of financial supervision. With the merger of Bank of America and Merrill Lynch, as well as the sale of Lehman Brothers to Barclays Bank, the American financial industry might return to mixed operation and financial supervision might reform with it.

3.4.4 Evaluations on the effect of response policy to financial crisis

In terms of the financial crisis response policy, we need to know its functional process and evaluate its future result in advance. For example, in the long term, injection of public funds to fragile banks might not improve their structure of assets and liabilities, because if these banks do not adopt corresponding reforms, the bailout policy might generate bigger moral risks, and risks brought about by the activities of these banks would be transferred to taxpayers. It is the ordinary taxpayers that bear the losses, instead of the banks and other financial agencies who take the risks. Moreover, the response policy of financial crisis may also bring out negative effects, which may, with the deepening of reform, become the major power to influence financial stability and economic growth. Therefore, evaluation of the response policy to financial crisis is also important.

One of the Keynesianism policy suggestions is to take the change of the interest rate as the guidance for monetary policy, adopting the "Against The Wind" policy, adjust the interest rate, and regulate investment according to the change of business cycles, so as to mitigate the fluctuations of business cycles and then stabilize the economic growth. This contingent monetary policy mechanism, which fully reflects the flexibility of policy, has been widely used in financial crisis. However, with this plan, it is more likely that the monetary authority might make the wrong judgment or change its attitude, which would result in discontinuous change or exceed the increase of money supply, and that becomes one of the main causes of economic instability (Friedman, 1991). Taking the United States as an example, the positive actions that the Federal Reserve took to prevent the market from sharp and continuous drop, namely Greenspan Put, made the risk activities of financial agencies "secured" to some degree, but its bailout activity did not change the risk preference of financial agencies. Rather, it made the moral risks worse and crisis emerged. Therefore, after the issuance and implementation of a policy, the government should evaluate the influence of the policy on the activities of financial agencies, especially its influence on financial risk management and financial stability.

In terms of ensuring the rationality of the response policy to financial crisis, several principles should be adhered to. The first is that it should have an appropriate driving effect to economic growth, without leading to an overheated economy. The second is that it should not trigger rising prices, to avoid inflation. The third is that it should coordinate investment and consumption and make sure that they would not crush each other; the fourth is that it should have good sustainability. But, taking China's policy and measures after the financial crisis in Asia as an example, the response to financial crisis had much negative influence: (i) excessive investment led to overheated economic growth. At the end of 1997, China experienced fast economic growth and prices rose rapidly, which was directly related to the proactive fiscal policy, and stable and loose monetary policy after the financial crisis in Asia. In particular, the large-scale fixed-asset investment, and the investment-driven mode that was formed in this stage was the direct cause of overheated investment. (ii) Investment has replaced consumption as the major power of stimulating economic growth. After the crisis, China started to fuel economic growth with fixed-asset investment and export. The excess increase of investment downplayed the role of consumption in pulling economy. The contribution rate of capital formation rate to economic growth increased from 23.7% in 1999 to 63.7% in 2003, and the contribution rate of consumption fell from 65.1% to 35.3% (Statistical Bureau, 2008). (iii) Government-led investment occupied the space for social investment. Long-term action of proactive fiscal policy generated a big crowding-out effect and the oversize scale of governmental investment replaced social investment. The lack of strength of market-led investment and the surge of deposits from residents in the early years of the 21st century is a direct reflection of this effect.

3.5 THE CHINESE GOVERNMENT'S EFFORTS TO MAINTAIN FINANCIAL STABILITY AMID DIFFICULTIES AND CHALLENGES

In practice, "one bank and three commissions" (specifically the PBOC, the CBRC, the CSRC, and the CIRC), the Ministry of Finance, and local governments have their own emphasis and strength in maintaining financial stability. The reconstruction of China's financial stability system is essentially the redefinition and repositioning of the functions of the aforementioned departments and a kind of institutional arrangement for their overall collaboration.

3.5.1 The functional orientation and difficulties "one bank and three commissions" have in maintaining financial stability

On December 27, 2003, the sixth session of the tenth Standing Committee of the National People's Congress (NPC) passed the amendment to the Law of PBOC. Article 2 states: "the PBOC shall, under the leadership of the State Council, formulate and implement monetary policies and exercise supervision and control of the financial industry." Article 5: "the PBOC is free of interference from the local government, government departments at all levels, social groups and individuals in the implementation of monetary policy, in performing duties and carrying out business." Therefore, as a functional department of the State Council, the PBOC has a certain independence, which means that it is independent from financial departments and local governments. At the same time, the new functions of the PBOC are officially presented as "develop and implement monetary policy, prevent and defuse financial risks and maintain financial stability." Since then, the concept of financial stability is formally put forward in China for the first time in the form of law, which symbolizes the transformation of the functions of the PBOC from micro finance risk supervision to macro financial risk supervision.

In recent years, the PBOC has put much effort into maintaining financial stability; however, it still has some difficulties and challenges. Firstly, the existing law on the role the PBOC has in keeping financial stability is too vague, and has not yet formed detailed, feasible rules and regulations, or an implementation process. If the PBOC could explore a theoretical system and an operational framework suitable for China's national conditions, which can monitor and analyze financial risks, assess and judge the financial situation, take prevention, rescue and disposal measures, then the maintenance of financial stability will be more effective. Secondly, its coordination mechanism with other departments has not yet formed an effective system arrangement, and the separate responsibility of each party in maintaining financial stability is still not very clear. Some blank areas or cross management problems exist. Thirdly, the lack of effective deposit insurance and the arrangement of the market withdrawal mechanism, resulting in the accumulation of the financial institution's internal risk, increased the instability and vulnerability of the system. In reality, few financial institutions were ordered to withdraw from the market due to operational risk; therefore, more clear and strong rules should be made.

Under the current situation, the CBRC, the CSRC, and the CIRC carry out their duties and have their own focus, constituting the Chinese financial regulation subjects. Overall, this pattern is compatible with the current separate operation system, but with the opening up and the acceleration of the reform, the existing supervision mode is facing many challenges.

First is the challenge the financial holding companies face with the separate supervision mode. In order to cope with the fierce market competition, financial institutions do everything possible to avoid financial regulation and bring forth business domains, while the emergence of financial holding companies adapted to this need. By combining institutions and businesses, a financial holding company can achieve the sharing of resources and complementary advantages, and produce a tremendous synergy of advantages that have improved financial services in terms of hardware resources and financial products. These advantages have also increased the holding company's complexity in organizational structure, internal control, related party transactions, etc. Therefore, the financial holding company is a typical case in avoiding the legal regulation. The regulatory issues encountered in the current system of separate supervision are representative and universal.

Second is the challenge of the coexistence between separate supervision and fragmented regulatory framework. The typical case is still the financial holding company's regulatory issues. The financial holding company has to accept the National Audit Office, Ministry of Finance, Inland Revenue Department and the supervision by "one bank and three commissions," though the regulation is focused on different aspects, the most popular keywords being asset quality, financial, profit, risk, etc. Thus, separate supervision will face the issue of a fragmented regulatory framework. Different regulatory authorities would affect the financial stability of operation due to various regulatory goals, different means, self-containment, and a lack of coordination, which make it difficult to form a unified institutional framework.

3.5.2 The role of the financial departments in the maintenance of financial stability

We need the government to use financial resources to compensate for the lack of market mechanism when financial institutions have huge losses and cannot resolve them through the market mechanism. The Ministry of Finance and its agencies' position, functions, and means in maintaining financial stability are relatively vague. In recent years, with economic growth and fiscal revenue growth, the Ministry of Finance has taken various measures to provide strong financial security for the maintenance of financial stability. Specifically, (i) speed up state-owned commercial banks to write off bad loans, reform the method of extracting and reversal allowance for doubtful bank accounts, and change the tolling years for commercial banks' overdue interest since 1997. (ii) In 1998, commercial banks separated from their shareholding security and trust investment companies to adopt the free transfer mode; meanwhile, the Ministry of Finance issued 270 billion *yuan* of special treasury bonds to enrich the four state-owned banks' capital. (iii) In 1999, a new loan asset classification method was introduced, going from "one overdue — two slacks" to a five-grade judgment system (FGJS) since four asset management companies were set up and stripped state-owned commercial banks' non-performing assets of 140 million *yuan*. In the restructuring of financial institutions, the Ministry of Finance has taken various forms of financing and relief measures. With China's rapid economic growth and increasing number of central fiscal revenue under the current international financial crisis, the Ministry of Finance has the ability to take continuous necessary measures and provide strong security for financial stability through the joint implementation of various fiscal policies.

3.5.3 Local government's function in the maintenance of financial stability

The local government's function in the maintenance of financial stability mainly lies in leading, organizing, and coordinating the judicial authority, financial service department (or competent department), and financial regulator to develop cooperation, and form a coordinate–supervise mechanism. No matter the present or the long-term conditions, or from the part or the whole, one bank and three associations share the same benefit with the local government. However, even though a national finance regulation department's branch office regulates the local and non-local judicial entities, all kinds of financial enterprises rely on, take root, or mix with the local economic environment. Therefore, local government intervention is inevitable, but the problem for the financial regulator is that risk management is the rigid constraint and economic development is soft constraint, while this is just contrary for the local government.

As a result, some local governments excessively pursue the thriving development of economic finance, while ignoring the necessarily precautions for financial risk. This makes a convenient environment for the local financial departments' unlawful acts and allows them to accumulate financial risk at the same time. Local government does not need to take the responsibility for state-owned commercial banks' financial risk, so it often uses its governmental authority to influence commercial banks to grant relationship loans and issue loans directly, even by using unlawful means.

In recent years, with commercial banking law and other laws and regulations being implemented, local government's direct intervention to large financial enterprises has been restrained. Nevertheless, how are we to regulate local government's direct intervention to local financial departments, such as commercial city banks, rural cooperative banks, rural credit cooperatives, and bonding companies?

3.6 STRENGTHENING THE GOVERNMENT'S CAPACITY FOR MAINTAINING FINANCIAL STABILITY THROUGH CAPABILITY TRAINING

3.6.1 A stable financial mechanism — including early warning, supervision, prevention, and remedy

From the lessons learned from the American financial crisis, it can be seen that good institution organization is the most important thing. To build a long-term, financially stable mechanism, its design will include early warning, daily supervision, crisis prevention, and crisis remedy capabilities to avert crisis. China once defended the Asia financial crisis in the late 1990s comparatively successfully; now the government is trying to deal with the present crisis. We need to further refine the prevention mechanism, for example, in the aspect of financial crisis' early warning, we cannot just stay at the level of simply analyzing data — and we also need to increase indexing and quantification.

Further research about the concrete implementation of preventing fiscal financial risk recommends that we strictly limit the requirement for aid or nationalization, and then make the aid to financial risk more public, more transparent, and more effective. Meanwhile, under the circumstance of economic globalization and integration, government departments should constantly focus on the international economy and finance-developing trend, and try to win some rights of speech and initiatives. After this round of financial crisis erupted, it is necessary for senior officials from the PBOC and the Ministry of Finance to put forward the demands for international currency system reform in a timely fashion, and this voice should be louder and greater. Only after we eliminate the unreasonable factors from the current international currency system and build a more reasonable, equal international currency system, and a new international financial order can we really reduce the loss of developing countries and effectively prevent the quick spread of a crisis.

3.6.2 Make the best of the PBOC to sustain financial stability

The final lender system arrangement can play a role in sustaining financial stability, but it still has the problem of the ambiguous standard of reloan and lack of supporting measures. In practice, these lead to most of the financial institutions that are going bankrupt to turn to loan and aids support, and only few financial institutions exit from the market. This objectively indulges banks or other financial institutions that are excessively engaged in high-risk acts and cause the increase of morality risk and adverse choice, so the unstable financial factors accumulated. When the PBOC exercises the function of final lender, it should notice two points:

(i) Introduce a decision standard for reloan requirements, which should: clarify the requirements of reloan, detailing the contents and specific conditions; change the historical experience that the commercial banks can always be supported by the central bank when encountering problems; encourage financial banks to rely on their own level of operating management, capital management, and risk management to defend possible financial risk; and to reasonably deal with or eliminate any unqualified and unhealthy financial banks.

(ii) Build multi-level frames to sustain the financial stability, and actively exploit the hierarchy effect to realize regional and global areas' effective interaction and supervision. According to the demand to sustain the regional financial stability, the PBOC can reasonably divide the duty of the central bank and affiliated groups in aiding the crisis, and build a reasonable divided, efficient cooperative organization frame and duty system. The rights of using the reloans and deposit reserves are divided between the central bank and their branches in the light of amount. This can enable the opportunity to aid and cut the delay cost, prevent the spread of the crisis and reduce depositors' loss utmost, and prevent a single bank's crisis developing to systematic crisis.

3.6.3 Build financial stability coordination mechanism and improve financial supervision mode

Currently, the range and depth of China's financial business globalization are comparatively limited, and the scale and proportion of financial businesses are small. Among the banking system, securities businesses and insurance industry, independent financial institutions are in the majority, and the intersect businesses that completely break through the boundaries are few. Therefore, business-based supervision remains China's mainstream financial supervision method. However, as the pace of financial innovation quickens, the financial institutions' combined operation increased progressively. All of this challenges the current business-based supervision mode. We can take two measures, as follows:

Firstly, make clear that the PBOC is the main provider of financial stability to institutions and correspondingly this gives it the right to coordinate. Under the circumstances of combined operation and differential supervision in China, coordination must be strengthened in order to avoid the overlapping and vacuum of supervision at utmost, and effectively prevent the infection and spread of financial risks among each supervisory institution, or between a supervisory institution, the central bank, and the government. It is especially important to clarify that the PBOC is the defender of financial stability and stands in the dominant position of the financial stability coordination committee, and has the power to coordinate financial stability.

Secondly, establish information sharing mechanism and work communication system to achieve the combination of financial regulation and prudential supervision. The "one bank and three commissions" should establish an information sharing mechanism, master the mutual supervision of financial institutions, and obtain information about financial supervision-related work. The "three commissions" deliver all kinds of information within their supervision area to the PBOC regularly so that it can have access to the latest business situation, historical illegal situations, and its handling of financial institutions. The PBOC should notify the financial supervisory department of the national monetary policy and financial macro control policies and measures, as well as the economic operation of the country. Based on the need for supervisory function, functional departments can borrow and consult financial material, understand and master the supervisory situation of relevant financial institutions in time. The "one bank and three commissions" discuss the problems found during the financial market supervision, and study and solve the problem of cross penetration of financial institutions in business innovation. They should also agree specific work cooperation, coordinate the cross-sector supervision management of financial institutions, and establish a rapid response mechanism to deal with different types, scope, and the degree of financial risk, jointly developing a joint emergency plan. Through these measures, "one bank and three commissions" wish to achieve the combination of financial regulation and prudential supervision, improving the efficiency of supervision and level of risk prevention.

3.6.4 Strengthen the supervision of foreign financial institutions

With the entry of foreign financial institutions and the faster internationalization of Chinese financial institutions, the supervision of these and the institutions' branches overseas should be strengthened. For China's financial institutions setting up branches overseas, financial regulatory authorities should take the following measures: strengthen the cooperation with the foreign financial regulatory agencies; set up a strict examination and approval system for setting up branches overseas and make a comprehensive assessment of these branches; strengthen the supervision of domestic financial institutions' headquarters, and urge the headquarters to control and manage their branches overseas. The measures taken to regulate foreign financial institutions in China include: bilateral or multilateral agreements with foreign financial regulatory authorities and establish a regular contact system to strengthen supervision; establish a scientific monitoring index system and the evaluation criteria of foreign financial institutions' credit rating; improve the legal system of the supervision of foreign financial institutions and improve the effectiveness and authority of the supervision; strengthen cross-border cooperation in financial supervision. According to the relevant provisions of the Basel Capital Accord, for cross-border banks, the home country supervisory authorities and their counterparts in the host country should conduct reasonable division of labor and cooperation. Usually, the home country regulatory authorities are responsible for the supervision of capital adequacy, final discharge capacity, etc. The host country's authorities are responsible for the supervision of the assets quality, internal management, and liquidity of the local branches. Therefore, the two authorities should consult and regularly exchange the issues found in the objectives, principles, standards, contents, methods, and problems.

3.6.5 Strengthen the organizational ability of regulators and develop modern regulators

As modern regulators, the organizational ability of regulators at all levels is crucial (He, 2004). Therefore, regulators must put much effort into self-improvement, establish clear incentives, restraint mechanisms and transparent, rigorous working procedures, improve the corresponding information support system, open up the channels of effective communication with the public, and strive to improve the quality of staff. Supervision is still a new management field in China, and its employees must be trained and screened before they can be competent for the job. The government should actively carry out professional training, develop an appropriate regulatory agency personnel system, establish the perfect knowledge structure, and competitive and incentive-compatible personnel employment mechanism, thus cultivating a group of employees with systematic knowledge of economy, finance, law, public administration, accounting, and auditing.

3.6.6 Give full play to the supervision of the self-discipline of the industrial organizations and social forces: Explore the mode of social supervision

The so-called socialized supervision mode mainly refers to the supervisory activities that use social forces to participate in the activities of financial institutions. Among them, the most important is to give full play to non-governmental regulatory organizations, such as self-regulatory organizations and social intermediaries, to form a good financial self-regulation mechanism. China already has a series of banking, securities, insurance and other fields of industry with self-regulatory organizations, but their function positioning, work pattern and many other aspects are not clearly defined, lacking the self-regulatory function of financial markets. The next step should be to speed up the establishment of rules and regulations, improve the organizational construction of industrial institutions, industry convention and regulations, as well as the inspection and disclosure system, and rewards and punishment system. At the same time, it should give full play to social supervision — with accounting firms, audit firms, and assets assessment firms to play the role of social intermediaries such as in audit supervision, improve the authenticity and authority of information disclosure and assets assessment. Next, media supervision should be strengthened; with media exposure encouraged to supervise and disclose illegal and corrupt behavior. Finally, investors, creditors, and other market participants should be allowed to take part in supervision.

3.7 IMPROVING THE LOCAL GOVERNMENTS' FINANCIAL MANAGEMENT SYSTEM

Local governments' financial management system refers to a system design[3] for local governments to be involved in the allocation of financial resources. This system attaches equal importance to the speed and quality of economic growth against the context of separated central and local government powers, and the government's dominance in

[3]The definition of local governments' financial management system in this book is based on the description of financial market management in Booth & Currie (2003). Financial market management means that public sectors intervene in economic matters, because of the requirements for rectifying market defects and unfair allocation of resources.

economic development.[4] However, according to the North Paradox,[5] apart from promoting economic growth, the local governments' financial management system also presents a problem, which is that of the financial system and actual economy being lagged and constraining each other due to improper and/or too much control or intervention. The system *per se* is a coexistence of power games and administrative restriction, and of supervision vacuum and functions overlap. As nowadays, there is an urgent need to change economic growth mode and to adjust industrial structure, to strengthen out the local governments' financial management system is a pending necessity. To address this issue, the fifth plenary session of the 17th Communist Party of China (CPC) Central Committee approved the Suggestions on Establishing the 12th Five-Year Plan for National Economy and Social Development, where the requirement of "improving local governments' financial management system" was made for the first time. Thus, it is a crucial and instant task to identify problems in the system and their root causes, and to explore the efficient ways in which to improve the system.

3.7.1 Achievements and disadvantages of local governments' involvement in financial management

Now that financial resources are an indispensable factor that contributes to value augmentation in economic development (Zeng, 2005), the local governments have a strong motivation to gain a leading position in allocating

---

[4]Wei (2010) proposes that the Chinese government, instead of stepping out of the market, has been getting involved in the market while it was practicing in the market economy in the past 30 years of its reform and opening up. The government commanded, manipulated, controlled and dictated the market, as well as directly participated in the market's operation. From Wei's point of view, China is forming a mode where a powerful government dominates and even steers the market. Moreover, such power grows ever stronger, and as a result, the government is involved in the market even deeply. (Retrieved from http://www.caijing.com.cn/2010-04-09/110412911.html.)

[5]The North Paradox is coined by Douglass C. North, an American economic historian. See more in North (1981). *Structure and Change in Economic History*. W.W. Norton & Company.

those resources.[6] However, the right of financial management in China has long been highly concentrated by the central government. As economic reform keeps advancing in China, organizations under the central government have been streamlined and the administrative approval authority has been canceled, which allows local governments more rights to independently decide their own economic affairs and obtain more profits. Nevertheless, the dominance in allocating financial resources between central and local governments, such as the examination and approval authority for the opening of financial organizations, the decision authority for the scope of business of financial organizations, and the system of authority for approving credits is still grasped by the central government. To acquire and allocate credit capital as much as possible, local governments are doing their best to pursue financial management authority, and obtaining more or less the right to govern financial resources through setting up a large number of organizations that serve financial service. Under the circumstance where governments lead economic reform and development, the function to allocate resources endowed with the financial system attracts unprecedented attention. The trend of financial resources' being foreignized as fiscal capital for central and local governments and the finance industry as the "secondary finance" is getting increasingly obvious from day to day. With deepening financial reform, we have witnessed the reorganization or banning of the trust business, once the profit tool for provincial and municipal governments and of rural cooperative funds, which governments at county and village level were involved with. At the same time, the banking system gradually advances the reform to a vertical management system, with the bond that connects local governments and local branches of state-owned banks being weakened. Despite this, GDP index is still an important indicator for performance check on local governments. In this case, local governments are giving up contending for resources directly from state-owned banks. Instead, they resort to an indirect approach by

[6]According to the types of financial system summarized by Zysman (2009), China's belong to the second type, which takes credit as the basis and keeps key prices under the control of the government. Zysman believes that this type of system promotes and advocates the intervention of the government in industry-related matters.

helping, indulging, or acquiescing in dodging or invalidating the debts of enterprises under their administration. In the meantime, taking advantage of the restructuring of city commercial banks, they supplement their unsatisfied need for resources in state-owned banks by controlling local financial resources. Moreover, some of the local governments have to go beyond their original boundaries to get more power of control over financial resources.[7] In the past few years, the appeal and competition for financial resources among local governments has grown intensive and fierce. The local governments have gone through great changes. In the beginning, they blindly vied for the resources, leaving defaults and problems to the central government. Later they optimized the financial ecosystem, built up financial centers, and offered favorable policies to support the establishment of new financial agencies and branches. As a result, it becomes widely acknowledged among local government officials that they should get considerable local finance by issuing regulations and official files. In this way, local governments stand out to be a crucial factor that renews financial organizations and product forms, alters financial structure, management, and operating patterns, and then influences or changes the path and efficiency of financial development. This indicates a strengthened status of local governments with the renewed allocation of financial resources.

(i) Positive effects of local governments' intervention in financial management

As the link between the institutional supply of the upper structure (or a nation) and the need for institutional innovation of the lower structure (or the society), local governments can define financial property rights through institutional innovation.[8] From practices in recent years, we can

[7]For example, Bohai Bank was established under the support of the Tianjin municipal government in 2006. Another example is that of the Shide Group in Dalian City, which subscribed 66 million shares worth 82.5 million *yuan* issued by Yinchuan Municipal Business Bank in its second increase in capital and share on August 13, 2005.

[8]For example, Yin (2001) holds that the places that are with stimulus and capable of arranging local finance must have superior economic development level and a wider market. These allow those places to achieve Pareto optimal allocation of financial resources even when they are faced with deposit-loan gap effect, due to the monopoly of state-level financial arrangements.

see that the financial coordination of organizations in local government not only make the overall planning for local financial growth, but also contribute a lot to developing local financial organizations, guide and promote financial industries, set up local credit systems, establish financial ecological environment, standardize behaviors of financial agencies, and release financial risks.

Firstly, the environment for operating finance is improved and local economy is promoted. Local governments have taken multiple measures to perfect policies in order to attract more financial organizations and more capital. On the one hand, they have applied more effort to build financial ecology, advance regional finance integration,[9] defuse financial risks,[10] encourage the construction of a good credit environment, assist bans or corporations dealing in financial asset management by accelerating the disposition of local non-performing asset, improve financial structure of enterprises, and activate or enhance the financing ability of enterprises. Take municipal commercial banks as an example. In order to resolve the risks that municipal commercial banks have faced since the year 2000, local governments of all levels have paid nearly 100 billion RMB to slash the NPL rate in these banks from 30% of four-grade category in the peak time to 5% of five-grade category, lifting up the asset adequacy rate from minus to over 8% (Tang, 2010). In fact, governments at village and town level acted as the guarantor for enterprises to raise capital as early as the initial period of reform and opening up, strongly facilitating the development of local enterprises (Ma *et al.*, 1994). On the other hand, local governments take steps to strengthen environment building, such as by promoting construction of a credit environment, helping banks and companies in dealing with non-performing asset of enterprises, and accelerating policy environment building. This has played a key role

[9] For example, the Financial Affairs Office in Chengdu, Deyang, Mianyang, Suining, Leshan, Ya'an, Meishan, and Ziyang in Chengdu Province signed a Financial Cooperation Memorandum (hereafter referred as MOU) on December 22, 2010. Since then, the eight cities have commenced cooperation in 21 financial fields, including financial management, organizations, markets, businesses, and ecological environment building, pushing forward financial integration in the Chengdu economic region. (Retrieved from http://search.snxw.com/2010/e/action/ShowInfo.php?classid=54&id=107110.)

[10] For more examples, please refer to Liu & Ji (2008) Review and reflections on Guangdong Province's defusing financial risks. *Journal of Financial Research*, 8.

in improving financial operation conditions, establishing a united and an efficient financial market system, and ensuring financial safety (Li & Jiang, 2008).

Secondly, the structure of financial markets is optimized. The competition for financial resources among local governments stimulates the initiative to advance economy in relevant regions and encourages a series of institutional innovation, with the aim of reducing trade cost and boosting the economy. At the same time, the intervention of local governments in credit intermediaries boosts transaction efficiency. Besides, local governments strive to develop local financial organizations, promoting — to some degree — financial competition, and the optimization of the Chinese banking market structure, enhancing the overall efficiency of the banking system (Wang, 2010a, 2010b).

Thirdly, the costs for central government to control finance are reduced. The costs include four aspects, namely payment for information and supervision, increased running expenses of state-owned financial organizations, the loss due to low-efficiency allocation of financial resources, and mounted loss caused by non-performing assets (policy-related bad debts and abnormal business-related ones) (Lin, 2000). Experience shows that with financial supervision, the grass root levels will counter great difficulties without the close coordination of local governments. On the contrary, the participation of local government into allocating financial resources is conducive to cutting down the costs of the central government in its financial control. For example, under the framework of the Yufu mode, the local government sponsored the establishment of asset management corporations and made them the bridge that connects creditors and debtors, and local government. This is also another way to share the cost burden of reform.[11]

(ii) Negative effect of local governments' intervention in financial management

To promote local economy, the local governments exercise undue financialization and transfer the function of finance from deposit to investment.

[11] For further information, please find Lu (2006) Sharing reform costs, local government financing, and asset bubble. Caijing Magazine7.

This to some extent leads to a unilateral understanding that highlights finance's functions of supporting economic growth, and neglects balance development and financial ecological environment construction. The potential negative effects of local governments' intervention in financial management can be described in three aspects, described as follows.

Firstly, it weakens the performance of monetary policy. At the same time as when the growing power of local governments to control financial resources arouses the enthusiasm to develop finance and the economy, it also weakens the strength of central government's macro control. Local governors try to achieve the maximum levels of GDP and fiscal revenue during their administration, so the governments possess strong motives of contending for financial resources and expanding economy, but in the meantime, they lack the power of active adjustment and contraction. When it comes to local financial management, this negative effect manifests as the local governments' selective following of financial policies, especially monetary ones, set up by the central governments. In other words, the local governments often act more cooperatively toward an easing monetary policy than a restrictive one. The game between local and central governments significantly impairs the implementation effect of monetary policy, creating fluctuation risk of both economic and financial operation, while the operating costs of macro control and of maintaining financial stability largely mount. According to related studies, local governments' immoderate intervention in financial development results in 30% loss of conduction efficiency for monetary policy (Zhang, 2010a,b,c).

Secondly, it affects financial stability. Local governments competitively place pressure on financial organizations by taking advantage of their political impact. For instance, they may abuse their administrative power to carry out taxation checks on commercial banks or financial organizations, tactically consent to illegal evading payment of debts to make assets in banks unable to be withdrawn,[12] or attract financial organi-

---

[12]According to the analysis of Zhou (2004), bad policies issued by local governments accounted for nearly 30% of non-performing bank assets. (Retrieved from http://www.people.com.cn/GB/jingji/1040/2459998.html on April 21, 2004.) Besides, the distribution of non-performing asset rates in banks is closely related to certain regions (2003). The eastern coastal areas like Shanghai, Zhejiang, and southern Suzhou Province appear to

zations or banks by administrative resources, e.g., deploying deposits of fiscal institutions to the degree that branches of the central bank become affiliated to local governments to some extent, and the quality of local financial assets goes down. Moreover, to address the financial crisis in the United States, local governments borrow too much and abuse local credit resources. Local economy grows too fast to constrain the rocketing capital needs for city construction. Nowadays, investment and finance regarding city construction are not clearly defined and distinguished. Therefore, it is inevitable that a large number of projects with uncertain investment return turn out to be the objectives of fiscal financing and local governments have to bear most of the burden of providing money supply for construction. The direct consequence of these behaviors would be financial risk once local governments can no longer pay for the construction projects.

Thirdly, it lowers the efficiency of financial market. After local governments intervene in the allocation of financial resources, they excessively pursue economic growth rate, prefer projects that cost less, yield quick returns and require short-term operation, support listing and financing of local enterprises, and practice inappropriate actions when building local credit system. These behaviors have boosted local economy, although they have led to bad allocation and efficiency loss of the overall financial resources (He, 2005). What is worse is that the local governments, by making administrative commands, impede credit funds from being dispatched internally in commercial banks or from flowing between regions and places. Thus, local protectionism is formed, which lowers the efficiency of financial resources allocation and discourages

perform better than those in western and central China. Several problems need solving in the central and western areas. Firstly, economic marketization is at a low level with more economic intervention by local governments and more severe regional protectionism. Secondly, local governments are beset by heavy debt and local financial sectors are lacking enough independence. Thirdly, those regions lag behind concerning the construction of legal system, showing little consciousness of property rights protection and hard law enforcement. Fourthly, honesty and integrity are not widely advocated in society. Lastly, more severe financial law breaching happens in these regions (Institute of Finance of Chinese Academy of Social Sciences, 2005).

the development of financial industries. At the same time, the segmentation between regions results in discrepancy, in terms of target functions between local and central governments, and therefore affects the performance of macro control upon finance (Wang, 2010a, 2010b). Financial markets in many regions, regardless of scale or type, are largely government-shaping entities and communicate little between one another, leading to separated allocation of financial resources. In a study of the situation in the Wuling region of Hunan Province, Chen (2007) discovers several phenomena, including the "self-righting effect"[13] of the rural financial institutions and of the gradual-increase reform of rural finance. Other phenomena include the "crowding-out effect" of formal financial arrangements against informal ones. There is also the "Matthew effect" in financing, which is the polarization between the rich and the poor, where the accumulation of financial risks pushes the local governments' interference in rural financial resources allocation beyond the boundary of "market failure," thus causing distortion that is unfavorable to the efficient growth of allocation.

The 12th Five-Year Plan requires a relaxed control over market entry and advocates more participation of private capital in financial services and other domains. At the same time, the plan demands in-depth reform on rural credit cooperatives and encourages the founding of county-based community banks, so as to develop small-scale financial organizations in rural areas and petty loans, to perfect rural insurance system, and to improve rural financial services. Thus, it is not hard to predict that finance in China has an increasingly prominent trend of localization. Taking into consideration the dual aspects of local governments' intervention in resource allocation, it is necessary to clarify the current situation of local governments' financial management and the problems that need resolving, so that a solid foundation can be laid for improving the financial management system of local governments and making the best out of it.

[13]The "self-righting effect" is used when things turn out not as expected or what you get is not what you want to get. The essence of this concept is that things will turn out to be the opposite of our expectations if not controlled properly.

3.7.2 Local governments' financial management system: Current situations and problems

(i) Main methods of local governments' financial management

Local governments in China have different ways in allocating financial resources. Nevertheless, there are two main categories, which are overt management and covert intervention.

(a) *Overt management of local financial resources*

Some local governments have established sectors specifically in charge of the management and coordination of local financial resources, in order to attract more funds and other financial organizations. Since the Financial Service Office in Shanghai came into being in 2002, agencies of the same kind were founded in 222 out of 283 prefecture-level cities in 26 provinces of China by the end of 2009. Moreover, some county- or district-level governments have sponsored such agencies (Zhang & Wu, 2011). The agencies are called "Financial Affairs Office of (the name of region)," "Financial Service Office," or "Bureau of Financial Management." During the reform of local government organizations from 2008 to 2009, the functions, internal units, and manning quotas were enlarged. In some places, the financial offices became independent, upgrading from sectors affiliated to the General Office, Bureau of Finance, The National Development and Reform Commission (NDRC) and the like, to organs directly under the local governments. Take the provincial financial affairs offices as an example. Their functions include: firstly, to help reinforce the implementation of national monetary policy and to maximize the supportive role the financial industry plays in local economic and social development; secondly, to plan for provincial financial development, coordinate optimized allocation of financial resources, and promote financial industry; thirdly, to manage local financial organizations; fourth, to monitor, prevent, and resolve financial risks so as to maintain financial order and lay a basis for ecological environment construction; and fifth, to take care of the shareholding reform of local enterprises, developing listed companies, and standardizing work related to development.

The basic functions of financial affairs offices in counties and cities are pretty much the same. Apart from submitting a development plan for regional financial industries, putting forward relevant suggestions to policy making, and paving the way for a healthy development of China-invested, overseas-funded, and non-local financial organizations in its administrative region, local financial affairs offices also have another important function. This is communicating with central regulators to improve regulatory systems, establish a financial risk precaution system, and enhance the awareness of financial risks and prevention ability. Other sectors also bear specific financial management responsibilities, some examples of which now follow. Entrusted by provincial governments, provincial credit cooperatives are in charge of managing, directing, coordinating, and serving rural credit cooperative. The State-owned Assets Supervision and Administration Commission (SASAC) acts as a sponsor and regulator at provincial and municipal levels to trust companies of the same level. Pawnshops are under the supervision of State Economic and Trade Commission (SETC) (those of prefecture or municipal levels are supervised by the Trade Bureau), while the financing of bonding companies is managed by the Bureau of Small and Medium Enterprises. Local financial management organizations fill up the regulatory gaps[14] (for example, the supervision of equity investment, placing, and quasi-financial organizations such as equity exchanges, small loan companies, and financing bonding companies) of "one bank and three commissions" to some degree.

In recent years, the management of financial affairs in local governments mainly focuses on four aspects.

[14]The "one bank and three commissions" do not supervise directly over local quasi-financial organizations, making the supervision exercised by the local financial affairs office necessary. According to Interim Procedures for Management of Financing Insurance Company and Instructions on Small-Loan Company Pilots, regulatory sectors, small-loan companies, and insurance companies are appointed by local governments, which are usually provincial or municipal financial affairs offices. However, most cities have not carried out supervision upon equity firms, except for the municipal governments of Beijing, Shanghai, and Tianjin, which have determined that those firms registered as partnership funds should accept the supervision of the financial affairs office.

Firstly, by providing support to local financial organizations,[15] local governments have been dedicated to strengthening their structure, especially commercial banks in cities and rural credit cooperatives, since the reform and opening up. Moreover, they are also enthusiastic at accelerating the integration of these organizations, in particular the development of commercial banks into listed companies. For example, local governments were occupied with organizing their own provincial commercial banks after the establishment of Huishang Banks of Anhui Province, Jiangsu Provincial Bank, and Jilin Provincial Bank. The government of Hunan Province invited the China Huarong Asset Management Corporation as a strategic investor to sponsor the reorganization of four commercial banks in the cities of Xiantan, Zhuzhou, Hengyang, and Yueyang, and the Urban Credit Cooperative of Shaoyang City, making the foundation of the Huarong Xiangjiang Bank on October 12, 2010, possible. The Huarong Xiangjiang Bank determined its position in the market as "serving local economy, serving small and medium enterprises, and serving citizens of provincial capitals." Another example is that under the leadership of the government of Hubei Province, five commercial banks in the cities of Yichang, Xiangfan, Huangshi, Jingzhou, and Xiaogan emerged and reorganized to form the Hubei Provincial Bank. Moreover, local governments lavish their efforts on supporting the "lineal" financial organizations. More often than not, local governments would prefer positive measures when local financial enterprises are to go bankrupt in consideration of local stability. For instance, government sectors in Beijing screened and rectified rural credit cooperative foundations, applied administrative liquidation to Jinghua Trust Company, and reorganized Beijing Securities and China Securities.

Secondly, by establishing local financing platforms — in recent years, a trend of high-speed increase in the numbers of local financing platform has been witnessed. Since 2009, local financial management has focused in particular on providing funds for local financing platforms, achieving

---

[15]Relative to national financial organizations, local financial organizations refer to those which provide financial services for local or regional economic development and for residents and local enterprises, including regional commercial banks, security companies, credit cooperatives, trust companies, leasing companies, and pawnshops that are formed by local governments, economic organizations, or individuals.

over 30% of occupation rate of loans from the platforms in total newly added credits of long and medium terms. Local governments' finance platforms amounted to more than 8,000 and showed a loan balance of 7.66 trillion *yuan* by June 2010. Generally speaking, under the circumstances of scarcity of standardized financing channels and of funds for infrastructure construction, local financing corporations will help combine the advantages of bank capitals and of government credits and the power of markets, give support to weak links, promote local economic development, and moreover play a crucial role in building infrastructure. However, there are also issues that need attention, such as excessive growth in the scale of debt financing, non-standard operation, illegal or covert insurance offered by local governments, and increasing debt risks.[16]

Thirdly, by intensifying construction of software and hardware for financial development, local governments have, on the one hand, taken measures to build up financial functional zones and host financial forums or exhibitions about investment and financial management. This includes building a favorable atmosphere of public opinion, and developing service and support systems for financial organizations (e.g., renting call centers, information exchange and processing centers, client service centers, and technical support centers) in order to optimize the environment for financial growth. On the other hand, local governments made policies with favorable terms[17] to attract more financial organizations, including one-

---

[16]According to data up until June 2010 released by the CBRC, local financing platform loans account for 7.66 trillion *yuan*, of which 2 trillion of cash flow for loan projects can cover both the principal and interests, taking up 27% of the total government financing platform loans. This can be regarded as a regular loan pattern. The second pattern is when the first pay-off sources are not enough and second sources are needed. That accounts for 4 trillion *yuan*, taking up 50% of all funding. The third type is loans with illegal borrowers or guarantee, or with more severe paying-off risks (appropriation of loans and making loans as capital funds), taking up 23%.

[17]For example, according to the *Some Suggestions on Promoting Capital's Financial Industrial Development* announced in 2005 in Beijing, the new financial enterprises were awarded 5–10 million *yuan*. This meant their staff were eligible for 1,000 *yuan* per square meter of subsidy for buying or renting houses for one year; senior managers could receive a drawback worth 3,000 at most; staff could draw their housing provident funds free from a national upper limit; and staff could obtain a registered permanent residence in Beijing and their children could enjoy preferential terms when they attend school.

time bonus or subsidy, subsidy for workplace use, preferential tax, preferential personal income tax and accommodation subsidy exclusively for senior managers or business backbones, and awards[18] to encourage the organizations to support local economy. These policies helped reduce operating costs for the financial agencies and guide financial resources inward.

Fourth, to promote multi-level construction of financing and investment markets. Measures include encouraging enterprises to conduct direct financing through issuing shares and bonds, establishing a reward mechanism base on the amount financing listed companies have achieved at different stages, and advocating the founding and development of quasi-financial institutions such as industry investment funds and venture investment. Besides, some local governments actively develop a multi-level capital market system by promoting local equity markets and setting up pilot projects for the Agency Share Transfer System.

However, despite the fact that the local financial affairs offices have achieved many good results in aspects of planning, coordinating, supervision, and offering services, the gap between local finance development and economic development remains to be a serious issue needs solving. By far, most of the local financial affairs offices in China have no administrative powers such as deciding personnel, law enforcement, and allocating funds, leading to weak constraint of financial organizations and limited efficacy.

(b) *Covert intervention in concrete financial businesses*

As financial reform proceeds, there has been a sharp decrease in direct administrative intervention by local governments in specific financial

[18]For example, the local government of Shenzhen City offers one-off awards of a maximum of 5 million *yuan* for financial organizations who have participated in the reorganization of risk-based financial organizations and who have put money into it afterwards. Chengdu City gives awards to senior managers in financial organizations, which adds a yearly loan outstanding to enterprises — small- and medium-sized enterprises in particular. Besides, Shenzhen City also set up a Financial Innovation Award with a maximum of one million *yuan*, followed by Shanghai, Suzhou, Dalian, and Qingdao.

businesses, but in the meantime, covert intervention remains and even appears to be intensifying. By covert intervention, it means that local governments indirectly interfere into credit decision-making and operation of financial organizations. This means that the local governments make them serve local enterprises and economic growth by exerting political impact and administrative power, and by adopting methods such as persuading, inducing, and piling pressure on them, instead of dictating the organizations to issue loans according to the governments' will (Wang, 2007). However, when a project under the framework of local policy fails to receive financial support in regular ways, governments will resort to an administrative approach and order financial organizations under their control to provide funds. As Wu (2008) points out, governments of all levels are still holding the power of allocating credit resources. Some local governments inductively interfere in financial organizations by making use of resources in hand, like fiscal deposit, major projects' financial services, and fiscal fund subsidies. Some even disturb operation of the organizations with selective law enforcement if inductive methods do not work, in order to make them invest more on industries and projects the governments recommend (Liu & Shen, 2008). Most of the recommended industries are high pollution, energy intensive, and resource-consuming heavy chemical projects or industries of over capacity, which can contribute a lot to the GDP figures and local fiscal revenue in the short term, but may not meet the internal requirements of labor division on the basis of specialization and regional comparative advantages. In addition, local protectionism can be seen in the low winning rate in lawsuits where banks seek creditor's right protection and low implementation rate even after they win a case. Moreover, local governments often set stricter limits on transregional development of financial organizations, as they eagerly hope that these organizations can better serve the local economy and social development. Thus, more often than not, local governments require banks to set up branches in their own districts, and at the same time interfere with operation of the banks outside their administrative regions either overtly or covertly. Besides, covert financial intervention by local governments also includes carrying out service ranking among financial organizations to encourage good services and get financial planning in full swing to clarify developing targets of financial organizations. Inevitably, the covert interference will distort market allocation of funds, damage allocation efficiency and pricing mechanism in financial markets, and aggravates rent seeking in the financial domain.

(ii) Problems in current local governments' financial management

(a) *Blurred boundaries among functions of local financial management sectors*

The financial affairs offices differ a lot in their development. Some provinces have no such agencies. Names of government sectors relevant to finance are not unified, their functions not being identified clearly, and positions being wrong. In some places, several sectors join up to be in charge of financial management. These issues bring a question to our attention. Should the function of local financial management sectors be focusing on the prevention of financial risks, guaranteeing financial stability, or promoting local financing? The "three-determination plan," the determination of institution, of manning quota, and of functions, schemed by financial affairs offices either clearly states[19] or actually bears the function[20] of promoting financing. Nevertheless, this function contradicts the function of financial supervision, which is gradually included by the offices. In 2009, the rural credit cooperatives in Hebei Province provided 39.75 billion *yuan* for local financing platforms, which was supported by the provincial financial affairs office and which was against the law. When it comes to the supervision upon financing-based guarantee industry, conflicts between the functions of financial affairs offices are even more severe. As a financing and credit-increasing agency, a guarantee company

---

[19] For example, the Beijing Municipal Bureau of Finance has functions that include participation into planning of major government-sponsored financing projects, coordinating a comprehensive use of financial instruments and platforms, and offering financing services to the capital's economic construction — in particular, the development of major projects, mainstream industries, key districts, and small- and medium-sized enterprises.

[20] For example, the yearly conferences on financial work at provincial or municipal levels mainly aim for the requesting banks to ask from the head offices for more lines of credit and to issue more loans to local companies.

is under the supervision of the financial affairs office. A government-controlled guarantee company will probably be used to serve the loans at local financing platform and this illegal behavior is usually hard to discover. Researches show that several government-controlled guarantee companies in Guangxi Province, Sichuan Province, and Beijing have illegally aided local financing platforms (Zhang, 2010a,b,c). Besides, the CBRC advocates the establishment of small-scale financial organizations and provides guidance regarding supervision and management for local governments, although the latter is still scrupulous in actual action, because the central government requires that a local government have total responsibility over the risks of its financial organizations. In order to reduce risks as much as possible, local governments intentionally raise the entry requirements to small-scale financial agencies (some provinces doubled the required minimum amount of registration funds) and increase the difficulty for them to get the approval, impeding the development of such agencies.

Moreover, the blurred function boundaries also results in the author of "one bank and three commissions" being challenged at grassroots. Compared with financial affairs offices which act on behalf of local governments, the branch organs of the "one bank and three commissions" have to seek coordination of local governments, even though they are not under their control. For that reason, those organs have to rely on financial affairs offices. What is more, the financial affairs offices in some provinces also act as a local SASAC, deciding personnel appointment and removal, exerting influence on the daily operation of local financial organs. A financial affairs office of that variety just resembles a "super shareholder" that renders the board of directors useless and undermines management of a company, which runs opposite to the principles for the reform of financial organizations set by the central government.

(b) *Covert intervention functions more than overt management does*

There exist management vacuums in the local financial management system. For example, provincial credit cooperatives are both a government management agency and a legal entity without separation; new quasi-financial organizations are not clearly supervised — the licensing authority does not supervise and the administrative authority does not take care of approval — some local banks and rural credit cooperatives issue financial products without effective control over the associated risks of doing so. Taking into consideration of the vacuum in management, as well as the blurred functional boundaries and eagerness of local governments for boosting economy, some provinces have established close relations with financial organizations. In most cases, they take various favorable measures, like awards and tax reduction or exemption, to attract financial organizations to set offices or branches in their regions. When banks need more deposits, they would seek help from government officials; while when enterprises cannot get enough loans from banks, they would also ask for help from the government. Therefore, governments and officials are in a sense a bridge of communication, and sometimes a guarantee for enterprises to obtain loans. Under these circumstances, the free credit contracts between banks and companies turn out to be governmental-will-based contracts rather than maximum-profit-based. There is no doubt that this disturbs the normal operation of financial organs and weakens their independency.

(c) *The quality of management and operation in most of local financial organs is not good*

Low asset quality is a general issue that local financial organs are faced with. The reasons for those low-quality assets are rather complicated. Apart from constituents in support of a part state-owned economy and mistakes in operating, factors such as policy changes, local administrative interference, and merging with municipal credit cooperatives and some rural foundations are also crucial.[21] Local financial holding companies are usually held by local financial organs, which were originally established

[21]The occupation of resources in commercial banks by local governments has generated bad results. In 2003, 73% of 110 banks had zero profits, some of them technically going bankrupt and others reaching a non-performing rate of over 50%. The loan rate of single clients was surprisingly thousands of times over the normal rate. None of the 110 banks achieved a profit rate of more than 1%. Quoted from Ba, *et al.* (2005). Researches on local management and bank reforms in Chinese financial system in transitional period. *Journal of Financial Research*, 5.

or affiliated to government sectors. Moreover, governments often hold shares in most of the local corporate financial institutions and combine their functions as administrators or investors. This phenomenon hurts the interests of other shareholders and disturbs the fair competitive order of the market. There are also cases in that the local financial organs release loans to strong shareholders due to interpersonal relations or offer guarantee illegally, and even take financial businesses as instruments of conveying interests. In addition, due to dispersive shares and deviation from original intention of the cooperative system, financial organs practicing joint stock cooperative systems, such as rural credit cooperatives, often give little opportunity for small or medium shareholders to supervise and manage the affairs of the organs. This is the likely result of an absence of shareholders and monopolistic manipulation by insiders.

(d) *Excessive overdraft of local governments' credit*

The lack of national-level policy-based financial organs leads to the appearance of a large number of non-conventional policy-based financing platforms. Currently, the local financing platform is faced with problems like an overdue use of short-term loans, fixed use of floating loans, displacement of loans and loans being not put into use. Consequently, there are many risks, such as a government's difficulty of paying off debt (loans outnumbers fiscal revenue) with scarce risk easing methods (loans are credit loans in most cases with the low realization ability of pledges). Other risks include the existence of many illegal operations (mainly referring to government offering guarantee or decisions made by the local NPCs), low ability in price negotiation, and weak system risk control (closely related to platform loans and land finance).[22]

What is worth noticing is that while at the same time, the local financing platforms support local economy, they bring along problems as well. The "fiscal credit" introduces local governments into the competition over financial resources, squeezing out folk investment. In the long run, in

---

[22] See more in the interview with Mr. Wang Junshou, Deputy Director of Tianjin Bureau of Banking Regulation in "Improving local financial management system under the framework of the Twelfth Five-Year Plan," *Financial Times (China)*. (Retrieved from http://finance.stockstar.com/JL2010121300000700.shtml.)

particular the cooperation between banks and governments based on government credit will accelerate the flow of credit funds into local financial platform and make investment by state-owned sectors surpass that by private sectors when the monetary policy is loose. While once the monetary policy becomes tight, financial organizations are likely to withdraw short-term loans issued to private small or medium enterprises, as the loan projects of a local financing platform are usually of a large size and long validity. Besides, since local financing platforms often pay off loans by non-tax revenue, e.g., charge of public utilities and land transfer, local governments are prone to raising charges on public services, facilities, and prices of real estate in order to enlarge or maintain its credit scale. Thus, pressure is placed back onto monetary policy and the difficulty of control over potential inflation is increased.

3.7.3 The main reasons for the defects of the local governments' financial management system

Nationally, the local government's financial management system is different from that of the local government in the development areas, as well as the emphasis of management. For example, in some capital cities such as Tianjin, Hangzhou, Jinan, and Chongqing, the local government emphasizes putting finance to support and introducing capital to finance for the local economic development. The local government aims to build up the regional finance center and provide direct finance for regional economic development; the undeveloped areas have purer motive to join the regional economic development because of their local-limited development that is to finance more bank loans for local companies (Li & Jiang, 2008). Overall, the defects of the local government financial management system are in some degree affected by the following factors.

(i) The assessment mechanism of the GDP Championship

The local government's one-sided emphasis on the assessment mechanism of GDP is the main reason for the defects of the local government financial management system. For a long time, the government's targets of economic development for China multiplied, but the primary goal is to ensure economic growth. Its other targets include the growth rate of the central and local fiscal revenue, consumer price index (CPI), urban unemployment population, energy conservation and emissions reduction, education, health care, social security, promoting consumption, narrowing the gap between urban and rural areas, the development in the central and western regions, etc.

In spite of these important goals, the actual result of their implementation is the exceeded completion of the GDP and fiscal revenue, but with annual debts of other indicators. "Put the growth of GDP as a major sign in the works of government at all levels, not only for the assessment of cadres, but also for the public opinion. This notion should be a form of the whole society" (Wu, 2008).

The promoting of competition by the local officials is mainly for regional achievements; the competition of regional achievements is for economic growth; the competition of economic growth is for the investment; thus the competition for the financial resources. The reason is that for the local government, the implementation of short-term targets or a medium-term plan needs capital. To realize the targets that require money where needed by putting pressure and influence on local financial institutions is not only the most efficient way of development and allocation of local economic resources, but also the main method of getting a better control of the financial resources for the local government, which make GDP performance as standard. The methods of controlling financial resources include setting up financial institutions, as well as putting influence on the business of these institutions — mainly on the arrangement of the rights of personnel administration and equity. Besides, an important feature of the GDP Championships is that the promotion of an official will reduce the opportunity of another official, which leads to local officials competing against each other for economy, creating politics, and hindering each other by setting barriers of element flows and market segmentation as far as costs allow. Consequently, the regional allocation of the financial resources becomes inefficient. At the same time, the one-sided pursuit of achievements leads to the inefficiency of some financial institutions of local government. These practices include the attraction and building up of financial institutions through policies on subsidies, executive tax relief, listed preferences for branches, and so on. "The local governments do not practice well in many aspects, but waste time, energy, and resources."[23]

(ii) Inequality between the rights on finance and rights on personnel administration of the local government

The inequality between the rights on finance and the rights[24] on personnel administration of the local government under the system of tax distribution leads to the competition for opportunities between the central and the local governments and between the superior and subordinate government, as well as "weak revenue, strong finance" (Zhou, 2003) in the transition period. All of these factors are main reasons for the local government to intervene in the allocation of financial resources. In recent years, the constant deepening of financial reform in China, "one bank, three commissions" (PBOC, CBRC, CSRC, and CIRC) and state-owned financial institutions have all strengthened the longitudinal-vertical management system. With the practice of this system, the local government and regional financial institutions are facing increasingly prominent contradictions, which have become awkward problems for the financial regulation of the central bank and the development of the financial industries.

One problem is the increasingly weakened local financial services, which have suffered due to the streamline of the four state-owned commercial banks and the withdrawal of rights back to the superiors. Another is that after the central financial regulators create a vertical leadership system over the local branches and place financial regulation as the focus, and the local financial industries' development becomes

[23]Quoted from the speech of Wang Jun, Chief Financial Expert of the Bureau of Asia and Pacific Financial Development of the World Bank, on National Financial Affairs Offices Development Forum on October 31, 2010. (Retrieved from http://www.360doc.com/content/10/1104/16/1661689_66580065.shtml.)

[24]The statistics show that local fiscal revenue took up an average 47% of total national revenue from 1995 to 2008, but created 74% of total expenses. At the end of 2008, in particular, the central government and local governments took, respectively, 1.18 trillion and 2.82 trillion *yuan* of the 4 trillion *yuan* of the economic incentive plan after the global financial crisis. However, the local revenue totaled only 2.77 trillion *yuan*.

increasingly incompatible with the financial services. The severe situation makes it embarrassing for the local government to face and make progress. On the one hand, although the local government takes complete responsibility for regional, economic, and social development, it is still powerless when the local economy is blocked by the insufficient supply of effective credit services. On the other hand, though a lack of voice, let alone decision-making power on the financial problems, the local government has to take the "obligatory responsibility" of ensuring a party's financial security. Therefore, setting up financial office under control of the local government to help the central government strengthen the regulation of the local financial institutions is necessary. On the one hand, because of the devolution of powers from central government, the local government is not only responsible for developing the economy and making policies for education, employment, agriculture, rural areas and farmers, but also responsible ensuring local stability. There is a "time lag" between the hysteresis of fiscal revenue and the need for construction projects (e.g., bridge financing, which is paid in stocks by contractors after a project is listed), of which it should be aware. On the other hand, allocating financial resources nationwide based on the market often leads to the resources flowing to the wealthier areas, whereas the government of the poorer areas has to control the financial resources through administration or other diplomatic strategies. The local government is able to control the price of labor, land, and other elements; in fact, this means the local government has the right to allocate the regional financial resources, because the "newer" preferential policies on land, tax, and market access have been the most trusted guarantee of banks and governments at present. Therefore, the financial resources are naturally allocated through administrative power and the combination of the capital and power achieved.

(iii) Policy-oriented financial decline and the narrowed channel of local government finance

The decline of policy-oriented finance and the narrowed channel of local government finance is another example of the defects of the local government financial management system. Due to the lack of nationally supported and policy-oriented financial institutions (Jia, 2010), many fields that need these policy-oriented financial services are short of large capital. These fields are of great significance for the development of national economy and social stability, mainly including "agriculture, rural areas and farmers," small- and medium-sized enterprises financing, coordinate regional development, post-disaster restructure, technical reform, innovation, and so on. At present, the local government can commercially finance some profitable projects by indirectly setting up investment companies or balance of trade (BOT) or trust, but the majority of public goods are of poor profitability, have a long construction period, and big risk can only be supported by the government.

Compared with the mature bond financing method of the government overseas, and the "Budget Law of the People's Republic of China" rules, the budgets of local government at all levels should be planned with the principle of making ends meet and avoiding deficit. The local government could not issue the governmental bonds otherwise stipulated by law or the State Council. In spite of 400 billion dollars of local bonds indirectly released by the Ministry of Finance successively, the limit on local bonds definitely affects the issued scale and quantity of local bonds. Since revenue growth could not meet the needs of local development, the policy-oriented financing decline and financing channels become narrow, and bank credit has been a key link of the financial system, besides, "local government as enterprises" (Walder, 1998) has to intervene to support the whole system and make decisions for financial allocation through administration. As a result, the local economic development cannot be supported by financial resources through effective channels, then the strong need for funds comes into being, catalyzed by some factors including the GDP Championships, inequality between financial powers and administrative rights, policy-oriented finance turning to enterprises, and the competition of the local government for the financial resources becoming fiercer. To solve the aforementioned problems and achieve harmonious development between local finance and economy, the local government definitely needs to face the local demand for financial resources, improve the financial management system, and play a positive role in the allocation of financial resources.

3.7.4 Some thoughts on improving local governments' financial management system

The 12th Five-Year Plan emphasizes that China should focus on the transformation of economic growth pattern, the structural adjustment in economy, industry, and urban-rural regions, the improvement of people's well-being, the in-depth reform and opening up, and closer regional collaborations. As to local governments, they should on the one hand enhance financial ecological environment in line with the requirements of national regional development plans, and on the other hand, taking the concept and development of local financial industries as the main thread, accelerate industrial structural adjustment and the fundamental transfer of industrial growth pattern. At the same time, it is of equal importance to improve local governments' financial management system, which requires the local governments to promote market-oriented allocation of financial resources as principle, establish institutional guarantee for economic development of the areas served by the financial organizations, and harmonize local economic development and overall efficiency of financial resources allocation. Moreover, three transformations also need to be realized. First is the transformation from covert intervention to overt management. To realize this goal, there should be a clear segregation of the duties of central government, local governments and financial regulatory sectors, specific boundaries for the actions of local governments in terms of financial management, standardized and decided functions of organs in charge of local financial management, and a well-established supervisory and incentive mechanism. The second is the transformation from heavy dependence on bank credits to multiple ways of financing. It demands the establishment of a multi-level regional financial market system and a municipal bond market, as well as advocating innovation of local financial products with controllable risks. The third is the transformation from government dominance to a combination of government and market dominance, and from direct financial interference to indirect guidance of the flow of financial resources by marketization.

To achieve this transformation target, the structure of the financial market should be optimized; private funds are supposed to be guided into local finance under the premise of the institutional guarantee of economic growth to the area served by the financial organizations. To sum up, there are several tasks, which need to be done as follows.

(i) Establish a scientific outlook of financial development and determine the conduct boundaries of local governments' financial management

In the first place, local governments must set up a scientific and rational outlook of financial development, diverting the attention of local financial management from the pursuit of funds to coordination and service. With the market-oriented allocation of financial resources as the leading force, local governments should not interfere in the normal and regular flowing of funds between regions, or in how financial organizations perform in specific businesses. They should make plans for local financial development in the light of regional situations and rules of economic development, and develop local financial industry by attracting private funds. Moreover, the proposed policies should offer preferential conditions to guide financial resources to flow toward underdeveloped rural areas in order to average financial services, bridge the gap between urban and rural regions, contribute to ecological and credit environment construction for local finance, and to create favorable exterior conditions for making the best out of the local financial system.

Secondly, it is necessary to re-determine the duties and powers of financial regulation between the central and local governments and make their duties virtually correspond to each other. The authorities of licensing approval for the branches of financial organizations should be segmented to form a dual-supervisory mode, where central government has the approval authority of founding an organization, while a local government has that of the entry of an organization. Meanwhile, the business tax of branches will be included in the revenue of a county or a city. Moreover, the local governments have the right to decide whether preferable terms should be granted to the branches by considering their service performance. This measure compels the organizations to take the balance issue of attracting deposits and releasing loans into account, so that the local financial resources will not go into overdraft. In the United States, the state governments have such financial functions as formulating and enforcing the state-level financial surveillance act, taking care of the registration and management of state-level financial agencies, monitoring the legal operation of those agencies, protecting the rights of consumers, optimizing local financial structure, making local financial operational information public, and maintaining local financial stability. Given that China has a unitary system of government, but fiscal arrangements among local governments show characteristics of the federal system (Huang, 2003), we can learn from America to transfer the approval authority for the market entry of financial organizations down to provincial governments, and confer them the corresponding duties of management. Institutional construction is strengthened to offer improved laws and regulations, to avoid vicious completion of supervision, and to promote supervisory cooperation. In this way, not only can the process of private capital entering financial industry be shortened, but also the stability of the financial system is kept.

Thirdly, sort out the relations and duties of governments at all levels and of financial regulators. Local governments should attach importance to the reform and coordinative service of local financial organizations. Financial regulators are responsible for supervision. While promoting reform and coordinating services, any approach, as long as it does not go against financial regulations and policies, is allowed. Furthermore, the relations between local governments and local financial organizations should be identified. Local governments should focus on servicing, protecting the legitimate rights of local financial organs, and advocating the foundation of chambers of commerce and associations of relevance in the financial industry, which will be responsible for communicating between governments and financial organizations after the reform on financial organs is basically complete. Local financial management sectors are supposed to help financial regulators by directing and supervising chambers of commerce and associations. Financial regulators must exercise powers in an appropriate way and strictly monitor asset quality, asset adequacy rate, market entry and exit, certification of employees, legitimacy and legal operation of local financial organizations.

(ii) Establish and improve the incentive constraint mechanism and guide administrative conduct of local governments

To begin with, an institutional guarantee should be offered for the economic development of places served by the financial organizations. Through reforming the credit funds management system, it should be clearly specified that a certain proportion of available funds be designated for economic growth. The scopes of businesses and services of different types of financial organizations should be identified. Moreover, governments should also encourage state-owned commercial banks and stock-holding banks to change their management mechanism, and in the meantime create new financial entities to provide a system safeguard for financial resources serving the local economy.

Secondly, governments' budget management must be perfected and the scope of local credit properly controlled from a macroprudential perspective. The central government should guide the budgeting of local governments to take into account local economic goals, investment plans and fiscal capacity, to make governments' balance sheets, and to accurately calculate indicators like debt ratio and debt service ratio, to gain awareness of risk and of debt paying willingness, and to realize the balance of projects, land use, and funds. At the same time, local governments should scientifically estimate the available financial resources, properly control the scale of credits, prevent possible risks to financing platforms, and avoid contending profits or loans with residents. Financial regulators should adopt counter-cyclical methods of supervision, offer advice on and resolve issues like the "individual rationality triggering collective non-rationality" induced by financing platforms, urge financial organs to moderately and properly participate in the financing of government-based enterprises or platforms in line with the principles of "risk foremost" and "compliance first," so as to ensure an organic unification of development and risks.

Thirdly, the laws and regulations necessary for financial management should be established and improved. The Budget Law and Tax Law of China currently in force are already outdated, so the amendment of certain terms is urgently needed to keep up with the times. For example, the new law can allow local governments to be in moderate debt by issuing bonds, borrowing from banks, and distinguishing its "powers of the purse," so as to constrain their impulse of investment and financing preference, and at the same time to carry out their duties properly and efficiently.

Lastly, weaken the institutional incentive of excessive GDP pursuit by local governments and avoid the risk that a government may fall into the temptation of specific profits or narrow interests. The performance check on local governments and officials should add to its criteria certain indicators, including the level of social development, the happiness index of residents, environmental protection, and ecological balance. In other words, economic development is not the only target to be examined, but also social development, stability, and harmony, by which way the functions of governments will be diverted from economic activities to public services.

(iii) Regulate the functions of local governments and financial supervision organizations; improve the level of specialization and marketization

Firstly, a financial supervision office should be set up within the local governments. Its functions are: to make the overall planning for local financial industry development; to guide the reform and development of local financial institutions; to be responsible for the guidance and coordination of the financial institutions that are wholly or partly funded by local governments; to promote the establishment of a local credit system and improve the financial ecology construction; to establish regional financial risk monitoring; and to establish a coordinated risk warning and crisis emergency intervention platform mechanism for the development of overall financial stability. Its final purpose is to promote the communication and exchange of information between local governments and basic central banks, financial supervision departments and financial institutions, improve the consciousness and prevention ability of financial risk, and jointly deal with the problems in financial operation.

Secondly, the financial office's management functions must be strengthened, and gradually stripped of its financing functions, highlighting its stability functions. Under the current financial framework, its functions should be to assist "one bank and three commissions" in financial supervision. This entails being responsible for supervising certain fields that "one bank and three commissions" are unable to cover, such as small loan companies and financing guarantee companies, to maintain local financial stability, and prevent and assist "one bank and three commissions" resolve the local financial risks. The existing financing functions of the financial office should be gradually stripped and transferred to institutions like the Investment Promotion Committee. At the same time, the economy's stability should be strengthened, while local governments should support the financial office to establish and improve the financial stability fund for mergers, restructuring, rescue, withdrawal, and other financial risk disposals of financial institutions. The financial office should enhance its financial risk aversion and disposal ability, and promote the development of local financial institutions.

Thirdly, strengthen the management system of the financial office; improve the ability of the financial office's screening, decision-making, and coordination. Establish a standardized and effective local financial institutions supervision system, and give the financial office certain administrative powers. These include the right to make recommendations in the selection of financial savings institutions, major projects financing institutions, the municipal state-owned listing and financing intermediaries, etc.; the right to evaluate the appointment and removal of personnel, performance appraisal of municipal financial institutions; and the right to supervise financial industries. At the same time, local governments should promote the greater use of economic, legal, and marketing means to supervise the lawful operation of local financial institutions, preventing the occurrence of illegal operations and other acts that endanger local financial security. The local government can supervise the legal compliance of the financial institutions by the administration of directors and supervisors, implementing a strict management responsibility system and perfecting their supervision mechanism, based on the reform of the property rights system and improvement of the operator's outgoing audit system, the annual financial audit system, and the major audit system. The Communist Party and external supervisors can manage those local financial institutions without government ownership. The government should establish the entry and exit mechanism of local financial institutions, clean up unqualified local financial institutions, improve stock reform, reform existing institutions, pay attention to incremental development, and take effective measures to enable the qualified local financial institutions enter the market, develop, and grow.

(iv) Establish a diversified multi-level regional financial market system; broaden the financing channels of local governments

At present, the capital market in most regions of China lags behind, its way of financing too dependent and risky on the banking system, thus increasing the vulnerability of the financial system, which is not good for its overall function. Therefore, the local government should place effort into promoting a diversified regional financing structure, and vigorously develop venture capital investment,[25] as a beginning. It should also establish a diversified multi-level capital market system involving more small and medium indirect financing institutions to ease the pressure of their financing. The promotion of the development for the financial service industry is also needed — with reduction of the transaction costs between the enterprises and financial institutions — as well as further improvements to the proportion of direct financing to help the enterprises within their jurisdictions get financing through the stock listing. This should include issuing bonds and asset-backed securities, issuing industry funds, BT or BOT mode, introducing risk investment, etc. In particular, from the experience of the United States, Japan, Germany, France, and other devel-

[25]Global experience shows that the emerging capital markets, such as venture capital and the securities market are more suitable to promote the innovation and the development of emerging industries with high risk and unbalanced distribution. The experience of China's reform and opening up has also shown that the current financial system is more effective for large-scale infrastructure and general industry development projects, but relatively not beneficial to the development of technology innovation, and small- and medium-sized enterprises. The financing difficulties of small- and medium-sized enterprises — especially those that are high-tech — have been a prominent problem in China for a long time. During the period of the 12th Five-Year Plan, with the change of supply and demand of the labor force in China and the gradual reduction of the "demographic dividend," the demand for innovation dividends will gradually get attention. In addition, the demand for financial services, such as venture capital, will also increase and their development will usher in real historical opportunity.

oped countries, the local bond market is an important means for local government financing. It plays an important role in the development of local economy. Therefore, a local public institution bond financing system that is suitable for China should be explored and established, (so as to continue to improve the central agency-issued local government bond system). Local public institutional bond markets must be developed in order to respond to the normal financing needs of local urbanization, and standard financing channels provided for local governments and their subsidiaries. In the meantime, the local government should try to avoid the various risks caused by informal financing, promote the rationalization of local governments' economic behavior, and create the necessary conditions for the adjustment of industrial structure.

(v) Improve governance structure of local financial institutions: Enhancing their risk management and control capabilities

For the existing local corporate financial institutions — especially those with government equity participation — the government should improve their corporate governance as soon as possible, clarify the relationship of property right, and safeguard the long-term stability of the independent legal person status. On this basis, the government should introduce the appropriate external pressure of competition and sustainable supporting policies, closely combining the insiders' rights and long-term interests of financial institutions, and strengthening the incentive constraints mechanism to avoid the risk of moral hazards and adverse selections. For all kinds of new financial institutions and quasi-financial institutions, on the one hand, the government should strongly support and encourage their innovation; on the other hand, this innovation needs prudential management. The government should constantly improve management rules, standardizing the management by external supervision norms, and pay attention to the possible risks in the growth process. It should also strengthen supervision, which shall not be limited to the mastery of its data, and discover any violating behavior through on-the-spot inspection, urging rectification of any such indiscretion.

(vi) Promote the policy-based financial reform: Optimizing the total efficiency of social funds allocation

The government should deepen the reform of policy-based financial institutions, improve their operational level, and gradually build a sound policy-based financial system. This must involve the motivation and utilization of financial resources to meet the needs of certain fields and industries such as agriculture, rural areas and farmers, the science and technology industry, and small- and medium-sized enterprises. This would trigger industrial structural transformation, filling the intermediate zone between direct financial expenses and commercial financing for the pursuit of converting the government financial support mechanism.

For "the market failure" participating for the allocation of funds and resources, the government can mobilize and explore various potential key elements that may be available. Optimizing economic structure and improving the quality of development can reduce the costs of national strategy and policy objectives, optimizing the total efficiency of social capital allocation Jia (2010).

Chapter 4

Real Estate Price Fluctuation and Financial Stability

The subprime mortgage crisis of 2007 resulting from the burst of the USA real estate bubble was the most serious impact on the global financial system and economic system since the Great Depression between 1929 and 1933. It warned us once again that real estate price stability has great importance to the financial system. With economic globalization and financial liberalization, great fluctuation, such as inflation and tightening, has taken place in the asset market related to stocks and real estate, which resulted in serious financial crisis. The Japanese bubble economy in the 1980s, the Asian financial crisis in the 1990s, and the American subprime mortgage crisis in 2007, have all related to the wide price fluctuation of real estate. Real estate price fluctuation has become an importation factor influencing financial stability.

4.1 THE MECHANISM OF HOW REAL ESTATE PRICE FLUCTUATIONS AFFECT FINANCIAL STABILITY

The real estate industry is a capital-intensive industry, which cannot develop without credit fund support from financial institutions. Moreover, the undue fluctuation of real estate prices result in frequent bubbles, while the banking industry has innate vulnerability due to its own management features. The combination of these two industries makes problems more serious; a real estate industry bubble makes asset prices unstable. Many financial resources are deployed in the real estate industry, which results in a large number of bad debts and is a cause of financial system instability. Furthermore, it may easily create a broken bank fund chain and initiate a systematic financial crisis threatening the sound development of the whole economy. Among these, information asymmetry is a key factor of real estate price fluctuation affecting financial stability.

4.1.1 Information asymmetry in the real estate market

(i) Information asymmetry theory

According to the analysis paradigm of new classic economics, the general competitive commodity market belongs to a perfect market of pure competition. There is no access barrier in such a market. Enterprises can come and go at liberty, realizing a free allocation of resources. Most enterprises supply the same products with no big difference between them. The buyer and seller possess complete information and knowledge in trade. In the analysis of market trade and operation, complete information hypothesis is an important premise. In accordance with the theory of new classic economics, the credit market belongs to a perfect market such as this, having no difference with other competitive commodity markets.

There exists a certain difference between the simplified and abstract analysis on the general competitive goods market of new classic economics and actual market operation; in particular, the complete information asymmetry is difficult to recognize in actual economy. Information asymmetry is very common in the market. Due to the cost of collecting data, both trade parties have a differing amount of information concerning demand and supply relation, price, and quality, etc. Generally, the buyer knows some related information. Classic economics theory ignores the asymmetric information condition; on the one hand, it is assumed that there is no information difference between traders in the market against the corresponding monopoly factor, to build an analysis from a perfect competition market; on the other hand, there is no obvious social division of labor and profession at that moment. With the development of social labor division and improvement of specialization degree, moreover, the information asymmetry phenomenon will be widespread due to knowledge limitation between economic bodies, the cost of collecting data, and information being blocked purposely by parties with priority access to information. It will seriously prevent the basic economic function of the market from working. Information asymmetry is a factor that cannot be ignored in social production and distribution; its effect on allocation effectiveness is it is already common knowledge in the field of economics research.

The party with information, or with more information (which is called the agent), is in an advantageous position. It is possible to obtain most profit in the trade by the use of information; the party with information, or less information (which is called the client), may therefore lose profit. According to time, information asymmetry may have happened before a business contract is signed, which is called prior asymmetry, resulting in adverse selection; information asymmetry may have happened after a business contract is signed, which is called post asymmetry, causing moral risk.

Adverse selection refers to that situation when the party with less information makes an adverse choice for itself in the trade before a contract is signed, due to information asymmetry. The American economist, George Akerlof, illustrated incomplete information theory in 1970 and proposed the model of the well-known used car market. In any commodity market, as in the used car market, the seller is the person who really knows the product quality. The seller with poor quality products does not tell the truth about product quality to obtain abnormal profit. The buyer can only make a decision on purchase quantity and price according to the average quality available in the market. In this case, faulty goods take advantage in being low cost, while good products with high cost will be eliminated out of the market. The average quality of trade product is declining in the market. When the buyer realizes product quality in the market is worse than expected, he lowers the amount he is willing to pay. Finally, good products may be eliminated from sale by the market adjustment. Consumers lose confidence and would rather not buy, than by taking a risk that creates market shrinkage.

Moral risk generally refers to that one party acting against the other party in order to increase profit to the maximum in the execution of a business contract. For example, in the principal–agent relationship after a business contract is signed, if the principal's benefit relies on the agent and the principal is not sure whether the agent would like to actively realize the benefit for him or not, the realization of benefit is facing moral risk. The agent possesses private information in contrast to the principal, and at the same time, the incompleteness of the contract protects the responsible agent from bearing full loss or profit, therefore they will not be culpable of the end result. There is also no internal incentive for them to realize the principal's benefits. The agent tends to act to improve his or her own income or benefit, while damaging the principal's.

Information asymmetry is typified by social labor division and specialization in the economic information field. It is also a basis of information economics and game theory research. Using information asymmetry to analyze economic operation is to build a model with asymmetric information. The most common-use analysis method is to build a countermeasure model with asymmetric information using the Bayesian Nash equilibrium to explain economic phenomenon and action in the actual market.

(ii) Information asymmetry of the real estate market

The real estate market is very professional; however, heterogeneity of product causes information asymmetry in trade. A real estate dealer has all the information related to the real estate process. He has the obvious advantage, compared with the purchaser of a house. The purchaser can only get limited knowledge of the real estate he purchased with time, knowledge, and information sources, etc. Under the circumstance of the pre-sale of commercial housing, the purchaser of the real estate under construction has no way to know the quality and condition of his property until the construction is finished and supporting facilities are equipped. Information asymmetry is obviously evident here.

First, information asymmetry is embodied in the cost and profit of real estate development. Commercial housing involves particularly large sums of consumption and investment. With the flow chart of a real estate project, the dealer himself is quite clear on various input cost and taxation expenditure in term of the land tender, construction and installation cost in construction stage, infrastructure, and supporting facilities and sale, whereas the common purchaser has not enough time, energy, and sources from which to collect relative information. Information asymmetry of real estate cost leaves the dealer with a lot of room for fixing a price. Because a purchaser has nothing to refer to or compare with in this situation, price fixing is more private and optional. The dealer can obtain large sum of profit by having that information advantage. In August 2005, Fuzhou Municipal Price Bureau published a commodity housing cost list of a representative development project in an interview with a reporter from the Xinhua news agency, taking the lead in the country to open out the profit ratio of cost of housing industry, which has an average value of above 50%. Information of this kind was seldom published after that. The profiting group in the real estate industry would not publish information on cost and profit, in order to obtain monopoly profit by keeping commercial house price high.

The second is information asymmetry of house build quality. House build quality is mainly expressed by structure, living space, layout design, supporting facilities, construction quality, and residential landscape, etc. It is very complicated to construct a building involving various professional fields, while at the same time, it is very hard to tell whether the work is completed or the quality good or not from outside appearances. The real estate dealer has the totality of information of all the processes including planning, construction and sale, whereas the purchaser is totally in an inferior position. The dealer often highlights the advantages and hides defects, by highlighting the supporting facilities or surroundings of the commercial housing in publicity materials, or even by providing false information in order to expand sale or improve price. For example, the real estate dealer changes the apartment design to minimize usable floor area and increase the pool area without permission from the purchaser; or cheats by cutting down on materials for the project and makes a false report on the grade of these building materials, or by occupying green belt, etc. In particular, under the system of pre-sale housing, the landscape and green belt are often far away from the promised planning at the time of sale. The purchaser can only make purchase decision from the information (e.g., advertisement) provided by the dealer. Even if a completed apartment is sold, it is difficult to tell whether the building material and equipment are good or not, or whether there is any defect in foundation or structure from the appearance of the building. Information asymmetry of apartment quality makes it easy for the party with full information to increase self-benefits to the maximum and do harm to the other party at the same time.

The third is information asymmetry of apartment supply in the market. Residential housing has a long production cycle, which needs a large amount of money in the construction stage. If the constructed residential housing cannot be sold, it will not only be a great waste of social resources, but also bring financial risk; therefore, it is permitted for a real estate dealer to sell housing under construction in many countries and regions. Because a project is under construction, the real estate dealer has a longer time before the actual sale of the constructed apartment, which will choose a best time to fix a top selling price. In order to achieve such purposes, a real estate dealer will corner apartment sources or arrange on-site sales staff to create an atmosphere that demand exceeds supply, leading to a upsurge of market in order to raise prices and obtain more profit.

The fourth is information asymmetry of commercial housing prices. The heterogeneity of housing commodity makes it different from general commodities. There is no batch of products sold at same price. Even if several apartments are in one building, their prices vary because of different floor, orientation, access to daylight, and the individual preferences of each different purchaser. However, such microscopic factors can only affect unit price, but not the average price of real estate. Regional economic development conditions and macroeconomic factors can influence housing price, resulting in fluctuation of average price of real estate. Therefore, it is hard to grasp all the information that affects real estate price. As the information asymmetry of housing price exists between real estate dealer and purchaser, the former has the advantage in fixing price by these factors. In general, a real estate dealer will use such a pricing policy in a residential project for which the construction is done in stages; the price of buildings constructed later is higher than those constructed earlier. The purchaser generally neither buys up nor buys down, and the dealer exploits this to create a buyer impulse to purchase the house sooner rather than later. As a necessity, house demand price has a low flexibility. Raising the selling price has less impact on rigid demand; moreover, speculative demand will emerge. It helps a real estate dealer to get monopoly on profit by raising the price constantly. Therefore, it is hard for the cost of real estate to reach an equilibrium point in market price.

(iii) Information asymmetry of the real estate financial market

As a large sum of assets is needed in real estate construction and transaction, it is a high cost to bear, no matter who is the real estate dealer or apartment purchaser. External financing is often taken into account, particularly by obtaining indirect financing from financial institutions, whether to enable project construction or to buy an apartment. In addition, the real estate industry is one of the highest profit industries in the past few years. Besides, since real estate market reform in 1998, price, and sales volume has been going up steadily. Real estate enterprise is capable of making profit and repaying loans. It is also safe to give a mortgage loan to a house purchaser. Therefore, real estate industry is the main fund investment field for financial institution in the country. Credit funding from banks has already become main fund source of real estate enterprise, as well as the funding source for the house purchaser with a mortgage. Nearly all the commercial banks have made real estate credit fund a major business. A large quantity of credit fund has been made available to the real estate market.

Analysis is made in terms of the information asymmetry that the financial institution as a fund supplier has less information about financial condition and solvency of the fund requesters (real estate dealer and house purchaser) in the real estate financial market. The real estate developer knows about its own business condition and financial situation, while it is hard for financial institution to collect full information about real estate enterprise, due to being a different professional field and the cost of data collection. Information asymmetry exists between financial institution and house purchaser as well. Due to the variety of mortgage borrowers, it is hard for a financial institution to check carefully the actual income and solvency of each borrower. A limited check is done according to the information provided by the borrower.

Therefore, it is difficult to distinguish and eliminate applicants with bad credit before a loan is issued. Information asymmetry between the financial institution, real estate developer, and house purchaser results in a game between all economic bodies in the real estate market and financial market. This will affect the transaction price and total credit fund input.

4.1.2 Analysis on the real estate transaction and credit market deal based on information asymmetry

(i) Game analysis on main bodies in real estate transaction market

As the main bodies in the real estate transaction market, both real estate dealer and house purchaser have their own interests and targets. Their individual behaviors are limited rational. Each stakeholder is pursuing maximum interests in the transaction. The real estate dealer realizes best economic benefit by way of improving land-use rate, plot ratio, and building density, as well as raising selling price. The house purchaser collects information from housing sources to buy a suitable apartment for residence or investment at lower price. However, the real estate dealer has more market information than a house purchaser, but it is not complete. In accordance with Harsanyi's transformation theory, the real estate market is divided into prosperity and recession by natural selection; the probability is q and $1 - q$, respectively. The real estate dealer has two strategic choices of reducing price or not; the consumer has two strategic choices of entering into the market, or to wait and see. Under the condition of information asymmetry, both parties play the game around transaction price. The payment function of the real estate dealer and house purchaser is shown in Figure 4-1.

In the recession period of real estate industry, the dealer reduces a price for sale promotion. If a house purchaser enters into market, the profit of the dealer at the time is $x - c$: x stands for the income from house sale; c stands for its development cost; the house purchaser's profit is $u - x$. The u stands for the effectiveness gained by the purchaser from house purchase, i.e., an expected price for the house purchased, while x stands for

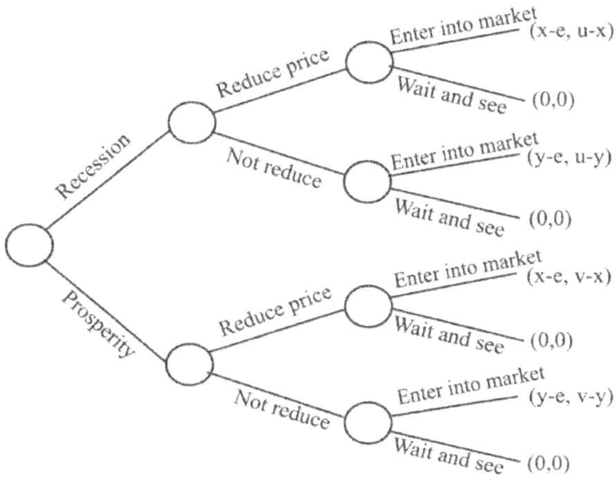

Figure 4-1. The information asymmetry game between real estate developer and house purchaser.

the actual payment for the house. If a house purchaser takes a "wait and see" attitude, the profit is zero for the real estate dealer, and the same is true for the house purchaser. When a real estate dealer does not reduce a price, if a house purchaser enters the market, the dealer's profit is $y - c$; y stands for the income of the house sale and c stands for development cost. Meanwhile, the purchaser's profit is $u - y$; u stands for the effectiveness the purchaser gets from house purchase, i.e., the expected price for the house, while y stands for actual payment. If the purchasers wait and see, the profit is zero for both dealer and purchaser.

In the prosperity period of real estate industry, when a real estate dealer reduces price, if a purchaser enters into market, the profit is $x - c$ for real estate dealer at this moment and $v - x$ for the purchaser. While v stands for the effectiveness the purchasers get from the house purchase, i.e., expected price for the house purchased, x stands for the actual payment for the house; if the purchaser waits and sees, the profit is zero for both real estate dealer and house purchaser. When the real estate dealer does not reduce price, and if a house purchaser enters the market, the profit is $y - c$ for the dealer: y stands for sales income; c stands for development cost; and profit is $v - y$ for the house purchaser. At the same time, we assume $y > x > c$ (sales income before price reduction is bigger than that after price reduction; sales income is bigger than cost of development, otherwise real estate enterprise exits from the market); $v > u$ (i.e., the price the purchaser would like to pay in the prosperity period is higher than that of recession period).

The Bayesian equilibrium under incomplete information static game conditions is shown as follows:

(i) When $u - x > 0$, $u - y > 0$, $v - x > 0$, i.e., $v > u > y > x$, no matter whether the real estate market is prosperous or recessive, the house price that the purchaser is able to pay is higher than the actual price of the house, and the purchaser will choose to enter into market. The expected profit is $x - c$ if the dealer reduces the price, which is $y - c$ if the dealer does not reduce the price, therefore $y - c > x - c$ is the Bayesian equilibrium at this time. The dealer may even try to increase the selling price according to rigid demand for housing.

(ii) When $u - x > 0$, $v - x > 0$, $u - y < 0$, $v - y < 0$, i.e., $y > v > u > x$, no matter whether the real estate market is prosperous or recessive, the price the purchaser is able to pay is lower than the sale price when the dealer does not make a reduction. Only if the dealer reduces the price, the purchaser would like to pay higher price than the selling price. The expected effectiveness at the time of purchase is higher than the expected profit when adopting a "wait and see" attitude, and the purchaser will enter into market. The dealer's expected profit is $x - c$ when he reduces the price, and zero when he does not reduce the price, because $x - c > 0$. Therefore, the dealer will reduce the price in such a game (the dealer reduces price and purchaser will buy), which is the Bayesian equilibrium satisfying the aforementioned conditions.

(iii) When $u - x < 0$, $v - x > 0$, $u - y < 0$, $v - y < 0$, i.e., $y > v > x > u$, the purchaser will buy when he is able to pay a higher than selling price, if the market is prosperous and the dealer reduces the price. The expected profit is $q(x - c)$ when the dealer reduces the price, which becomes zero when he does not reduce the price. Because $q(x - c) > 0$, so the dealer will reduce price. At this time (the dealer reduces price and the purchaser buys when the market is prosperous), the Bayesian equilibrium satisfies all conditions. When the real estate market is in recession and house purchasers choose to wait and see, then complete strategic Bayesian equilibrium does not exist at this time.

(iv) When $u - x < 0$, $u - y < 0$, $v - x < 0$, $v - u < 0$, i.e., $y > x > v > u$, no matter whether the real estate market is prosperous or recessive, or if the dealer reduces price or not, the price that the house purchaser is able to pay is always lower than the selling price, and the expected effectiveness of purchase is lower than the expected effectiveness of waiting and seeing. So at this time, the purchaser would not buy and the profit is zero whether the dealer reduces the price or not. Complete strategic Bayesian equilibrium does not exist at this time.

(v) When $u - x > 0$, $v - x > 0$, $u - y < 0$, $v - y > 0$, i.e., $v > y > u > x$, excepting situations where the dealer is determined not to reduce price in the period of recession, the purchaser will buy if the price he is able to pay is higher than the selling price. The expected profit in the prosperous period is $x - c$ when the dealer reduces the price. When he does not reduce the price, the expected profit is $y - c$, because $y - c > x - c$, which is the Bayesian equilibrium of the game (the dealer does not reduce the price, but the purchaser buys).

(vi) When $u - x < 0$, $v - x > 0$, $u - y < 0$, $v - y > 0$, i.e., $v > y > x > u$, at the time of market prosperity, the purchaser is able to pay a higher price than the selling price, and the expected effectiveness at the time of purchase is higher than that of a "wait and see" moment, the purchaser will enter into the market. (For example, at the time of market recession, the purchaser is able to pay lower than the selling price, and the purchasers would like to wait and see.) The purchaser chooses to enter the market when it is prosperous. The expected profit is $x - c$ if the dealer reduces price and, $y - c$ if he does not reduce price at the time of market prosperity. Because $y - c > x - c$, the dealer would not reduce price. Then that is Bayesian equilibrium of game (the dealer does not reduce price, the purchase buys). The purchaser chooses to wait and see at the time of market recession; there is no Bayesian equilibrium.

It is known from the aforementioned game result that the transaction of real estate is not only affected by the development cost and price-fixing policy, but also by the effectiveness gained from the house purchase by the purchaser, i.e., expected price of the commodity. As long as the expected effectiveness of the house purchase is bigger than that of the "wait and see" moment, no matter whether the real estate market is in prosperity or recession, the purchasers will choose to buy. When the house price goes down at the time of market recession, the expected price from the purchaser goes down as well, and a "wait and see" attitude will be taken. When the market is prosperous, the expected price goes up; more purchasers will choose to buy. The real estate dealer will try to improve house price. The game between various parties in a house transaction results in an obvious internal impulse to force the house price going up. Credit fund support from banks will turn it into a reality.

2. GAME ANALYSIS ON MAIN BODIES IN CREDIT MARKET

In terms of bank credit, there are two main bodies in the real estate market, i.e., bank as credit fund supplier and real estate enterprise and house purchaser as credit fund demander. The bank and the borrower, as game players in the real estate credit market, choose to act in order to realize effectiveness to the maximum. We assume that there are two types of fund demander, i.e., a borrower with good reputation and a borrower with a poor reputation. A borrower with a good reputation refers to real estate enterprises, which carry out development based on full research and assessment of the real estate market; it also refers to house purchasers who have a down payment and are capable of repaying the loan. Both borrowers are fully guaranteed to pay back the loan. The borrower with poor reputation refers to those real estate enterprises that have only blind optimism for the real estate market, having neither further analysis of market trend nor repayment ability. They just follow the upsurge of the real estate market. It also refers to those house purchasers who buy the house based on an expectation of price increase without consideration of their own payment ability. Borrowers cannot guarantee the repayment. Both supplier and demander of credit funds are not quite sure about the real estate market trend, and whether it is prosperous or recessive. Judgment is only made by individual analysis.

In game theory, individual effectiveness function relies on not only its own choice, but also relies on the choice of other players in the game, i.e., individual optimal choice is a function for others' choice. There is interaction between banks and borrowers in the borrowing and lending game. In order to get the loan from the bank, it will show its cooperation and honesty in applying a loan. Due to information asymmetry, it is hard for the bank to distinguish among borrowers with good or poor reputation based on the borrower's behavior. It can only make a judgment to issue the loan by the credit records of the borrowers. At the same time, the borrower will adjust its tactics according to the bank's requirement to realize maximum effectiveness. In this game, the borrower at first chooses to make a good reputation action (i.e., a real estate developer selects a project with less risk, a house purchaser buys a house according to his repayment ability), then the bank will decide to issue the loan on the basis of credit analysis of the borrower. In a single stage game, both parties of the loan take action according to prior knowledge of similar type to maximize one's effectiveness; in a multi-stage game, both parties correct the other's expectation according to the action in previous games to achieve maximum effectiveness.

At first, we define the player's faith in his counterpart in the real estate credit market. We assume that ψ_e stands for the faith that a borrower is a high risk to a commercial bank, i.e., $\psi_e = h_e$. ψ_f stands for a borrower's faith on a commercial bank's judgment on a market situation, i.e., $\psi_e = h_f$. We use *ai* to stand for action that both parties take. In $a_i \in (0, 1)$ and $i = (1, 2)$, various activities of players are defined, respectively: $a_1 = 0$ stands for a borrower taking low-reputation action; $a_1 = 1$ stands for a borrower taking good reputation action; $a_2 = 0$ stands for commercial bank taking less support action for loan; and $a_2 = 0$ stands for bank taking more support action for loan.

For those rational participants in the game who aim to obtain maximum effectiveness, payoff is the key point that each player really cares about. As it is shown in Table 4-1, $u_i(\pi_1, \pi_2)$ stands for game player payoff between bank and borrower, among which $i = 1, 2$. $u_i(\pi_1, \pi_2)$ stands for the borrower's payoff when a borrower takes π_1 action and the bank takes π_2; on the same condition, stands for a bank's payoff when the bank takes financial support (π_2) action and borrower takes π_1 action.

In the game, we assume the borrower takes action first. Under normal circumstances, if the borrower takes good reputation action, the commercial bank will take full-support action, therefore the payoff function $u_1(1, 1)$ is established.

Table 4-1. Real estate loan payoff matrix of commercial bank.

		Loan applicant	
		Good reputation	Poor reputation
Commercial bank	Issue loan	$u_2(1, 1), u_1(1, 1)$	$u_2(0, 1), u_1(0, 1)$
	Issue no loan	$u_2(1, 0), u_1(1, 0)$	$u_2(0, 0), u_1(0, 0)$

The borrower makes a choice to take action in the game based on the bank's judgment for the market situation, in order to maximize its own payoff. It is shown as follows:

$$\zeta_1(\psi_f) \in \arg\max_{\psi_b} \sum p(\psi_f) u_1(\pi_1, \pi_2, \psi_e). \tag{4-1}$$

In the formula, p stands for the probability of certain action the bank will choose under different condition. When the borrower takes good reputation action, the payoff function is $u_1(1, 1)$; when the borrower takes low-reputation action, the expected payoff function is

$$\begin{aligned} u_1(0, \pi_2) = \psi_1[h_1 u_1(0, 0) + (1 - h_1) u_1(0, 1)] \\ + (1 - \psi_f)\,[h_2 u_1(0, 0) + (1 - h_2) u_1(0, 1)]. \end{aligned} \tag{4-2}$$

With this formula, h_1 stands for the probability that the bank takes less credit support when the borrower takes low-reputation action under the condition of a prosperous real estate market expected by the bank, i.e., $h_2 = h(\pi_2 = 0,\ \pi_1 = 0,\ \psi_f)$. h_2 stands for the probability that the bank takes less credit support when the borrower takes low-reputation action under the condition of a depressive real estate market expected by the bank, e.g., $h_2 = h(\pi_2 = 0|\ \pi_1 = 0,\ 1 - \psi_f)$. We assume that $h_1 < h_2$ all of the time, i.e., the commercial bank prefers less credit support in market recession than in market prosperity. Likewise, we assume $u_1(0, 1) > u_1(1, 1) > u_1(0, 0)$; further explanation follows here.

First, the borrower's payoff is $u_1(0, 1)$ in the case of a borrower taking low-reputation action, while the bank taking high-credit support is bigger than the payoff $u_1(1, 1)$ in the case of the borrower taking good reputation action and the bank taking high-credit support. When the borrower takes good reputation action, he needs to get a detailed investigation on the real estate market to make sure that his project can make a profit to pay back a loan. At the same time, taking into the consideration of the costs of management, personnel and sales, etc. in the construction period, the cost of borrowing goes up certainly. Therefore, $u_1(0, 1) > u_1(0, 1)$ is reasonable.

Second, the borrower's payoff $u_1(1, 1)$ in the case of a borrower taking good reputation action, while the bank taking high-credit support is bigger than the payoff $u_1(0, 0)$, the borrower obtains in the case of the borrower taking low-reputation action and the bank takes in less credit support. When the borrower takes low-reputation action, the commercial bank will take a strict check of the loan application, which is quite possible to be refused; the borrower may lose his chance for investment because of fundraising failure. Therefore, the assumption that follows is reasonable: if $u_1(1, 0) > u_1(0, \pi_2)$, the borrower will take good reputation action; if $u_1(1, 0) < u_1(0, \pi_2)$, the borrower will take low-reputation action.

No matter what aforementioned action the borrower takes, the profit is completely dependent on what kind of judgment he made with a commercial bank. We make $u_1(1, 0) = u_1(0, \pi_2)$, and a critical value of bank's faith can be calculated.

$$\psi_f^* = \frac{[h_2 u_1(0, 1) + (1 - h_2) u_1(0, 0) - u_1(1, 0)]}{\{[h_2 u_1(0, 1) + (1 - h_2) u_1(0, 0)] - [h_1 u_1(0, 1) + (1 - h_1) u_1(0, 0)]\}}$$
$$= \frac{[h_2 u_1(0, 1) + (1 - h_2) u_1(0, 0)] - u_1(1, 0)]}{(h_2 - h_1)[u_1(0, 1) - u_1(0, 0)]}. \tag{4-3}$$

When the borrower confirms that the probability of the bank's judgment on market prosperity ψ_f is bigger than the critical value ψ_f^*, he will take good reputation action. In the period of market prosperity, the borrower, who is capable and willing to take good reputation action, can obtain better profit from real estate investment. Moreover, the good reputation action will gain a follow-up loan from the bank, which provides fund support for large-scale investment later. When the borrower confirms that the probability of the bank's judgment on market prosperity ψ_f is smaller than the critical value ψ_f^*, he will take low-reputation action. Because a bank is often reluctant to issue loans in high-risk cases when the real estate market is in a depression period, it is hard for a borrower to obtain loan or it will cost a lot at that moment. The borrower's profit will drop off if he takes good reputation action. The borrower prefers low-reputation action in the consideration of cost and profit.

The commercial bank's payoff $u_2(1, 1)$ is the net income gained from a loan issued to a good reputation borrower; $u_2(0, 1)$ is the net income of the bank gained from a loan issued to a poor reputation borrower. $u_2(1, 0)$ is the effectiveness the bank gained when it rejects a loan application to a good reputation borrower. Because opportunity cost is $u_2(1, 1)$ when the bank does not support a good reputation borrower, so $u_2(1, 0) = -u_2(1, 1)$; $u_2(0, 0)$ is the bank's net income when a loan application from a poor reputation borrower is rejected, which is zero at this time.

Due to information asymmetry, the commercial bank can only judge a borrower with good or bad reputation according to the information obtained and then decides to issue the loan to the real estate enterprise or house purchaser or not. If the borrower is judged to have a good reputation and the real estate market is prosperous, the commercial bank will issue the loan based on credit risk evaluation, otherwise the loan application may be rejected. However, a real estate enterprise and a house purchaser know better about their own assets and credit. It is impossible for the commercial bank to fully understand a borrower's credit and possible risks, which can only rely on various financial statements, the income sheet submitted by the borrower and other collected sources, to evaluate the borrower. Therefore, a single game belongs to a static incomplete information game, for whether a commercial bank's strategy can be issuing a loan or not.

ψ_e refers to a bank's faith that regards a borrower as being high risk, while the probability for the bank to regard the borrower as good reputation one is $1 - \psi_e$. A bank tends to issue loans to low-risk borrowers and not to those of high risk, where the probability for the bank to issue a loan is is $1 - \psi_e$, and ψ_e for it to not release a loan.

If the expected effectiveness for the bank to release a loan is E_1, and for it to not release a loan is E_2, then

$$E_1 = (1 - \psi_e)u_2(1, 1) + \psi_e u_2(0, 1), \quad (4\text{-}4)$$

$$E_2 = (1 - \psi_e)u_2(1, 0) + \psi_e \times 0 = -(1 - \psi_e)u_2(1, 1). \quad (4\text{-}5)$$

On the critical point of deciding to issue a loan or not, $E_1 = E_2$, then we get

$$\psi_e^* = \frac{2u_2(1, 1)}{2u_2(1, 1) - u_2(0, 1)}. \tag{4-6}$$

The commercial bank can make an optimal choice on loan application. A loan is released when $\psi_e < \psi_e^*$, and rejected when $\psi_e > \psi_e^*$. There is no difference for loan issue or not on the critical point.

It is shown from the commercial bank's choice in the game of whether it issues a loan or not relies mainly on the comparison between its faith in the borrower (who may be high or low-risk) and its faith at that critical point. When real estate price remains steady or goes up, real estate enterprise's profit goes up, the value of the house purchased increases, and the borrower is more able and willing to pay back the loan. So it is less probable for the bank to regard the borrower as being high risk, i.e., the optimal choice for the bank in the game is to issue the loan. At the same time, when the borrower thinks ψ_f^* (bank's judgment on market condition) is bigger than ψ_f^* (critical value), a high-risk borrower will take good reputation action, and therefore credit risk goes down. In addition, the borrower provides the bank with information that helps the bank's credit check process. Under the circumstance of information asymmetry, the commercial bank prefers to provide credit support and increase loan issue to real estate industry when house prices are set to rise. When real estate price falls, the market is in recession, the profit of real estate enterprise declines, and the market value of the house purchased goes down, it is more probable for the commercial bank to judge a borrower as being high risk, i.e., $\psi_e > \psi_e^*$. The commercial bank will reduce credit input to the real estate market, which will cause the real estate industry to decline further.

Analysis is made from real estate transaction and game playing in the financial market; games between various parties involved in the real estate market will result in the increase of house prices. Under the circumstance of house price increases, the commercial bank will tend to release loans to real estate enterprises and house purchasers to further promote house prices. There is competition between commercial banks in issuing loans for real estate. (Loose, and loose) is the only Nash equilibrium between banks in the game. The bank will lower credit issue standards to attract more clients to gain market share, and increase loans as well (Cao & Xu, 2010). The real estate market is confronting the pressure of house price increase due to investment and speculation caused by supply constraints, rigid demand, and excess liquidity. In this context, it is an optimal choice for the bank to provide credit fund to real estate industry in the game. In case of obvious bubble or policy change related to real estate, players in the market begin to lose confidence in the market and the commercial bank will supply less credit funding, which will result in the burst bubble and bad debts of previous credit fund input, and may cause financial crisis.

4.1.3 Unusual fluctuation of real estate price impacts financial stability mechanism

(i) Accumulation of financial risks in the process of real estate price increase

Information asymmetry of real estate market and the resultant game between market players will cause house prices increases. Real estate is a typically fund-intensive industry. Among all the funds involved in real estate development and sales, funds from the bank directly and indirectly take a large proportion; in terms of the bank, when house price is steady and on up trend, with less risk for bad debts, a real estate loan is one of the best loan types. It is therefore the main loan input way for the bank and a main source of profit.

Credit funding into the real estate industry is less possible to become a bad debt in a prosperous market. The market value of an investment house keeps going up, and a purchaser can obtain profit when the investment house is sold and repay the loan; a mortgage loan takes less and less proportion in the house market value for an occupied house. A house purchaser will not be in arrears with a mortgage payment against agreement. Even if some passive default of contract happens due to a purchaser's repayment difficulties, the bank can repossess mortgaged property to reclaim funds; when purchasers are active in the market and a developer sees flourishing in both production and sale, high profit and enough cash flow can guarantee a timely repayment of loan.

When housing prices go up, the real estate industry affects the banking system by the source allocation and balance sheet effects of financial departments. In terms of resource allocation, in recent years, traditional industry obtains low profit in China, while the real estate industry has a high investment income rate when house prices go up. Most idle funds among people enter into the real estate market. The bank is also willing to input funding into the real estate industry. In terms of the balance sheet effect, if house prices go up, at first, the market value of mortgaged property increases and it is safer for loaning. Better asset quality makes banks increase input into the real estate market. House prices will be further promoted.

When house prices go up, credit funding risk will not be obvious, but instead hide inside the bank and accumulate potential. Real estate price increases, in particular irrational prosperity, will bring more direct and indirect risks for the financial system, including unbalance of economic structure and long-term inefficiency of resources allocation, enlarging the gap between the rich and poor. A quite large proportion of social funds are from commercial banks that promote house price increase in the real estate upsurge. Risks from such funds also shift to banks, which bear all the risks brought by real estate industry. When real estate prices go down, various problems will stand out gradually, for example, price will decline by a big margin in a short time, which will be a threat to financial system.

(ii) Transmission mechanism of price fall of real estate impacting financial stability

(a) *Real estate price fluctuation impacts bank steadily through credit issue*

The irrational prosperity of real estate cannot continue indefinitely breaking away from economic fundamentals and social purchasing power. Deviation of market price and value at a certain degree is bound to return to value. Real estate price sways from abnormal high level to real level are decided by supply and demand. Price correction by a big margin gradually reveals the risks covered by market prosperity and becomes a threat to financial stability. A study on historical financial incidents shows that there is a close relation between the price fluctuation of real estate and stability of the banking system. The financial institutions underestimate the effect of price fluctuations on their own business and stability. A serious bubble appears in real estate prices; moreover, the commercial bank allocates a high proportion of credit source to the real estate industry. If the bubble bursts, the rate of bad debts from credit funding increases, which is a treat to financial stability, and even results in a collapse of the financial system.

A price fall will firstly affect real estate enterprises, whether they can pay back loan according to contract or not, and will then further impact on banks' asset quality and system stability, so it is important to analyze the impact process of house price decline in terms of developer and banks. Under negative impacts of difference intensity (λ_i), the real estate industry has impacts of price decline degree (δ_i), loan loss (β_i) and financial stability, which is shown in Figure 4-2. Regarding the dividing line of contract breach, real estate enterprises that run business normally and pay back loans on time are in a safe and stable area; when the price declines to λ_0, there is a loss due to price decline, covering all the profit of real estate

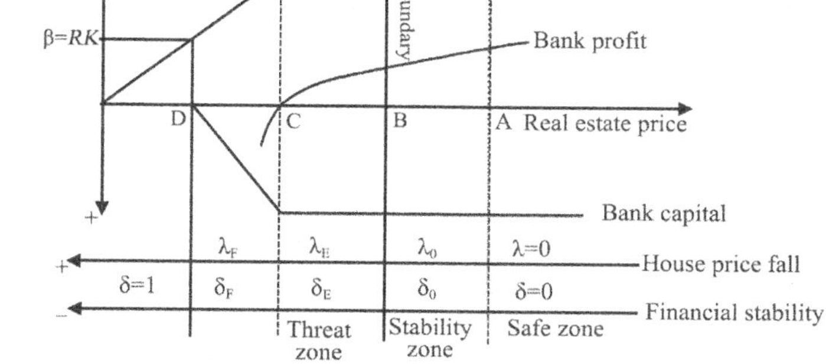

Figure 4-2. The price fall of real estate affects financial stability.

enterprises. Should prices continue to decline between B and C, loss of loan has gone beyond the enterprises' affordability. The enterprise suffers a loss and breaks the loan contract, while the bank has to bear the loss and profit decreases due to bad debts. The normal business and stability of the bank have been affected to a certain degree. If the real estate prices go down to $\lambda_{E,}$ the loss of bad debts equals the bank's profit, so the profit of the bank is zero at this point; if prices continue to decline, between C and D, the bank has to use capital to hedge its loss in real estate loan, the fragility of financial system is obvious and financial condition deteriorates; if prices continue to decline, the bank's capital decreases gradually, which will initiates a financial crisis.

With this mechanism, a smaller loss due to the price fall of real estate is undertaken by the real estate enterprise; the bank undertakes a bigger loss. If bubble burst causes bankruptcy and financial crisis, the loss will be undertaken by the whole society. The degree of impact on bank capital and financial stability shows nonlinear variation according to the price fall and loan loss; the commercial bank can use dynamic provisioning, profit and cash capital as a buffer, which can undertake certain bad debt loss from price correction. Due to the pro-cyclicality of credit fund supply and change of cash capital, when exogenous shock causes loan loss and increase of bad debts, the reduction of cash capital will induce multiple credit crunches. High house prices will accelerate price fall, while conversely it will promote credit squeeze and capital squeeze, and finally result in a spiral circulation mechanism of price fall and credit squeeze, and deterioration of the financial system. It may finally cause bankruptcy and financial crisis. There is also risk present in mortgaged loans from house purchasers, in particular, when there is a big fall in house price, the balance of the mortgage loan is higher than the property's market value, and repayment of the mortgage loan might stop, which is a threat to financial stability.

(b) *Analysis on conditions that real estate price collapse initiates financial instability*

In economics literature, "bubble burst" is directly translated from English words, which means a bubble disappears very rapidly and market price falls sharply. In theory, there are probably many types of bubble burst.

First, the bubble bursts when prices fall a great extent in a short time; second, prices fall gradually, close to value and by and by, the bubble tends to burst; the third, the market enables bubble existence. There are bubbles in the irrational increase of real estate price in China.

Analysis is made in terms of the following conditions to decide whether price fluctuation causes financial instability or not from now on, which will provide some reference for positive research and policy control in real estate.

First, whether the price will increase dramatically before the price collapse of real estate, i.e., the bubble phenomenon. If there is a continuous bubble before price collapse, moreover, many credit funds were injected into the real estate industry in forming that bubble. Then, the price bubble burst brings not only bad balance sheets but also non-performing assets to financial institutions, even causing bankruptcy and initiating banking and financial crises.

Second, the extent and speed of real estate price fall. If the price gradually falls over a longer time period, real estate enterprise's profit declines, but there is no large-scale loss and bad debts. Real estate industry and financial institutions can take such negative impact. The bubble is broken and disappears gradually. If the price falls sharply in the short term, then the real estate industry must confront the deterioration of the business environment and the steep rise of bad debts. Meanwhile, the bank can only make decisions such as improving loan rates and reducing loan amounts, which will cause serious information asymmetry and various problems to flare up, intensifying financial instability and affecting economic stability.

Third, the status of an enterprise's assets and liabilities at the time of price fall. If the finance of an enterprise is in good condition with a low rate of liability, then the enterprise is more capable of taking the pressure from price fall, which will cause less impact to the financial system. While if an enterprise has a high rate of liability, and the bank had enlarged credit fund rapidly, then price fall will result in further deterioration of liability and great loss to the bank.

Fourth, whether the central bank can take proper currency policy before or after real estate price collapse. When the bank confronts the increase of bad debts, less liquidity, and even bank crisis due to bubble burst, it should provide enough liquidity support for financial institutions. It might not prevent the attack of price collapse on the financial system, but ease the tension of negative impact and delay, or avoid, bank crisis and financial crisis.

4.2 A REVIEW OF THE DEVELOPMENT AND RISK OF THE CHINESE REAL ESTATE INDUSTRY AND RISKS IN REAL ESTATE FINANCING

After the urban housing system reform in 1998, the year of implementation of the Policy of Housing Monetization Allocation, the real estate market experienced fast development. The financing of real estate changed also from granting enterprise development loans to providing financing support to investment and sales, and the real estate loan became the fastest developing business for financial institutes. Chinese real estate industry and real estate financing experienced a swift development; meanwhile, they come along with some evitable risks.

4.2.1 Development of the Chinese real estate industry and house price fluctuation

(i) The Chinese real estate industry's three stages of development

At present, the real estate industry is experiencing the most severe regulation and the first thorough adjustment in its history. This regulation and adjustment are related to the positioning and development of the industry after the Reform and Opening. After 1978, with the reform and the establishment of the market economy system, the Chinese real estate market experienced a process of sprouting, development, and perfection, and real estate became a pillar industry from scratch. Combining historical and theoretical analysis, from 1978 to 2008, the Chinese real estate market experienced three stages of development.

(a) *Stage one: 1978–1991. Theory preparation and testing of the real estate market*

In September 1978, at the urban housing construction conference, Deng Xiaoping gave a talk on the problems of housing. The main idea was to broaden the solutions available to solving these housing problems, such as allowing private individuals or companies to build housing with nationally available financial help, using installment payment systems thus motivating people to spend money, and the government can resolve the problem of materials shortage.

On April 2, 1980, during another of Deng Xiaoping's speeches about the construction industry and housing problems, he said: "In most Capitalist countries, the construction industry is one of the three pillars of the national economy, which makes sense. In the past, we did not pay more attention to the construction industry and only treated it as the issue of consumption and held the thought that the buildings are for people to live. However, the field that produces the consumption goods is a key industrial field that can make product and increase revenues. We need to change our mind that the construction industry does not make money. We should realize that it does make money and increase the national revenue and it is a key industrial field. In the long-term planning, we have to put the construction industry at a major position because if the construction industry develops, it can create a large number of employment positions and build more houses for people to live in. As for the housing problem, we should consider a series of policies about the urban housing and house allocation" (Yang, 2010). Deng also pointed out those urban residents could purchase houses privately with a single payment or by installments. The price of rent should be regulated so that people would believe that buying a house is more economical than renting a house. With the rent increases, the low-income workers should be subsidized. Deng's speech did not cover housing commercialization and marketization, but it mentioned the housing policy regulation and the basic idea of direction for the real estate market development.

Following Deng's thought, in the early 1980s, theorists and relevant departments had very deep conversations on land commercialization and compensated land use, and came to an agreement on some problems. These conversations broke the ice for housing commercialization and the real estate market and provided the theoretical basis for forthcoming policies. In 1984, the government working report brought up that the urban housing construction should be merchandized and the real estate business should start. In the Thirteenth National Congress of the CPC held in 1987, the government explicitly pointed out that "the socialistic marketing system should not only contain the consumption goods and production goods, but also has capital, labor, technology, information, and real estate." It determined the validity of the Chinese real estate market. In 1998, the rent raising reform of the state-owned housing was the first step of the housing commercialization, and selling old state-owned houses was prevalent, which is the embryonic form of the housing market. In 1991, the investment capital on real estate was 33.62 billion RMB, the built housing area in urban areas and towns was 0.192 billion square meters, the sold commercial residential building area was 30.25 million square meters, and the sales value of the commercial residential building was 23.79 billion RMB. All of these signified that the real estate market was beginning to take shape.

(b) *Stage 2: 1992–1997. Coexistence of urban housing allocation and real estate market transaction*

After Deng Xiaoping's south tour speech in 1992, the 14th People's Congress determined the target of establishing the socialist market economic system reform. The third session of the 14th people's congress explicitly determined the content of rule and requirement for land market development, which promoted the development of the real estate market and triggered the first development zone and real estate booms. In 1993, the year after the boom, the real estate investment accounted for 5.6% of the GDP.

In 1996, the 9th Five-Year Plan for the development of national economy and society focused on resolving the people's housing problems, and created a "residential project," which accelerated the path for housing commercialization. In 1997, the total investment in real estate development reached 317.84 billion RMB, which accounted for 4.02% of the GDP and 12.74% of the investment in the fixed assets. The urban built housing area was 0.167 billion square meters, the sales area of the commercial residential housing was 90.1017 million square meters, and the sales value of the commercial residential housing was 179.948 billion RMB.

(c) *Stage 3: 1998–present. The fast development of real estate, and its important role in the national economy*

In order to stimulate consumption and increase domestic demand, in July 1998, the government issued *Further Deepening the Urban Housing*

System Reform to Speed Up Housing Construction Notice (File 23). This emphasized that the residential housing market should be the new economic growth point and the reform of the Chinese residential housing was initiated, characterized by the annulling of the welfare-oriented public housing distribution system. File 23 also emphasized that, after stopping housing distribution, the new national housing guarantee system should gradually allow allocation for housing monetization, and establish and perfect a housing supply system characterized by economical housing. Based on the conservative calculation at the time, the lowest income and highest income families accounted for 10% of the urban residential families, and the middle-low-income families that were able to purchase the economical housing accounted for 80% or even 95% of the urban residents.

At the end of 1999, the welfare-oriented public housing distribution system was eliminated and the housing monetization distribution system formally started. Public housing was largely sold, which signified the real residential housing market. Since 2000, the Chinese real estate market developed rapidly as its operation and rules improved, and then it was booming. In 2001, the government started to support residential consumption, and in order to reduce the amount of unsold commercial, office, and residential housing sold before June 30, 1998, all business tax, contract taxes, and administrative fees were canceled. Since then, the real estate market entered a swift development phase, and was prosperous.

The notice on *Promoting the Continuous and Healthy Development of the Real Estate Markets* (File 18) specified for the first time that the real estate industry is linked to and can promote many other industries, and it has become the pillar industry of national economy. It signified that the real estate market development should be kept healthy, and based on the progress of the urban housing policy reform, residential housing and income level, the ordinary residential housing should be increased. It also meant that the housing supplying policy should be improved, the macroeconomic control of the land market be enforced, and the amount of credit loan support increased for the qualified real estate development companies and the real estate projects. File 18 reduced the control of the real estate market by File 121 (*Further Strengthening the Administration of Real Estate Credit*), and the real estate sales increased dramatically.

Table 4-2. Major indexes of the real estate industry 1998–2010. Unit: %.

Year	GDP growth rate	Fixed asset investment growth rate	Real estate investment growth rate	Ratio of real estate to GDP	Ratio of real estate to fixed asset investment	Growth rate of average commercial housing
1998	7.8	13.9	13.7	4.28	12.72	3.28
1999	7.6	5.1	13.5	4.58	13.74	−0.48
2000	8.4	10.3	21.5	5.02	15.14	2.88
2001	8.3	13.0	27.3	5.79	17.05	2.75
2002	9.1	16.9	22.8	6.47	17.91	3.71
2003	10.0	27.7	30.3	7.48	18.27	4.86
2004	10.1	25.8	29.6	8.23	18.67	15.02
2005	10.4	26.0	20.9	8.69	17.92	16.72
2006	11.6	23.9	22.1	9.17	17.66	6.29
2007	11.9	24.8	30.2	10.13	18.42	14.77
2008	9.0	25.9	20.9	10.17	18.05	−1.66
2009	9.2	30.0	16.1	10.63	16.14	23.19
2010	10.4	23.8	33.2	12.03	17.36	7.51

Data source: China Statistical Yearbook 2011.

In 2004, the housing sales prices rocketed anomalously, driving investment in real estate.

After 2005, in order to control the overheated the real estate market, control policies were issued on credit loan, taxation, and land control, but the real estate market still grew. In stage 3, the effect of the real estate market on the national economy was obvious; as shown in Table 4-2. In 1998–2010, the growth rates of national society fixed asset investment and real estate development investment were higher than the GDP growth rate. The rapid growth of real estate pushed the economic development. Based on calculation, in 2007, the GDP growth rate was 11.9, 1.86 of which came from real estate development investment — the real estate industry played an important role in the national economy. Based on the Research Group of National Bureau of Statistics (2005) calculation on the effect of real estate to other industries, every 100 RMB of real estate demand (or construction industry output) could bring up 34 RMB of mechanical equipment manufacturing demand, 33 RMB of metal product manufacturing demand, 19 RMB of construction materials and other non-metal product demands. Combined together, every 100 RMB of real estate demand affected 215 RMB of all other industries, and this strengthened the position of the real estate industry as a pillar industry in the national economy.

(ii) Analysis of the problems in the development of real estate industry

The basic problem in Chinese real estate industry development is the inadequate development of protective residential housing, meaning that we tend to let the market push the development of the real estate industry. In 1998, the target of the residential housing system reform was to establish and perfect the residential system that was characterized by economical housing. To be specific, the lowest income families (10% of all) live in low-rent housing — such housing comes from the abandoned public housing built by the government or companies. The middle-to-low-income family (80% of all) can purchase the economical housing, which is sold at a low profit. High-income families (10% of all) can purchase and rent the market price housing. This is because in China, its material foundations are not yet adequate for the government to fully provide social (protective) housing, and the government cannot provide the "financial inflection" point for low-income families (Cao, 2011). However, during the development of the real estate market, some local governments have not paid much attention to economical and low-rent housing, and so the construction scale of these housing is small.

In 2008, the economical housing investment amount was 98.264 billion RMB, which increased 17.9% but only accounted for 3.21% of the real estate investment amount of the same period. In 2009, among the minimal assurance families in China, only 7% of them had their housing difficulties resolved by the government; among the cities that have started low-rent housing schemes, this only account for 1% of all housing. In contrast to the investment into social housing, in 2009, the national real estate investment was 3.6 trillion RMB (16.1% increase); the total income from the land leasing of all local governments was 1.59 trillion RMB; the profit of the real estate merchants was more than 1 trillion RMB. In 2009, China's economical housing was less than 4%, whereas in Singapore the figure was 86%. The inadequate development of social housing made demand focus on the commercial housing market, which results in the pressure of long-term price increases for commercial housing (Lu 2011).

The key problem in Chinese real estate industry development is rapid price increase. The foam of real estate brings financial risk, and its social problems have become the focus of the world. Since Reform and Opening to the world, the growth rate of Chinese GDP is almost 10%, and the disposable income of the urban residents has increased rapidly. Meanwhile, the cost of land, construction materials, and labor force has increased, so the commercial housing price rise is, to a certain level, meaningful. However, since 2003, the real estate price increased dramatically rapidly. In 4 years, the growth rate was over 14%, and in 2009, it was over 23.19%. The prices among major cities (in terms of population density from high to low, such cities are named level-1, level-2, and level-3) were quite different. Even in 2010 when the control was intense, the real estate prices in some cities were increasing dramatically. In Figure 4-3, except Wu Han, in the 10 major cities, the housing growth rate was over 15%; in Hangzhou, it was 35%.

In China, as a whole, the increasing price of housing has lowered the purchasing ability of residents, and the house price to income ratio used

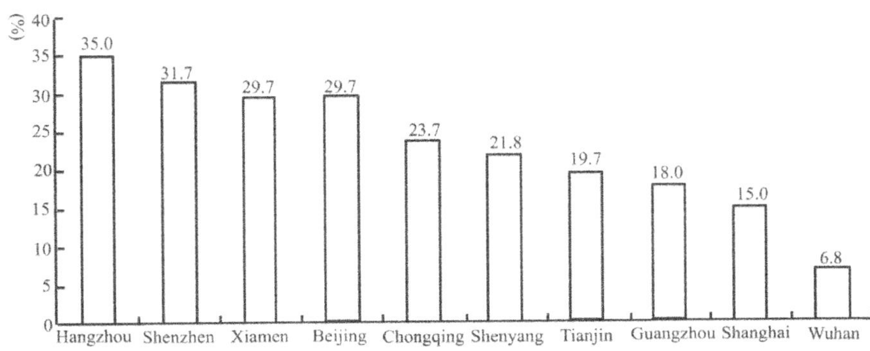

Figure 4-3. The housing price growth rate in 10 major cities, 2010.

Data source: China Real Estate Information Corporation (CRIC).

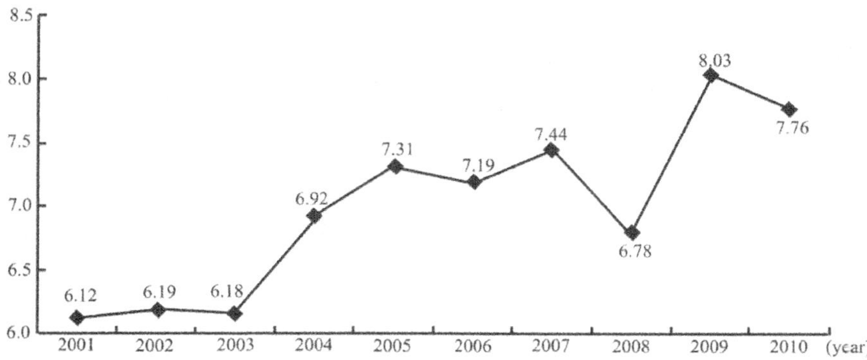

Figure 4-4. National housing price to income ratio.
Data source: CRIC.

to determine the rationality of the housing price is high. The house price to income ratio has different calculation methods, and we adopt the method by Yang Hongxu from Yiju Research Institute (ratio = unit price of residential housing sales price × residential housing building area per capita/disposal income of urban residents per capita). As shown in Figure 4-4, the disposable income of Chinese urban residents per capita and residential area per capital increased in 2001–2003, and the housing price increased rationally; the national house price to income ratio was stable at 6.2. From 2004 to 2007, the real estate price exceeded the disposable income per capita, and the ratio increased to 7.44 in 2007. In 2008, with the real estate control policy, the housing price decreased a little, the disposable income per capita also increased a little, so the ratio reduced to 6.78. In 2009, the Chinese real estate market became over heated again, the newly built commercial residential housing sales price increased by 23.2%, and the ratio went up to 8.03. In 2010, under the governmental control policies and the rapid increase of urban residents' disposable income, the house price to income ratio decreased. Based on reality, the ratio is rational at 6 ~ 7. In 2010, it was 7.76, which is rational but a little higher than normal.

Compared vertically, some of the cities, especially the level-1 and level-2 cities, have significant real estate foam. From 2001 to 2010, these cities' house price to income ratio increased dramatically. Figure 4-5

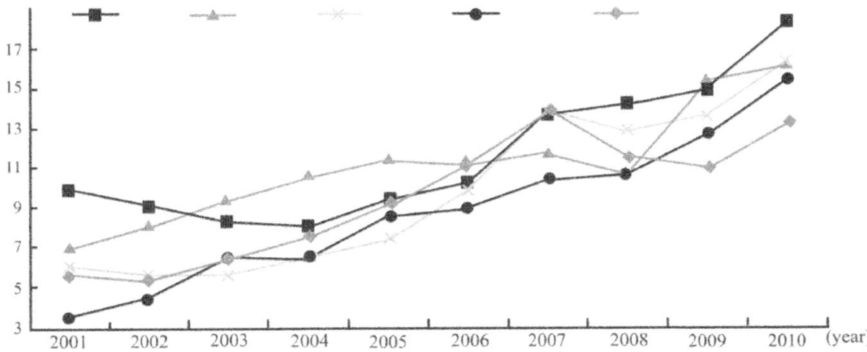

Figure 4-5. Housing price to income ratio in Beijing, Shanghai, Shenzhen, Hangzhou, and Xiamen.
Data source: CRIC.

illustrates the first five cities whose ratios were the highest: Beijing, Shenzhen, Shanghai, Hangzhou, and Xiamen — their ratio was 17.44, 15.62, 15.45, 14.65, and 12.75, respectively. The high housing prices hinder the talented people and middle-to-small companies from developing in these cities, and bring a threat to real estate credit loan security and its financing. The governments should take measures to control the housing prices in order to lower the high house price to income ratio problems (Shen & Zhang, 2011).

Ni (2011) used the parameter estimation method to estimate the benchmark price and the foam index of the ordinary residential housing in normal areas in 35 major cities in China. The foam index = (real price — benchmark price)/real price, which represents the ratio of the foam in the real housing price. In Figure 4-6, the foam index was high, and the cities where the ratio was over 50% are: Fuzhou, Hangzhou, Nanning, Qingdao, Tianjin, Lanzhou, and Shijiazhuang. The ratio was between 30 and 50% in: Beijing, Shenzhen, Wuhan, Changchun, Ningbo, Haerbin, Dalian, Guiyang, Shanghai, Zhengzhou, and Chengdu. Then, it was between 10 and 30% in: Nanchang, Jinan, Hefei, Xian, Guangzhou, Kunming, Xining, and Changsha; and under 10% in: Nanjing, Taiyuan, Huhehaote, Shenyang, Xiamen, Haikou, Chongqing, Yinchuan, and Urumqi. The aforementioned two statistics have differences in objects and methodology, but the results

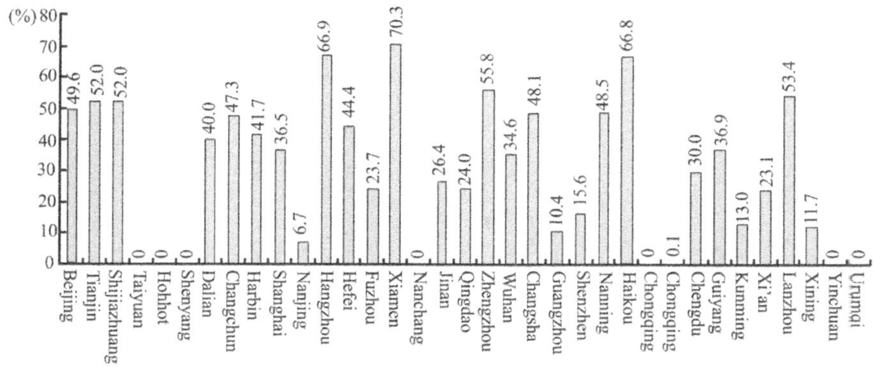

Figure 4-6. Price foam of ordinary commercial residential housing on normal areas in 35 major cities, September 2010.

Data source: *China Residential Housing Development Report (2010–2011)*, Ni Tengfei, Social Sciences Academic Press, 2011. Page 214–216.

show that in some cities, there are obvious real estate foams. The housing price should be controlled at a stable level.

4.2.2 Chinese real estate financing review and analysis

(i) Chinese real estate financing development process

(a) *Stage 1: Chinese real estate financing recovering and regulated development (1978–1997)*

Real estate financing encompasses the real estate development and sales process, plus the credit financing and other financial services. It includes financial institution housing saving loan, real estate loan (real estate development loan, and mortgage loan), real estate investment, trust, insurance, and the issuing and transaction of securities.

In the beginning of the 1980s, a thorough economic system reform started in China, and the real estate market began to develop. In order to adapt to this development, the banking system launched the real estate financing business. In those years, real estate reform implemented the state-owned construction and private construction subsidized by the government for general urban development. To adapt to these changes and support the housing policy reform, some banks started offering housing credit schemes. In 1981, the China Construction Bank established the China Housing Development Company, which specialized in real estate projects. In 1982, this bank enlarged its real estate financing business by issuing private housing loans. In 1984, the Chinese State Council issued the *Meeting Memo of Management System Reform for Basic Construction and Construction Industry*, which regulated that every region should found real estate comprehensive development companies, and the China Construction Bank supplied the liquid capital to enable this to happen. Since then, real estate financing became a major business of China Construction Bank. At the end of 1984, this bank has issued 1.763 billion RMB in loans, part of which was used on land development and operation.

In 1986, Benbu, Yantai, Tangshan, and other cities were nominated by the State Council to be the first trial cities for national housing system reform; in 1987, the State Council approved the Bengbu Housing Saving Bank and the Yantai Housing Saving Bank. Both two banks played important and positive roles in early real estate financing business development in China. The housing capital settlement center was formed, which was responsible for the flow of housing reform capital and ensured that it was carried out smoothly. The center also opened the long-term low-interest mortgage for private housing purchase, which offered great support to personal housing purchases. In addition, the center started the real estate development loan business, and participated with the development and construction of commercial housing.

In February 1988, the leading group for housing reform under the State Council established *Implementation Plan for a Gradual Housing System Reform in Cities and Towns,* and proposed that the local government should entrust banks to establish the real estate credit loaning department that is responsible for the financing and credit loan settlement business for the residential housing construction. Since then, the China Construction Bank and the Industrial and Commercial Bank of China (ICBC) established their own real estate credit loan departments, and some new founded banks, such as Shanghai Pudong Development Bank and Shanghai Bank, also established this capacity and entered the real estate credit loan market. The real estate financial business in China, characterized by housing financing, was also developed. In 1993, at the third national urban housing system reform meeting, some policies were implemented, such as the Housing Found, Housing Saving, Housing Purchase mortgage, and housing insurance. Forming these political and commercial systems reinforced the housing credit loan system.

In 1992, Deng Xiaoping's South Tour Speeches and the 14th National People's Congress (NPC) boosted the national economy that was entering into a high period. Many real estate development and operation companies were founded, and real estate investment was active. For instance, in Hainang Province, the number of provincial real estate development companies was 3,500 in 1994 compared with 351 in 1991, and the construction area increased from 1.878 million square meters in 1991 to 8.268 million square meters in 1994. The heat of real estate resulted in the expansion of investment and credit loan scales, which led to new inflation. As a result, since July 1993, the Chinese government began to control financial business and reduce the capital flowing into the real estate field. In order for a regulated development of the real estate industry, in December 1994, the leading group for housing reform under State Council, together with People's Bank of China and the Ministry of Finance, issued the provisional regulations for state-regulated residential housing loan management. Then in July 1995, the People's Bank of China issued the provisional regulations for commercial banks' housing loan schemes. Both sets of regulations maintained the state-regulated housing financing and commercial residential housing financing business.

(b) *Stage 2: Rapid development of real estate (1998–present)*

In order to cooperate with the housing system reform in 1998, the People's Bank of China issued the *Personal Residential Housing Loan Management Methods* in May 1998, which regulated the personal residential housing loan's credit object, approval conditions, procedures, loan period, interest, loan guarantee. Every state-owned commercial bank issued corresponding implementation details, which signified that the residential housing loan characterized by mortgage guarantee loan had already formed. The financial industry's support to the real estate industry transferred from the pure support to the real estate company's development loan, to the support of a company's investment and the provision of mortgage loans for individuals. In February 1999, the People's Bank of China gave some instructional opinions to the commercial banks about actively and stably expanding personal consumption loans, which signified that the personal housing loan expended to all kinds of residential housing loans for the borrower's personal use. These policies actively supported the financial development of the real estate companies in those years.

In 2001, File 195 confirmed the development mode of Chinese real estate finance, which signified that the credit loan capital of the banks could not become the major capital sources for real estate companies, but instead be an auxiliary support. This File regulated that the banks' credit loan capital could be used in real estate industry in three ways. (i) The real estate companies should use their own capital to pay the land-transferring fees and the compensation for demolition, obtaining the state-owned land-use right, the state-owned land use certificate, construction land planning use certificate, construction project planning certificate, and construction permit. The real estate company should have its own capital that is less than 30% of the total investment before obtaining the real estate development loan from the banks. (ii) Before the major parts of the construction project are finished, meaning the top level of a multiple layer building is complete and two-thirds of the investment has been obtained, the commercial bank can issue a mortgage to the house purchaser, and the loan amount cannot be more than 80% of the housing sales price. (iii) The commercial bank can issue little liquid capital loan to the real estate companies.

Since 2001, File 195 has not been effectively implemented, thus the loan capital was largely invested to the real estate industry from the bank; the land and house prices were increasing rapidly, which resulted in an overheated market. In the second half of 2002, the Ministry of Construction and the People's Bank of China examined real estate finance, and the result was released in *Monetary Policy Implementation Report of 2002* that the illegal loans were gathered in real estate development loan and personal commercial housing loan, but no relevant measures were adopted. In 2003, the File 121 made a new regulation to the issuing of development loans to real estate developer, which included land reserve loans, personal housing loans, and personal housing funding loans too. Shortly, File 18 regulated explicitly that the real estate market was the pillar industry of China, so this File pushed forward for its rapid development.

Since 2004, although the State Council, the People's Bank of China, and other departments adopted monetary, taxation, and land measures to regulate the rapid price rises in the real estate market, real estate became the main tool to push for economic development once there was a slow growth rate. In particular, when facing the global financing crisis at the end of 2008, the State Council issued the *Opinion on Healthy Development of Real Estate Market*, and a series of measures stimulating the real estate market were applied. A huge amount of money was released into the economy, so all of these factors resulted in an incredible rise to house prices in 2009. As shown in Figure 4-7, at stage 2 of the real estate financing development, the domestic loans to the real estate development companies increased from 105.317 billion RMB in 1998 to 1,256.370 billion RMB in 2010 — a total 11 times increase. Since 1998, the People's Bank of China took a series of policies stimulating residential housing consumption, and the personal mortgage balance increased from 42.62 billion RMB in 1998 to 6.2 trillion RMB in June 2011 — a total 144.5 times increase.

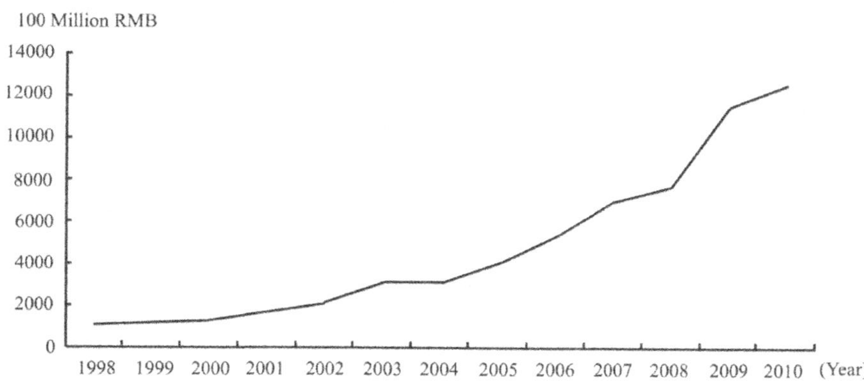

Figure 4-7. Domestic loans of real estate development companies: 1998–2010.
Data source: China Statistical Yearbook 2011.

(ii) Innovation and practice of real estate financing

Looking in retrospect at Chinese real estate financing development, we can see that the real estate financial market was far too dependent on commercial bank loans, which accounted for a large portion of the real estate capital source, and the risk of the real estate industry was mostly taken by the banks. Innovations should be made in financing methods and risk transferring systems to reduce credit risk, liquid risk and interest risk, and premature loan repayment risk on commercial banks' real estate credit loan capital. The real estate financing system should be improved.

James A. Rosenthal and Juan M. Ocampo released a book named *Securitization of Credit: Inside the New Technology of Finance* in 1988. In the book, capital-backed security was defined — a deliberately structured process, which means that the loan and the receivable debt are packaged and sold in security form (known as ABS or asset-backed securities). The MBS means that the commercial bank gathers its housing mortgages that lack liquidity (but are relatively stable) into a capital pool; the special units buy the capital in cash, which is guaranteed by government or other methods for credit upgrade, and then sold in the form of securities to investors. The MBS makes the real estate industry transfer from the traditional mode of "loan-receiving payment-loan" to the new mode of "loan-loan selling-loan." In essence, the MBS is the technical process of transferring future cash gains to the security of high credit on the financial market. With MBS, the mortgage's liquidity and cashing ability can be increased, and once such security is sold, the credit risk, liquidity risk, interest risk, and the premature loan repayment risk of the financial institution can be reduced. In this way, the liquidity supplement system of the residential housing market can be established. (Zhang & Lang, 2011). The long-term mortgage can be changed into short-term liquid capital by using MBS, which increases the liquidity of the institutions' capital and reduces the loan risks. In addition, since MBS is based on the residential housing mortgage, its security credit level is relatively high with good safety features, which are only lower than the safety of national debt, so in Western countries, it is called the bank security.

MBS was created in 1970s in the United States, when its interests were increasing, which made the commercial banks and saving institutions — characterized by short-term-saving-long-term-loans, absorbing float interest saving — to issue fixed interest loans, in order to increase their interest level higher than the loan interest; this resulted in significant non-matching of assets and liabilities. In the meantime, against the background of innovative financing, the gain rate of this new type of monetary market tool was so high that the saving source of commercial banks was diluted, resulting in the banks' liquidity difficulties. Consequently, a type of financial institute that specialized in purchasing residential housing mortgages from the commercial banks emerged. After purchasing these mortgages, these institutions sold them to the governmental credit departments or issued securities based on them, and these securities belonged to MBS. For the commercial banks, selling these mortgages helped them to improve their assets and liabilities structure, reduce risks, and obtain liquidity. Securitization of the real estate market is a trend for a country to develop to a high level. In 1990, the Nobel Laureates in Economics, Merton Miller and William Sharpe, analyzed real examples and drew their conclusion of price formation for financial assets, the so-called Capital Asset Pricing Model (CAPM).

During the start and initial development period of real estate financing, because of its special role in banking, the China Construction Bank had been the pioneer in real estate development and real estate financing business. As the credit loan capital increased, the China Construction Bank faced a new question on how to reduce the bank's real estate mortgage risk, dilute the risks, and increase the liquidity to ensure the safety of the loan. In 1996, the China Construction Bank established the residential housing loan security unit under its financial department, and it began to research the securitization issue.

In April 2002, the Trust Law was issued, which provided a lawful framework reference to the asset-backed securitization. The China Construction Bank submitted the mortgage-asset-backed securitization plan that was designed in trust mode and consisted mainly of balance sheet financing. Based on this plan, the China Construction Bank intended to transfer part of the mortgage to the trust estate and trust companies; also, it established the special trust that sold the ABS.

In February 2005, this ABS plan was approved, and (shown in Figure 4-8) the Jian-Yuan 2005-1 was issued as per the following steps.

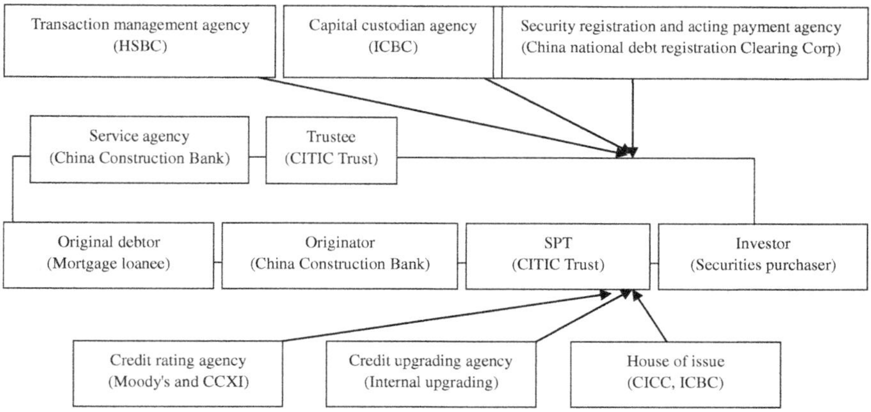

Figure 4-8. Personal housing mortgage support security flow chart (Jian-Yuan 2005-1).

Step 1: the China Construction Bank launched a 3 billion RMB mortgage into the asset pool. This 3 billion RMB mortgage was from three branches in Shanghai, Jiangsu, and Fujian, which had the best assets and management systems.

Step 2: the China CITIC Trust Co. (CITIC Trust in short), as the trustee with the special purpose trust mode, established a trust account that is managed by the trustee, but is accepted as the trust asset of the China Construction Bank and therefore independent to the trustee. For attracting investors and reducing the financing cost, the CITIC Trust carried out a credit upgrade for the securitized products, and divided the asset pool into four parts, in which class A, B, and C were optimal securities, and class S was the inferior security, held by the China Construction Bank. The investors of the three optimal securities had the highest repayment priority, and the investors of class S securities undertook any loss. Based on the rating of two agencies — Moody's and CCXI — the class A loan amount was 2.4 billion RMB with AAA credit rating; the class B loan amount was 0.3 billion RMB with AA credit rating; the class C loan amount was 0.21 billion RMB with BAA credit rating; and the class S loan amount was 90 million RMB held by the China Construction Bank, and not rated. The priority securities use the benchmark interest rate plus interest rate spread, and the benchmark interest rate was the 7-day repo weighted average interest rate issued by the China Foreign Exchange Center. The interest rate spread was 1.1% for class A, 1.7% for class B, and 2.8% for class C; and it had no interest rate upper bound for the three high priority securities.

Step 3: China International Capital Corp (CICC), as the issuing authority, sells the trust beneficiary certificate in the banking security market. By regulation, within 2 months of issue, the class A and B securities are allowed to transact in the security market, and contract transfer can transact class C security. As a result, after the personal mortgage-backed securitization, the property of the underlying asset belongs to CITIC Trust (SPT), so the underlying asset was separated from the organizer's bankruptcy.

Step 4: the China Construction Bank, as the service agency, receives the principal and interest from the housing purchaser, hands them over to the custodian agency, and reports to the trustee (CITIC Trust). The repayment of the Jian-Yuan 2005-1 is monthly-based interest, and the capital-received money of the underlying asset in the asset pool should pay the interest to, as per the following sequence: security of class A, B, C, and inferior class, and the same for the capital payment. During this process, after the China Construction Bank received the loan repayment, it should periodically pay the custodian agency (ICBC), and report to the CITIC Trust.

Step 5: the custodian agency is entrusted by the CITIC Trust to host the capital account, periodically provide the monthly report, and repay the principal and interest to the investors. The CITIC Trust should order the ICBC for security repayment when it is time to do so, and the ICBC should repay the security principal and interest to the China national debt registration Clearing Corporation, who shall make the payment based on the clearance sequence.

Since December 25, 2005, and the release of Jian-Yuan 2005-1, the China Construction Bank transferred 3 billion RMB personal mortgage credit assets into cash, which dramatically increased the asset liquidity and the efficiency of using capital. The China Construction Bank realized the low-cost financing and increased the capital adequacy, and optimized the accounting status. For other investors, the Jian-Yuan 2005-1 provided another investment choice. For the market as a whole, the issuing of 2005-1 promoted the active interaction between the financial market and the real estate market, realized the reallocation of the capital and risk in the financial market, and improved the efficiency of the capital allocation.

In January 2007, International Review of Finance, Asia (IFR Asia) rated the Jian-Yuan 2005-1 personal mortgage-backed security as the goal of Chinese ABS.

Based on the 2010 follow-rating report of ABS after Jian-Yuan 2005-1 personal mortgage-backed security, by the end of June 30, 2010, the unpaid principal balance in the asset pool was 699,838,249.32 RMB on 5,727 loan cases, which accounted for 23.2% and 37.77% of the money and cases when the trust was initialized. Then 87.38% of the class A security was repaid. The principal balance of classes B and C did not change. By July 30, 2010, CCXI tracked the securities and remained the class A security in Jian-Yuan 2005-1 at the AAA rating, and upgraded class B securities to AAA rating, and class C securities were upgraded to AA rating.

Although Jian-Yuan 2005-1 had the risk of being repaid ahead of time and of transacted in the banking security market, as the first personal housing mortgage MBS project, its issuing resolved a series of lawful, accounting, and taxation problems for Chinese housing mortgage MBS development. The China Construction Bank tried to normalize the MBS business and in 2007, it issued 4.16 billion RMB Jian-Yuan 2007-1 personal mortgage MBS. With the development of the real estate market in the past few years, a large number of loans were launched at the real estate industry. By the end of June 2011, the loan balance of most financial institutions' real estate sector was 10.26 trillion RMB, in which the personal housing mortgage balance was 6.26 trillion RMB. The risk of the real estate industry focuses on the banking system, so the experience of the China Construction Bank's MBS should be analyzed in order to promote the Chinese MBS development.

4.2.3 Chinese real estate financing review and analysis

(i) Analysis of accumulated financial risks during the rise of real estate prices

Since the real estate market reform in 1998, as with real estate prices, the credit loan scale of the commercial banks to the real estate industry grew rapidly; however, the real estate financial institution support system was not established. The three institution systems are commercial housing finance, cooperative housing finance, and policy housing finance. As for the support from these systems to the real estate development and consumption, the commercial housing finance took the leading role, and the policy only accounted for 15% of the personal housing loan, and the cooperative housing finance accounted for almost zero ratio.

In the real estate financial market, the main institutions are commercial banks. Two credit institutions that were founded in 1987, housing savings banks in Yantai and Bengbu, had transformed into commercial banks before 2003. At present, Tianjin Zhongde housing savings bank is the only operational one in the market, which was founded in February 2004 and had a fast business scale, but was confined by location and had less influence to the national real estate financial market. The commercial banks still take a leading role in the Chinese real estate financial market, and there is no real estate financial supplying system with multiple capital sources in China.

The depth of the real estate financial market is only the first-level market. The products available on the financial market mainly consist of real estate company development loans, personal housing mortgage loans, and housing funding loans, which reside in the first-level market. Other products, such as real estate investment trusts (REITs) and personal housing mortgage MBS are of the second-level market, except that the MBS was given a trial in two branches of the China Construction Bank. Meanwhile, additional products are still in the research and discussion process and have a long way to go before market operation.

Among the real estate financial products, the bank credit ones take the leading role. Real estate development capital comes from national capital in the form of budget, domestic loan, security, foreign capital, real estate company capital, and other capitals (deposit and advance payment). Based on the analysis of Chinese real estate investment capital sources conducted by the People's Bank of China, although the ratio of domestic loan to the capital source of real estate development dropped, the real estate company's capital and other assets have a big contribution coming from personal mortgages. Thus, the bank loan in the real estate development accounts for over 50%. If we put the capital source from the bank to the construction companies, this ratio is more than 70%. Despite the fast increase of policy housing loans in the past few years and that the personal housing funding loan balance was 507.433 billion at the end of 2007, the policy housing loan only accounts for 16.9% of the commercial personal housing loan (Ni 2011). From a certain point of view, the commercial banks are the major capital providers in Chinese real estate industry.

The real estate companies in the Chinese real estate financial market are quite dependent on bank loans, which signifies that Chinese financial market is not fully developed and that bank financing takes a leading role in the financial system. The intimate monetary relationship between the real estate companies and the banks results in the large credit loans of the commercial banks in the real estate market. The macroeconomic control of the real estate industry may have the chain reaction: tightened monetary policy — real estate loan dropping — real estate company capital chain tension — commercial banks' loan risk rising. In addition, if the real estate price dropped, the risk of bad debt from real estate loans could rise, which would threaten the financial system's stability.

(ii) Analysis of accumulated financial risks during real estate price rise

The Chinese real estate financial market relies mostly on commercial bank loans, which eventually transfer the risk of real estate price fluctuation to the banking system. This situation happened twice during the development of the Chinese real estate industry: the real estate foam in Hainan Province in 1990s, and the Shenzhen mortgage default in 2008.

(a) *Hainan real estate foam*

In the 1990s, the Hainan Province real estate foam was an important event in Chinese real estate industry development, and it affected the industry's development in later years. After the South Tour Speeches by Deng Xiaoping in 1992, the new reform started. The real estate market of Hainan, the so-called "free land," grew rapidly, and its prices increased accordingly. There were more and more institutions and private companies from all over the country in Hainan Province, which included large state-owned companies and private companies. A great amount of capital entered the Hainan real estate market. By the statistics of 1992–1994, the capital entering Hainan was 100 billion RMB, most of which came from bank loans.

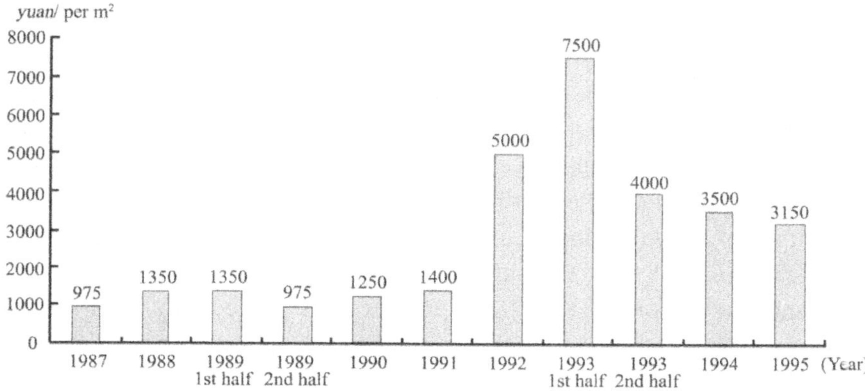

Figure 4-9. Hainan real estate prices: 1987–upper half of 1995.
Data source: China Real Estate Market Yearbook 1996.

Hainan's real estate price increased rapidly, as shown in Figure 4-9. In Hainan 1988, the average real estate price was 1,350 RMB per square meters; 1,400 RMB in 1991, 5,000 RMB in 1992 (257% increase), and 7,500 RMB by late 1993. The land value/Mu in Haikou was 980 thousand RMB in 1991 and 6.8 million RMB in 1993. Hainan, the province with the lowest population in China, ranked in 3rd place for commercial housing sales value in China and the 1st place of growth rate. In Haikou particularly, the economy increased by 83% in 1992. The financial revenue in the consecutive 2 years increased by one time than the previous year, but real estate revenue accounted for 70% of the total revenue.

In June 1993, the State Council issued the *Opinion about Current Economy Situation and Reinforcement of Macroeconomic Control.* It had 16 strict control measures, which included bank credit loan scale control, increasing deposit/loan interest and national debt interest, retrieving unlawful loaned capital, reducing capital construction investment scale, clearing up all the in-process projects, etc. After the stringency, huge capital in the Hainan real estate market was retrieved, and the real estate price started to drop from the second half of 1993. In 1995, the real estate price dropped to 58%. In 1996, it dropped 85% compared with previous years. The burst of foam resulted in Hainan having a huge amount of unsold commercial housing that accounted for 10% of that in China; Hainan's population only accounted for 0.6% of the whole Chinese population. The unfinished buildings in Hainan were more than 600 buildings with 160 million square meters. The idle land was 282.510,000 Mu. The idle capital was 80 billion RMB. The bad debt of four state-owned commercial banks was 30 billion RMB. In Beihai, sedimentary money was 20 billion RMB, and the area of unfinished buildings was more than that of Sanya. Beihai was named the "Chinese foam economy museum."

The burst of real estate foam led the finance and economy of Hainan into a hard time, and a great deal of credit capitals were trapped in real estate projects, which resulted in less liquidity and high financing cost, and some local financial institutions had payment difficulties. Some 34 city popular banks suffered, and nine trust investment companies were closed. In August 1995, the government of Hainan decided to found the Hainan Development Bank, hoping to resolve the capital difficulties of the provincial investment companies. However, this measure did not work. After 2 years and 10 months, a run on the bank was evident, and in June 1998, the People's Bank of China had to shut down the business of the Hainan Development Bank, which became the first provincial commercial bank in payment difficulty. In other provinces, some financial institutions encountered huge loss from investing in Hainan's real estate market. In Zhenjiang, there was a countryside foundation crisis; in Beihai, there was payment difficulty at urban popular banks.

The real estate foam brought the Hainan economy to an economic low point: the economy growth rate dropped to 4.8%, which was only 41% of what it was in 1993. Many residential buildings were left idle, real estate properties went unsold, plus the claims and liabilities controversies were frequent, which severely affected Hainan's economy and image. Up to 2003, the revived construction land accounted for 88% of that in that period, and 54.4% of unsold commercial housing were processed, and 42% of construction projects were recovered or disposed.

Hainan's real estate foam event negatively affected Hainan Province and other financial institutions. It was a warning to the entire development of the Chinese real estate market. Since 2003, the government started to control rapid growth of real estate to control its prices. In 2010, after the approval of Hainan as the international tourism island, the real estate was overheated again. However, this time, the Hainan government monitored the market change and controlled real estate project planning and approval in order to stabilize the land supply and construction speed, and guarantee the healthy development of the real estate development.

(b) *Shenzhen mortgage default event*

Before August 2008, through a series of measures — increasing interest and reserve requirement ratio, controlling real estate loan, strengthening land management and taxation — the control of the real estate market had made a good influence and the real estate prices started to drop. From the State Statistical Bureau data for the commercial housing prices of 70 major cities in China, in January, February, March, April, and May 2008, the growth rate from a month-to-month basis was 12.9%, 11.7%, 5.7%, 2.6%, and 1.3%. In 2008, the average real estate price decreased 1.66%. In 2007, the real estate price in Shenzhen was 14,000 RMB/square meter: the growth rate was 50% to the previous year; in 2008, the price decreased significantly. On July 9, 2008, the Urban Planning Land and Resources Commission of Shenzhen Municipality issued the *Development Situation Analysis Report of Shenzhen Real Estate Market in first half of 2008.* This concluded that the real estate transaction in the first half-year of 2008 was 54%, and the housing prices in May dropped by 36%, compared with the highest level in October 2007. As shown in Figure 4-10, in the months of

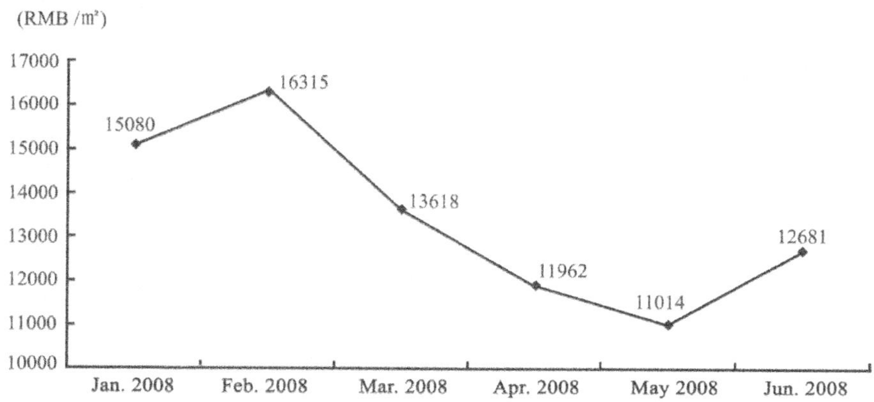

Figure 4-10. The month-to-month housing price drop.

Date source: Development situation analysis report of Shenzhen real estate market in first half of 2008.

March, April, and May, a month-to-month price drop was observed. From February to May 2008, the average housing price in Shenzhen dropped from 16,315 RMB/square meter to 11,014 RMB/square meter with a drop rate of 32.5%. In June 2008, the price increased a little, mainly because there were some low-density buildings entering the market, and the price was 12,681 RMB/square meter.

As the real estate price went down, the housing purchasers who entered the market in October 2007, the highest price period, could not accept this reality. From the point of view of the price threshold that generated the negative asset, calculated on 70% mortgage of the housing price, if the second-hand house price dropped 30% compared with the highest price, the bank could have negative assets. Some housing purchases with 30% of down payment also became negative asset holders. Under this background, in Shenzhen, there was mortgage default. The Shenzhen media reported this news and detailed many default cases. One of these cases is a building project name Bishui Longting. In 2007, during the price peak of the Shenzhen real estate market, the building price of this project was 13,000 RMB/square meters, but in 2008, it dropped to 8,000–9,000/square meters. There were 68 owners of this project, who became the negative asset holders and eventually refused to pay the mortgage with the excuse that the housing quality and landscape planning did not meet the description in the contract. These owners wanted to force the real estate developer to compensate their losses. It was reported that in the Shenzhen Baoan, Longgang, and Nanshan areas, the "negative assets" phenomenon was prevalent and rampant.

For the bank itself, the imprudent operation in mortgage business was one of the reasons for high housing loan risk. When the real estate market was overheated as the price of the deposited commercial housing was increasing, some banks did not evaluate the mortgage customers very strictly, which resulted in unqualified people obtaining loans. During the overheated period, some investors used these loopholes by making up the deposit housing price then obtaining the mortgage with 30% or 10% or even zero down payment.

The mortgage default event negatively affects Shenzhen banking industry. The Chinese Financial Operation Report 2007 revealed that in Shenzhen 2007, the mortgage balance was 359.46 billion RMB, which was an increase of 160 billion compared with the previous year; however, in 2008, the mortgage balance was only 5 billion more than that in 2007. The Shenzhen branch of the Bank of China was ranked the top place for personal loan business in Shenzhen, and its personal loan default ration increased from 0.2% in 2007 to 0.5% in 2008.

Shenzhen's mortgage default received even far more attention. The China Banking Regulatory Commission notified its local branch to report the whole story, and in addition, the State Council formed a research team that went to Shenzhen to investigate the risks this event caused for the local banking system. In order to resist the impulse of the international financial crisis, the Chinese government changed the attitude of the real estate market from "control" to "save." From October 2008, a series of policies intended to support the real estate development were issued. In 2009, the real estate price rocketed and the growth rate of Shenzhen's housing price was 31.7%, and the mortgage default was gone.

This event did not create too much bad debt loss for the financial system, and did warn of the current real estate price decrease after the macroeconomic control. The real commencement of the Chinese real estate market started from the second half of 1998. Until today, it has not completed one full circle, so there is no experience to compare for the domestic real estate price drop and how it affects the credit capital safety and financial stability. In this situation, we need to analyze and reference international experience and then use this to base how we get to know the real situation of financial risk of Chinese real estate. This will help us acknowledge the financial risk of the current real estate market, better control the real estate market, observe the amplitude and speed of the price decrease in order to realize a stable decrease of housing prices, and eliminate the potential risks in the real estate financial market.

Since the Chinese Reform and Opening to the world, the real estate market experienced startup, development, and booming stages. There were a series of policies that determined the Chinese real estate development path, such as the Government Work Report 1984 that proposed the residential housing commercialization trial, the 13th People's Congress that confirmed to establish the real estate market, the elimination of the welfare-oriented public housing distribution system in 1998, and the File 18 in 2003 that positioned the real estate industry as the one of the pillar industries that drove Chinese economic development. However, the development of the real estate industry deviated from the goal to create a housing supply system characterized by economical housing, resulting in the housing demand aggregation to the commercial housing market. This is indeed the reason for the long-term price rise in the Chinese real estate market. Under the background of excessive liquidity and rising real estate price, the real estate investment and gambling activities forced prices to increase. The rapid rising prices of the national real estate market increases the housing price to income ratio, and some major cities have severe real estate foam, which threatens the safety and stability of local real estate credit loan capital and finance.

Together with the development of the real estate industry, the real estate financing scale is increasing rapidly. The real estate financing innovations, such as MBS, are being developed. However, the financial institutions in this market are mainly the commercial banks, the market depth is only the major cities, and the financial product for real estate is mainly bank credit loans. Real estate financing is dependent on bank loans and no other financing channels are available, which results in the instability of the financing sources. Therefore, the real estate market has instable fluctuation and the commercial banking system has risks. If we look retrospectively at the real estate foam in 1990s Hainan and the mortgage default in 2008 Shenzhen, then we need to be prudent to the potential risks in the real estate financial market and properly control the market to gradually lower the price.

4.2.4 Analysis of examples that Chinese real estate price fluctuation affects financial stability

The startup of the Chinese real estate market was in the second half of 1998, when the residential housing reform happened. Since then, the real estate price entered a growth period, and even today, it has not finished a whole fluctuation period. However, if we analyze the examples that affect the mechanism and consequence of Chinese real estate loans and housing prices, research if there is intimate linkage between real estate price rising and rapid increase of loan supply capital, and study the effect of housing price fluctuation to the loan capital safety, we will get some very valuable information that is good for financial stability.

(i) Variable selection and data source

In this section, we will use the vector autoregressive model (VAR) to depict the dynamic relationship between a bank loan and the real estate price, and use the Granger cause-and-effect test, impulse response function, and other analytical methods to do some researches. The econometrician Christopher Sims (1980) advocated the application of the VAR model in his paper named *Macroeconomics and Reality*. In essence, it analyzes the dynamic relationship between different variables. Since the economic and financial time-series analysis has multiple variables, the VAR model is a good tool for monetary policy analysis and other macroeconomic finance. There are many parameters in the equations, but they are not our targets. We need to use the Granger cause-and-effect theory to test if certain variables' latencies can affect the current value of another or other variable(s), then we use impulse response function to fully reflect the dynamic response of all variables.

In order to research the relationship between Chinese real estate price and loan capital, we choose two indexes: the commercial housing sale average price (HP) and commercial bank real estate loan (L). HP equals to commercial sales amount over commercial housing sales area; L equals real estate development loan plus personal mortgage. The VAR model consists of three endogenous variables: HP; L_1; L_2. Considering the availability of the data source, especially the mortgage, we choose 66 data samples from January 2006 to June 2011, and the sources are from the *China Monthly Economic Indicators and Chinese Statistical Yearbook.* Since we do not have the January data, we use the data from January to February as the data for January and February. For the commercial housing sales amount, commercial housing sales area, and the real estate average sales price, we use the arithmetic average value of two consecutive months. The monthly data of the real estate development loan and mortgage loan have obvious seasonal changing rules, so in order to eliminate the seasonal effects, we use the X-11 method used by the United States Department of Commerce and United States Census Bureau to regulate the monthly data. For eliminating the data heteroscedasticity, we take the logarithm of the HP, L_1, and L_2, so we have L_nHP, L_nL_1, and L_nL_2.

(ii) Example testing

(a) *Unit root testing*

Because the traditional econometric method that works with a stationary time series is not available for non-stationary time-series analysis, if we use the ordinary least squares (OLS) method to estimate the econometric model, the econometric values of some parameters do not comply with standardized normal distribution and the non-stationary variable cannot accurately estimate the result. Before we analyze the L_nL_1, L_nL_2 and L_nHP, we need to carry out the stationary testing for the variable sequence in order to determine the stationary ability of each sequence. If the variable sequence is ordered and integrated, the cointegration analysis can be done; if not, then the cointegration analysis is not available and the unengaged VAR model should be used for analysis.

Table 4-3 shows the augmented Dickey–Fuller (ADF) testing result of the horizontal value and the first-order difference of the three mentioned variables. L_nL_1, L_nL_2 and L_nHP did not pass the threshold value testing, so we cannot deny the zero assumption, meaning the horizontal values of the three variables are not stable. First-order differences, denoted by $^{\Delta}L_nL_1$, $^{\Delta}L_nL_2$ and $^{\Delta}L_nHP$, all passed threshold value testing, meaning that they are stable. From this analysis, we conclude that $^{\Delta}L_nL_1$-$I(1)$, $^{\Delta}L_nL_2$-$I(1)$, and $^{\Delta}L_nHP$-$I(1)$, are of one order and integrated sequence and the cointegration method can be used on them for analysis.

Table 4-3. Unit root testing result of each time-series variable.

Variable	Testing type $(c, t\ n)$	ADF value	1% threshold value	5% threshold value	Testing result
L_nL_1	$(c, t, 2)$	−1.143989	−3.538362	−2.90842	Non-stationary
L_nL_2	$(c, t, 2)$	−1.971832	−3.536587	−2.907660	Non-stationary
L_nHP	$(c, t, 2)$	−0.886104	−3.538362	−2.908420	Non-stationary
$^{\Delta}L_nL_1$	$(c, 0, 1)$	−9.423187	−3.538362	−2.908420	Stationary
$^{\Delta}L_nL_2$	$(c, 0, 1)$	−8.924363	−3.538362	−2.908420	Stationary
$^{\Delta}L_nHP$	$(c, 0, 1)$	−12.66268	−3.538362	−2.908420	Stationary

Table 4-4. VAR model latency testing.

Lag	LogL	LR	FPE	AIC	SC	HQ
0	76.46898	NA	1.73e-05	−2.448966	−2.344249	−2.408005
1	238.0023	301.5288	1.07e-07*	−7.533409*	−7.114541*	−7.369567*
2	245.8430	13.85196	1.12e-07	−7.494767	−6.761747	−7.208042
3	249.4054	5.937347	1.35e-07	−7.313514	−6.266342	−6.903907

*indicates 10% significance level.

(b) *VAR model estimation*

For the latency testing with VAR model, the four determinant laws (FPE, AIC, SC, and HQ) all support the choice of the latency 1. Therefore, we determine that the latency is 1, and do the model estimation (Table 4-4).

$$\begin{aligned} L_nHP &= 0.92224547087 \times L_nHP(-1) + 0.0293628640186 \times L_nL_1(-1) \\ &\quad + 0.00269626355988 \times L_nL_2(-1) + 0.449290763415. \\ L_nL_1 &= 1.31600999198 \times L_nHP(-1) + 0.0196360388138 \times L_nL_1(-1) \\ &\quad + 0.249161965863 \times L_nL_2(\text{-}1) - 6.08216776927. \\ L_nL_2 &= 0.294617145352 \times L_nHP(-1) + 0.111712778758 \times L_nL_1(-1) \\ &\quad + 0.800675648684 \times L_nL_2(-1) - 1.96631104894. \end{aligned}$$

The fitting degree is good and the value of the three equations is 0.9841.

The goodness of fit of the three equations is 0.984101, 0.863077, and 0.939142, respectively. It shows a state of good overall fitting degree.

(c) *Johansen cointegration testing*

In order to determine if there is a long-term harmonious relationship among three variables, we carry out a cointegration test, as shown in Table 4-5.

Trace statistics and maximum characteristic value both prove that there is only one cointegration relationship vector among three variables: $\beta = (1, -0.7663, -0.2125)$. The cointegration relationship among three variables can be expressed by:

$$L_nHP = 0.7663L_nL_1 + 0.2125L_nL_2 + \varepsilon t. \qquad (9\text{-}7)$$

Table 4-5. Cointegration testing result.

Hypothesized no. of CE (s)	**Eigenvalue**	**Trace statistic**	**0.05 critical value**	**Prob.****
None*	0.395561	39.07466	29.79707	0.0032
At most 1	0.089675	6.853552	15.49471	0.5947
At most 2	0.013047	0.840518	3.841466	0.3592
Hypothesized No. of CE (s)	Eigenvalue	Max-Eigen Statistic	0.05 Critical Value	Prob.**
None*	0.395561	32.22111	21.13162	0.0009
At most 1	0.089675	6.013034	14.26460	0.6115
At most 2	0.013047	0.840518	3.841466	0.3592

* indicates 10% significance level.
** indicates 5% significance level.

For describing the relationship between variables, we take the Granger cause-and-effect testing.

(d) *Granger cause-and-effect testing*

The cointegration testing shown us that there is a long-term stable harmonious relationship among L_nHP, L_nL_1, and L_nL_2, but is this a cause-and-effect relationship? To find out, we do an additional test with the Granger (1980) cause-and-effect analytical method on the variable sequence, shown in Table 4-6.

From the table, we can see that the L_nL_1 and L_nHP have a cause-and-effect relationship; L_nL_2 is the Granger cause of the L_nHP, but L_nHP is not the cause of L_nL_2. For additional determining of the relationship between real estate price and real estate loan, we use the amount of real estate loan from bank L $(L_1 + L_2)$ and the real estate price HP to do the whole aforementioned tests and the Granger testing, and the result is shown in Table 4-7.

Table 4-7 denotes that there is Granger cause between L_nL and L_nHP, meaning that there is a cause-and-effect relationship between commercial bank credit loan to real estate amount and the real estate price.

Table 4-6. Cause-and-effect testing on L_nHP, L_nL_1, and L_nL_2.

Null hypothesis	Observation	F-statistic	Probability
L_nL_1 does not Granger Cause L_nHP	65	35.0347	2e-07
L_nHP does not Granger Cause L_nL_1		23.4261	9e-06
L_nL_2 does not Granger Cause L_nHP	65	17.3936	0.0001
L_nHP does not Granger Cause L_nL_2		2.20177	0.1429
L_nL_2 does not Granger Cause L_nL_1	65	25.9199	4e-06
L_nL_1 does not Granger Cause L_nL_2		2.89484	0.0939

Table 4-7. Cause-and-effect testing result of L_nHP and L_nL.

Null hypothesis	Observation	F-statistic	Probability
L_nHP does not Granger Cause L_nL	64	12.6715	3e-05
L_nL does not Granger Cause L_nHP		26.9874	5e-09

(e) *Impulse response function testing*

The impulse response function is used to measure the effect of a standard difference new interest from a random disturbance term to the current and future endogenous variables value. We first establish a VAR model, and then use impulse response to analyze. The result is shown in Figure 4-11.

Figures 4-11 and 4-12 depict the effect path of the new interest impulse to the commercial bank loan for real estate development and mortgage loan. From Figure 4-11, we can see that after giving a positive impulse to the real estate price, the real estate development loan increases in the short term. When it reaches its second peak, its value decreases gradually and eventually keeps the positive pulling effect of the development loan, which better explains that the expansion of the real estate price can trigger the investment impulsion. From Figure 4-12, when we give a positive impulse to the real estate price, the personal mortgage remains a steadily positive pull. As for the effect of real estate loans to the real estate price depicted in Figure 4-13, when we give a positive impulse to the real estate development loan, the real estate price will experience a rapid rise, and then drops and keeps a positive pulling effect. As shown in Figure 4-14, when we give a positive impulse in the current period to the mortgage, the

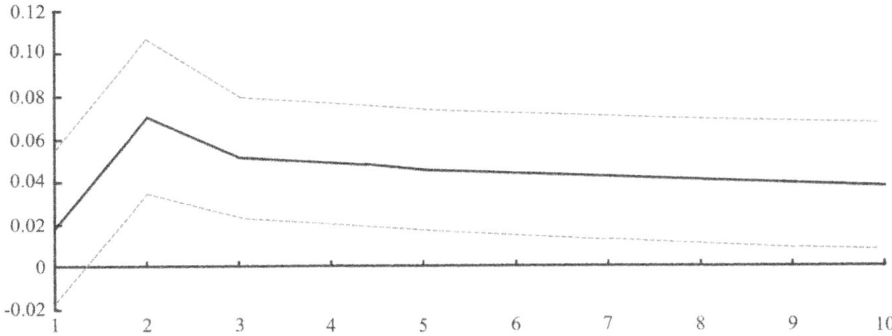

Figure 4-11. Response function of the real estate development loan caused by the impulse of new interest in real estate price.

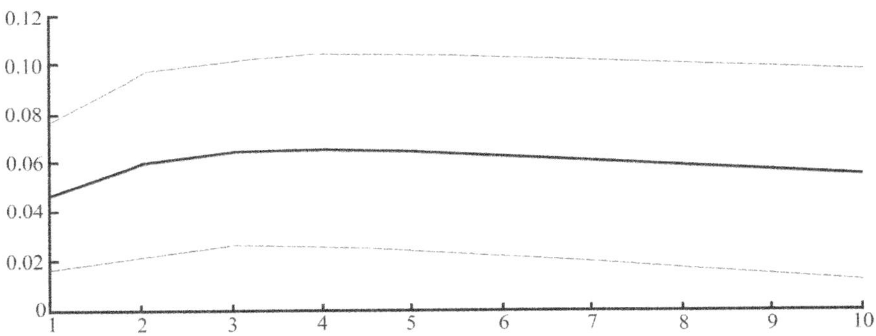

Figure 4-12. Response function of mortgage caused by impulse of new interest in real estate price.

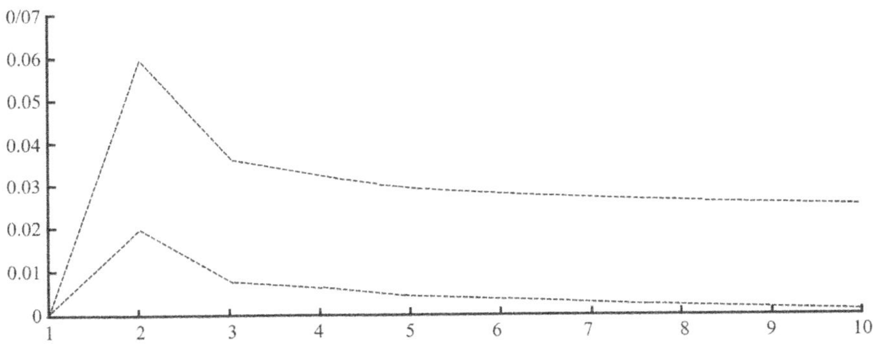

Figure 4-13. Response function of the real estate price caused by the new interest impulse of the real estate development loan.

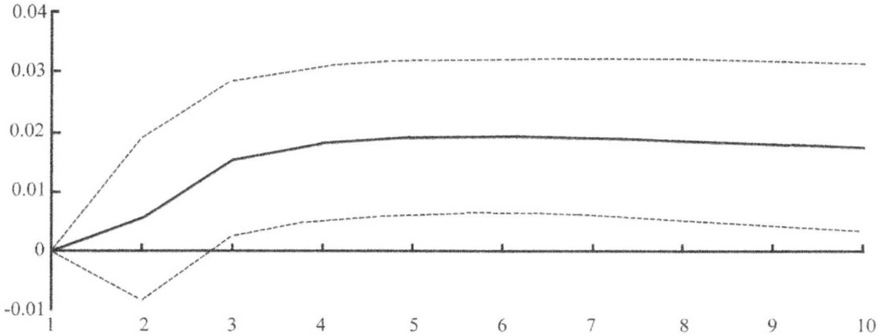

Figure 4-14. Response function of real estate price cause by new interest impulse of the mortgage.

pulling effect to the real estate price increases steadily in periods 1-4, and the positive pulling effect remains for a relatively long time.

It is shown by the aforementioned tests that there is an obvious cause-and-effect relationship between real estate price and bank loan to the real estate industry, and an obvious cause-and-effect relationship between mortgage and real estate development loan. During the period of real estate price rises after the real estate marketization, the commercial banks' real estate loan reached 10.26 trillion RMB at the end of June 2011. In Japan and the United States, the real estate foam made a huge impact on the stability of the financial market. The key is, during the forming process of the foam, the degree of the credit financing and the participation of the leverage department determine the expansion and break of the foam. At the time of Hainan's real estate foam, the rapid rise of the real estate price attracted more than 100 billion RMB into the Hainan real estate market; when the foam broke, the idle capital was 80 billion RMB, and the bad debt of the four state-owned commercial banks was 30 billion RMB. In Shenzhen 2008, the big housing price drop caused mortgage default and the increase of non-performing personal loans. As a result, we should pay more attention to the bank real estate development loan when the real estate price is rising, and the problems of the mortgage scale rising; we also should focus on the credit safety issues. Real estate control needs to be processed systematically in order to avoid the impact of a big real estate price drop to the banks' credit loan safety and the financial stability. The Chinese real estate market price is still in a high phase, and foam still exists in certain cities; therefore, we need to avoid the foam break that happened in Japan and the United States by using a stable and a steady control mode.

4.3 POLICY MEASURES FOR STABILIZING REAL ESTATE PRICES TO MAINTAIN FINANCIAL STABILITY

In order to maintain the stable development of the real estate industry, to attain the reasonable return of house price, and to eliminate the financial risks inside the real estate market, the strictest regulation and control policy implemented since 2010 has gradually played its part. The price increase of real estate has fallen stably, which lay a certain foundation for keeping down prices and maintaining financial stability. However, there are also many things worth exploring in depth in relation with how to further stabilize real estate prices and how to attain the goal of maintaining financial stability in the current domestic and international environment, and under the real conditions of our country.

4.3.1 The monetary policy choice for stabilizing real estate price fluctuations

(i) The monetary policy debate dealing with the price fluctuation of real estate

After the decade of the 1980s, the influence of stock and real estate price fluctuations on the banking system and macroeconomy became increasingly obvious. That if monetary policy should previously intervene in the volatility of asset prices and in what kind of way, has been an endlessly debated topic among the theorists. Before the USA subprime crisis, many academics and central bankers had not approved of direct intervention of monetary policy in a climate of volatile asset prices. The thought was that common stability of general price is the chief, or even the only goal for the central bank, which should classify as "benign neglect" (Bernanke, 2002; Greenspan, 2002) in dealing with the price fluctuations of real estate and other assets. This uses the ex post facto adaptive response in place of the pursuit of the previous positive policy response. This means that the response is made either only when the house price fluctuations affect the market's expectations of future inflation, or action is taken when the asset prices are shattered, to provide sufficient liquidity to the market as a lender of last resort, in order to avoid bank panic and financial crisis caused by lack of liquidity. A typical representative of this thought is Hessius, Deputy Governor of the Central Bank of Sweden, who believes that the central bank should not attempt to use the interest rate policy for controlling asset prices or piercing the bubble, and that the proper strategy is to restore financial stability after the burst that occasionally happens in the asset market.

Bernanke & Gertler (2000) put the asset price bubble into the financial accelerator model and compared it with the impact of asset price bubbles on the economy under the different reaction rules of monetary policy. They discovered finally that if the central bank's monetary policy concentrated on the inflation target, then reactions on the volatility of asset prices would result, but only when asset price fluctuations may affect inflation expectations and disturb the inflation target — for which the rules may well attain the target of controlling inflation and stabilizing output. However, the monetary policy rules that directly fix asset price bubble and make ex post facto reactions on the asset price fluctuations may cause bigger economic fluctuations. Therefore, they put forward the idea that it is not necessary for monetary policy to react to asset price fluctuations, nor is it feasible. In addition, the implementation of flexible inflation targeting, in which the central bank commits to use stable policy in relation to expected inflation, may provide an effective and unified framework for the realization of financial and macroeconomic stability. Under this method, monetary policy needs to respond to asset price volatility only when the influence of asset price fluctuations produced on price stability may lead to inflation or deflation pressure. Filardo (2000, 2001) discovered in his studies that if the analysis suggests that asset price fluctuations contain valuable information in anticipation of future inflation, the monetary policy targeting the control of inflation should make a corresponding reaction, regardless of any bubble factors in price fluctuations. He also put forward that the decision-makers do not need to react when the impact of asset price fluctuations on macroeconomy and inflation is uncertain.

Feng (2011) also put forward the idea that monetary policy should concentrate on real estate prices, because the latter contains the information related to economic operation. He states that if the increase of real estate prices causes the increase of consumption and investment, leading to economic expansion and rising inflation, the analysis of real estate price fluctuations may provide reference to China's central bank in formulation of monetary policy.

Most of the existing theoretical studies take the asset prices, or the stock prices directly, as the object of study — the documentations taking the real estate prices as the object of study are relatively fewer. Theorists analyzed the Japanese real estate economy bubble, factors of the real estate bubble in the Asian financial crisis, domestic real estate price rises in each developed country and the increasing proportion of real estate wealth in society's total wealth. They found that house price fluctuations have become an important factor that affect investment, consumption, and general prices, to which the economists and the monetary policy makers pay growing attention. In addition, more and more studies have taken the change of real estate prices as their research subject. Martha (2005) built a general equilibrium model containing real estate price bubble and credit market friction in order to figure out the possible reaction made by the monetary policy, taking general price stability as the target while facing the real estate price bubbles. The results of the study also show that it is more effective for the monetary policy to react when the rise of house prices makes inflation deviate from the expected target than to previously actively react to the real estate prices.

The reason why monetary policy makers do not agree with the previous positive intervention of monetary policy with regard to the rise of real estate prices is that they believe that previous interventions were faced with two inextricable problems, which cannot be avoided throughout the entire process of monetary policy implementation. One such problem is how to identify the presence of a bubble in the asset price volatility, or how to estimate the impact of real estate price bubble on future inflation expectations, while the central bank previously actively intervenes in the decision-making. A second problem is how to ensure effective control of the real estate price fluctuations by means of monetary policy, and how to effectively inhibit the development of asset price bubbles through the regulation of interest rates, without a simultaneous big negative impact on the macroeconomy, while the use of monetary policy intervenes in the real estate price bubbles. The previous positive reaction to the real estate price fluctuations can lead to either economic growth decline or recession, which makes the policy makers face the corresponding political risks and pressure.

Mishkin (2007) believes that the central bank should take measures to reduce the negative impact of highly volatile real estate prices on the general economy. However, he is opposed to excessive emphasis on the role of housing prices in monetary policy management. He believes it is impossible for the central bank to take action dealing with the bubbles, and the only right thing that can be done is to deal with the negative impact of asset price drop on the macroeconomy. Mishkin believes that asset price requires two assumptions to make itself effective in the process of monetary policy implementation: one is that the central bank is able to identify the asset price bubbles. Since the central bank has less information superiority than the market (Greenspan, 2002), the practice proves it is wrong that monetary policy makers know more than the market. If there is no information superiority, when the central bank is aware of the emergence of the bubbles, the market will also know this, so the change of market expectation will lead to a bubble burst. Therefore, any bubble that can be identified by the central bank is unlikely to expand further. Two is that the central bank is clearly aware of which monetary policy tool to use to inhibit the rise of asset prices. However, for Bernanke *et al.* (1999), Gruen *et al.* (2005), the rise of interest rates would lead to the bubble burst, which creates even more damage to the economy. The theoretical analysis shows that the impact of interest rate fluctuation on the asset price bubbles is uncertain. The practice of the central bank has proved that the policy means of raising interest rates might do more harm than good. The tool of using the interest rate is the optimal choice that the central bank uses in an expected period for attaining the target of inflation and employment. Changing the interest rate path according to the fluctuations of asset prices may produce a risk that deviates from the inflation target. The uncertainty of this hypothesis provides a strong support to the traditional view that "the monetary policy makers strive to maintain stable prices and employment rather than to pay special attention to the house prices."

Bell & Quiggin (2003) think that the reason why the central bank is unlikely to respond in advance to the asset price bubbles is that the monetary policy only has a single policy tool, in addition to the unidentifiable bubbles. Therefore, what needs to be done is to fix the single objective of price stability, within which the introduction of other targets will confuse policy focus, which will fail the target. At the same time, before the collapse of the bubble, dealing with the expansion of asset prices puts forward an important political issue to the central bank: the availability of asset boom and credit makes people feel that the economy is operating well. While people think there is no problem, taking measures to intervene in the rise of asset prices inevitably slows economic prosperity and this is not popular. If this response to intervention of policy leads to any economic recession, although the loss is less than a laissez faire bubble to the extreme, the market is not aware of the seriousness of the latter. Therefore, the political influence of the former is more serious, and the political and institutional risks caused by policy errors are very big. Since there is a great uncertainty in understanding asset market development and in affecting the real economy, policy makers are difficult to grasp this uncertainty and to make the right policy choice. Therefore, the monetary policy should maintain "prudence" on intervention in asset price inflation. The wise approach is that policy makers will take the inflation targeting framework as their basis, remain neutral to asset price volatility, or at most make tentative change of small scale to interest rates and thus affect the asset markets.

Although the traditional mainstream viewpoint takes inflation as a monetary policy target, considering the asymmetry of asset price boom and collapse on economic impact, some economists think that the central bank should go "headwinds" and prevent asset price bubbles by raising interest rates. Under the identifiable asset bubbles, the central bank may attain the target of suppressing asset price inflation, and maintaining the stability of financial system and macroeconomy through carrying high interest rates.

Christopher & Philips (1997) from the Australian Reserve Bank suggest that, through theoretical framework analysis, in the event of asset price bubble, under certain conditions and even if the expected inflation is below the target level in the short term, the central bank should tighten its monetary policy. This is in order to make the asset price bubble burst before excessive expansion and to avoid the formation of more severe asset price bubbles and the subsequent collapse, which may lead to long-term extreme effects. However, they point out that to attain these targets, monetary authorities shall subjectively strive to avoid the extreme negative impact caused by possible inflation. At the same time, as its monetary policy may prick asset price bubbles, the latter will not occur again in a period of time after the elimination of the bubble.

After simulating Bernanke & Gertler's (2000) models, Cecchetti *et al.* (2000) discovered that the active monetary policy which took a strong reaction and measures to the target zone deviated from inflation. Using inflation as the target for monetary policy led to greater fluctuations in output, although lower price fluctuations could be achieved. They believe that the continued, abnormal asset price fluctuations alienate investment and consumer behavior, resulting in extreme rise or decline of output. In order to prevent these kind of problems emerging, besides responding to expected inflation in accordance with traditional methods, monetary policy should also directly intervene in the volatility of asset prices in order to reduce the possibility of asset price bubbles, investment fluctuation in the boom and bust periods, and to better realize monetary policy goals. Therefore, whether the previous response to the volatility of asset price fluctuations should be made depends on the preference of the central bank between the fluctuations of output and price. They carried out a large number of simulation studies on various possibilities and proved that the monetary policy should make prior positive reaction on asset prices. Therefore, they believe that the asset variable contained in Taylor's rule is a more ideal policy response.

Bordo & Jeanne (2002) discussed the previous reactions and the necessity of intervention on assets prices from the angle of the burst bubble leading to financial instability. They argue that the fact that the central bank does not take intervention measures in asset price fluctuations is "benign neglect," because the impact of credit crunch, financial turmoil, financial crisis, and post processing may cause damage to the central bank's monetary policy objectives as soon as the central bank ignores or underestimates the asset price bubble. The central bank should not simply act as "lender of last resort," rather than intervening in the inflation bubble before the expansion of the bubble and eliminating it in the bud. Meanwhile, the so-called "accommodative monetary policy," favoring indirect intervention in asset prices, contributed more or less to the "financial imbalances" in the period of bubble economy. Therefore, they think the financial crisis is an endogenous instability caused in part by monetary policy rather than completely external shocks. The monetary policymakers should therefore not ignore the financial risks caused by their own behaviors.

Making amendments to the original monetary policy framework concerning the real estate price fluctuations may be the future trend of monetary policy response strategy. Some economists discussed how to revise the traditional monetary policy framework so that the monetary policy rules could properly deal with the real estate bubble, and the trend of macro adjustment and control. Jack & Carolyn (2007) from the Bank of Canada discussed how to add the flexibility in the framework of inflation target to deal with the abnormal asset price fluctuations. Having added flexibility measures dealing with asset price volatility into the existing inflation targeting framework and tested the changes of income and cost, they thought that the best choice for the monetary policy authorities was to keep consumer prices stable at a low level, which may promote the real economy and financial stability. The basis for this theory is that the flexibility inside the policy measures would give a certain responding space for the monetary policy to deal correctly with asset price bubble. They suggested that when the monetary authorities identified and judged the important influence of asset price bubbles on actual economic operation, they can take measures and go "headwinds," in the initial stages of the bubbles in order to better maintain price stability for a longer period of time.

After the USA subprime mortgage crisis, the aforementioned policy of pre-emptive active intervention to the volatility of asset prices, especially of real estate, obtained new support. This was suggesting that monetary policy should pay more attention to house price changes and go "headwinds" in the rapid rise of prices or deviation from normal price range (Cheng & Zhang, 2011). After the outbreak of the subprime mortgage crisis, the initiatives taken by some countries aimed at monetary easing, fiscal stimulus, direct support to the financial sector and housing market helped "clean up the mess." However, the evidence proved that policy effect is limited and could not stop the bankruptcy of financial institutions and crisis spreading. Although there are still some problems in the distinction between "bubble" from the real estate price changes, better indicators can be developed (such as price/income and price/rent index, credit growth and leverage rate) in order to assess the risks possibly associated with price increases and to decide whether to take action against irrational rise. The monetary authorities need to "save for a rainy day" with the innovation of monetary policy tools, in order to timely and effectively implement them in case of excess volatility in the financial market (Zhang, 2010a).

(ii) Limits of traditional monetary policy for regulation and control of housing price fluctuations

One of the reasons for the idea that the monetary policy should take a pre-emptively positive reaction to the asset price bubbles is that there is a lack of effective tools to deal with the fluctuations of the assets price. Since the role of traditional tools of monetary policy is relatively limited in the regulation of prices, even when the price fluctuations affect expectations of future inflation and the central bank makes adaptive response by raising the interest rate and the deposit reserve to intervening in the bubble, there are also great limitations. Japan's bubble economy and the USA subprime mortgage crisis show that it is a huge mistake to attempt to prick asset bubbles by monetary policy and interest rate rises.

In general monetary policy tools, the adjustment of the deposit reserve rate by the central bank can generate global impact on the commercial banking system and the money supply. However, if there is sufficient liquidity and higher excess reserves for commercial banks, the fact that the central bank raises the deposit reserve rate will not necessarily be able to reduce the credit loans of the banking system. Even if there is a certain effect for the control of the total amount, but the role for solving the partial overheat of real estate market and curbing the rise of real estate prices is also very limited. China's central bank has raised the deposit reserve ratio a total of 13 times from July 2006 to 2007. The deposit reserve rate paid by commercial banks was raised from 7.5% in the first half of 2006 to

14.5% by the end of 2007. Nevertheless, the amplitude of average prices in China's real estate sales was increased from 6.29% in 2006 to 14.77% in 2007. The practice shows that in China, the deposit reserve ratio has little effect for regulation and control of house prices.

The economists, whether being in favor or against the direct intervention of real estate price fluctuations, mostly emphasize the important role of interest rate policy in monetary policy. Theoretically, raising the interest rate of bank loans may reduce credit size in the real estate industry and ease the upward momentum of real estate prices. Nevertheless, during the bubble formation years when the real estate prices rapidly rise, the expected return of real estate may exceed the cost of raising interest rates. Since the rise of real estate market prices gives high capital gains, as long as the gains from real estate investment and speculations exceed the costs of raising bank loan interest rates, the measures of raising rates by the central bank cannot fundamentally prevent the flow of credit funds into the real estate market.

The open market operation has become an increasing favored monetary policy instrument of the Central Bank of China in recent years. It can either adjust the amount of money supply or lead the formation of market interest rates. But as foreign exchange flowed and grew very fast in China a few years ago (2003–2010), with an increase of more than 20 trillion dollars in foreign exchange reserves and an amount of 20 trillion *yuan* of corresponding money supply in RMB, the open market operation of the People's Bank of China aimed to offset the excess basic monetary supply. Moreover, even if the central bank can successfully control the money supply, the commercial banks will still increase real estate loans delivery by adjusting the credit structure when the real estate industry is hot. Therefore, the effect of controlling the real estate bubble using open market operation as a tool is also limited.

The fact that the adjustment of the general tools of monetary policy affects the amount of money supply and the capital loan costs of the whole social economy will inevitably have a negative impact on the other sectors of the economy. This is the case if say the aforementioned tools are used to control real estate prices, giving the policy effect more uncertainty and risks — that is to say, having higher costs of policy. Therefore, the People's Bank of China is very concerned about the real estate market. However, in the implementation of monetary policy, the regulation target of the general monetary policy tool is to achieve price stability and the stability of economic growth. Concerning the regulation of real estate price fluctuation, the target is to add flexibility in the existing policy reaction frame and to pay more emphasis on the selective monetary policy tool.

(iii) Easing housing prices by using the selective monetary policy tool

It is mainly through the real estate credit market that the real estate price fluctuations affect the stability of the financial system. Monetary policy tends to use real estate credit policy tools to control the real estate supply and demand, to effectively inhibit price fluctuations and to break the interactive relationship between real estate price and bank credit. The advantages of using alternative policy instruments for the regulation and control of real estate credit market can be explained as follows. One, compared with the general tools of monetary policy, such as interest rates and deposit reserve, real estate credit policy has stronger pertinence and higher effectiveness for suppressing housing prices. This policy takes into account provisions of the real estate credit qualification, loan value ratio of housing mortgage, the longest duration of loans, and loan fund price, which may directly influence the lending behavior of the real estate developers and purchasers. Two, the aforementioned selective policy tools aimed at the evolving real estate market and mortgage policies will not have a direct impact on other industries, and the indirect impact is also limited to the extent of the upstream and downstream-related industries. Therefore, in the response of monetary policy to the excessive volatility of housing prices, the selective monetary policy tools cost less than the general monetary policy tools.

Selective policy of the real estate market control refers to the central bank, which regulates the release of bank funds into the real estate market by way of controlling the credit amount, term, and price related to the real estate. The real estate selective control of the general national central bank is, basically, the demand management policy and the credit control for the real estate demand. Since China's real estate market system is not perfect, and real estate developers mainly rely on the capital source of bank credit and have insufficient awareness of risks, the central bank needs to make simultaneous regulations in dual aspects of demand and supply of real estate and proceeds with both for property buyers and real estate developers.

Regarding the practice of real estate regulation in China since 2003, the selective monetary policy tools used by the People's Bank are mainly four types: first, the financing main control, namely stipulating that only the main body in accordance with certain conditions can borrow or enjoy the preferential policies. Second, the constraints of financing proportion; on the whole, developers take the highest percentage of credit funds in real estate project financing, or use the lowest proportion of own funds; while property buyers stipulate the highest percentage of housing mortgage loans. Third is the deadline control, which stipulates the maximum repayment period, mainly for housing mortgage loans. Fourth is price control, namely the provision that is specifically aimed at the loan interest rate of real estate credit. The selective monetary policy tool is generally used in combination with the implementation process.

In 2007, warned by the subprime mortgage crisis in the United States, in order to prevent adverse housing credit from causing financial crisis, the People's Bank began to pay close attention to the real estate credit risk. On September 27, joined by the China Banking Regulatory Commission, it issued the "Notice on strengthening commercial real estate credit management," asking commercial banks to use mortgage loans for releasing capital to governmental institutions for land reserve. For this, the loan amount must not exceed 70% of the value of purchased land evaluation, for a loan period with a minimum of 2 years. Individual housing loans mainly support purchasers for the first apartment, or a small–medium-type house, to support living demands and are delivered only to the individual who purchases the apartment with a capped main structure. The buyer who has used bank loans for a housing purchase and who will purchase a second property and more shall pay a minimum proportion of 40% for the first payment, with a loan interest rate of no less than 1.1 times of the same grade benchmark interest rate announced by the People's Bank of China over the same period. The loan ratio of the first payment for a commercial housing purchase shall not be less than 50%, with a repayment time of

10 years minimum and a loan interest rate not less than 1.1 times of the same grade benchmark interest rate announced by the People's Bank of China over the same period. In the notice, one can find some provisions on mainly supported body purchasers; in proportion, deadline and price of land reserve loans, and loans for house purchase and targeted regulation through selective monetary policy tools in relation to various credit behaviors in real estate credit market.

In the most stringent real estate regulation and control policy implemented since 2010, selective monetary policy played an important role. On April 15, 2010, it was stipulated that the purchasers applying for loans to buy a second property pay 50% of the whole housing price for the first payment with a loan interest rate not less than 1.1 times of the same grade benchmark interest rate over the same period. The families purchasing their first property and a type of house over 90 square meters of construction area pay no less than 30% of the first payment ratio. In September, each commercial bank was asked to suspend the issuance of loans for households purchasing their third house and beyond. In January 2011, it was stipulated that the proportion of the first payment rise to 60% for loans for a second house. Severe regulation and control sustaining 2 years has achieved some results. In 2011, the average sales price of commercial housing increased 6.9% from 2010; lower than the GDP and the growth rate of per capita income. In December 2011, among 70 large and medium cities, the prices of the remaining new commodity residential homes dropped, flat, and raised were, respectively, 52, 16, and 2. Within these, the link relative ratio in Wenzhou, Hangzhou, and Shenzhen, fell more obviously, respectively, by 1.9%, 0.7%, and 0.5; in Beijing, Shanghai, and Guangzhou, by 0.1%, 0.3%, and 0.4%; only Guiyang and Yinchuan with their new commodity residential house price annulus rose comparatively by 0.1%, which meant that the regulation and control has achieved an obvious effect.[1]

[1]From January 2011 onwards, the National Bureau of Statistics began the implementation of the "Statistical investigation scheme on residential sales price." Since the new statistical survey scheme has made considerable adjustments in relation to the main factors affecting the price index, such as data sources, the index set, calculation method and effect, and so on, the data from January–November 2011 are not fully comparable to historical data.

The falling real estate prices conform to the spirit of the "promoting the housing price reasonable return" regulation called for by central government. But the dropping magnitude and speed should be properly held in order to avert the adverse impact on investment of sharply falling real estate prices, and to prevent the superposition of several unfavorable factors from causing economic hard landing under the background of external economic environment uncertainty and exports downturn. Therefore, on the basis of continuing to curb speculative demand, the real estate market selective monetary policy tools should be moderate, flexible in adjustment, and properly lower the first payment for buyers purchasing their first (and better) home. They should also suspend the increase of mortgage interest rates and stop giving certain groups preferential treatment, supporting the purchasers' rigid demand to pull the transactions of medium and low-priced commercial housing. This would ease the current slow destocking and the financial difficulties of real estate developers, to provide credit support for affordable housing construction and sales, to form a real estate supply pattern to both affordable and commodity housing.

4.3.2 Construction of macroprudential regulatory framework: Combination of monetary policy with financial regulatory policy

(i) Prudent regulatory policy is conducive to the prevention of real estate price bubble

Financial regulation involves comprehensive, regular supervision, inspection, and control of the financial supervision departments in the financial institutions to promote the steady operation of financial institutions, and to ensure the security and stability of the financial system. The focus and core of financial regulation are banking regulation, due to the core position of commercial banks in the social financing system.

The Dutch economist Jan Tinbergen was the first to propose the theory linking policy objectives with tools, pointing out that there needs to be at least several effective policy tools being independent from each other to attain several independent policy objectives. Later on, American economist

Bernanke (2002), on the basis of Tinbergen's rule, proposed that the proper tool should be selected according to the nature of the issue and that the central bank should concentrate monetary policy on attaining the corresponding macro targets, such as the stability of general prices, full employment; and to use its right of regulation, supervision, and last lender, in aid of maintaining financial stability. A large amount of evidence at home and abroad has proved that there exists an interactive relationship of mutual support and mutual promotion between the price bubbles of real estate and the bank credit. Meanwhile, the rationality and the effectiveness of direct intervention to the conventional monetary policy and fluctuations of real estate price have not yet been unanimously affirmed. The supervision and management imposed by the central bank or other regulatory authorities can assist banks with solving the deficiency of credit risk assessment; urge banks to setup the internal control mechanism of asset management of real estate credit; prevent internal risk; reduce the possible formation of real estate bubbles; or reduce the negative impact on the banking system after the burst of real estate bubbles.

Kent & Lowe (1990) thought that the asset price bubbles that have been found should be punctured as soon as possible, in order to prevent their bursting after auto-expansion from causing the economic recession and deflation, and approved the use of prudent financial regulation to prevent asset price bubbles. Good financial regulation can promote the healthy operation of the banking system, lower the exposure of real estate credit risk, reduce the loss caused after bubble collapse, and minimize the negative impact on financial system. Borio & Crockett (2000) thought that the prudential regulation toward financial institutions, such as commercial banks, could effectively avoid a generation of asset price bubbles. Even if strict regulatory or policy tool is not to the point, its cost is also less than monetary policy regulation. Moreover, the effect of the financial regulatory measures is predictable, while the monetary policy regulation and control has too much uncertainty and other factors under the influence of the transmission mechanism. Bordo & Jeanne (2001) emphasized that the regulatory requirement on capital adequacy ratio of commercial banks should be strengthened in advance, in order to deal with the loss caused by asset bubble rupture. They proposed that supervision and the deposit insurance system should be established to improve the robustness of the commercial banking system.

Borio *et al.* (2001) thought that the cyclical nature of financial system increased the fluctuation of the economic cycle, making the economy and the financial system unstable. During the rising phase of the economic cycle, as the return for the credit assets is considerable with lower risk, banks underestimate risk implicit in this part of the assets and release a lot of loans to improve the profit. As the economic cycle turns from rise to decline phase, especially after the economy falling into recession, the risk of stock credit assets of banks begins to emerge along with a large number of bad debts loss. At this moment, the bank must reduce the amount of credit and increase the level of provision to meet regulatory requirements. In addition, the banking system's credit contraction would further worsen the real economy. In the view of Borio & Crockett (2000), the effective regulation toward the banking system should be done in order to reduce or correct the financial system's pro-cyclicality, and to improve stability of the banking system and the macroeconomy. Greenspan (2001) also believed that financial regulation could strengthen the security and soundness of private banks, in order to ensure adequate banking risk management and to cultivate a banking system full of flexibility.

Ge *et al.* (2011) thought that although China's current overall system risk was in a relatively safe range, this risk was rapidly rising along with potential threat. These factors cannot be ignored, since the USA financial crisis happened under the influence of high-risk real estate credit, government debt, and of exchange rate fluctuations, bringing the decline of macroenvironmental stability. They propose that China should establish and improve its macroprudential regulatory framework, strengthen the counter cycle regulation, weaken the pro-cyclical behavior in financial institutions, set up an early warning risk system, and fundamentally prevent and resolve systemic financial risks.

(ii) Tool choice of macroprudential regulatory policy

Financial regulation before the subprime mortgage crisis in the United States emphasized microprudential regulation, which is based on the idea that with a single financial institution achieving sound operation, a financial system composed of all financial institutions should also be stable. Therefore, financial regulation only needs to pay attention on how to realize stable operation at the micro level. The subprime mortgage crisis showed that the formation and the burst of real estate market bubble have a significant pro-cyclical nature. The traditional microprudential regulation framework also has pro-cyclical features, which are insufficient to maintain the stability of the financial system as a whole. In this context, the concept of macroprudential regulation gradually formed. The regulatory authorities systematically evaluated the financial system risks on the basis of microprudential regulation from the perspective of the intrinsic links between economic activities, financial markets, and financial institutions, improved the design of the financial system and its regulatory measures in the macro aspect, and made correct policy reaction in a timely manner.

What is most important for the macroprudential policy is to redesign the existing prudential regulation tools and to solve the pro-cyclical problem. The IMF (2010) thought that the following measures could be taken to solve the pro-cyclical accumulation of financial imbalances.

(i) Control of the excessive increase of the leverage rate, increasing the requirements of minimum capital funding, capital buffers, provision of preventive expectation loss in addition to the minimum capital requirements in a period of economic prosperity.
(ii) Limit the accumulation of liquidity risks. In December 2009, the Basel Committee suggested the establishment of a flow quantification standard to limit the dependence of commercial banks on non-core capital financing, in order to avoid the excessive accumulation asset liability maturity mismatch in the economic boom stage and to prevent the excessive expansion of balance sheet.
(iii) Taking a prudent policy of loan pledge. Regulators can set a collateral maximum loan percentage in a period of asset price boom and relax the standards in recession in order to prevent the collateral prices drop from threatening the security of credit assets in commercial banks. These tools should be used in combination to reduce the accumulation of financial imbalances during the boom years, and the possibility of a financial risk would subsequently reduce in a recession. Peng & Miao (2010) believed that China should establish a high-level office of financial stability, the linking mechanism between monetary policy and asset price, develop effective macroprudential

regulatory tools, and construct a coordinated mechanism of macro-prudential supervision between China and other countries. From the analysis of macroprudential tools, according to China's financial system and the practice of supervision, the following tools can be used.

One is to adjust the capital requirements/risk weight. According to the standard method Basel Capital Accord II, the risk weight of the real estate loans is fixed (50% for residential mortgage loans, 100/100 for commercial real estate loans). Through the reverse cycle adjustment of capital requirements/risk weights, the bank is forced to hold more capital for real estate loans in a boom period in order to have ample capital buffer in the recession.

Two is to adjust the dynamic provisioning. The dynamic provisioning of real estate loans is a practice required for banks during the rise of real estate prices to improve real estate loan loss provision, which can be set as a specific function that varies along with housing prices. The bank increases the provision in case of the rise of housing prices and lowers it in case of recession. The additional buffer of provision that the bank is forced to establish (during the boom) may help deal with the potential losses in case of periodic variations.

Three is to adjust the first payment proportion of a mortgage and the monthly payments/income ratio. In the rising stage of real estate prices, the increase of the first payment proportion of mortgage will reduce the risk of falling housing prices. The higher the proportion is, the larger the dropping extent of real estate prices required for the formation of negative assets to the borrower. The proportion of the first payment may be declined during the dropping period of real estate prices in order to enable more potential buyers with the ability to pay the first payment transform into real demand. This is in order to balance the tension between supply and demand and to stabilize the trends of housing prices. The role of adjustment between monthly payment/income ratio is similar, which provides an "affordability" buffer when the purchaser repays the loans and a higher ability to deal with income decline or temporary unemployment.

Zhou (2011) believed that China's "constructing the frame of inverse cycle of financial macroprudential management system" is the stage of specific practical implementation and advance. Therefore, the macroprudential tools in view of the real estate market also need constant exploration and improvement. The adjustment of the mortgage down payment ratio as a tool has had a certain effect in China, but other tools face operational difficulties. These include the weight assets adjustment of real estate credit risk, for which the role would be weakened in case commercial banks own excess reserves, dynamic provisioning that covers no financial institutions or agencies outside the regulation, and so on. The macroprudential tools need further exploration and improvement for the future regulation of the real estate market.

(iii) Coordination and cooperation between monetary policy and macroprudential regulation

For the global financial crisis since 2008, the weakness existing in the financial regulatory system of the Western developed countries and the macroeconomic policy mistakes before the crisis was widely believed to be the reason for the generation and the spread of the crisis (Feng & Li, 2011). In China, under the frame of division between the central bank and the CBRC, the central bank emphasized the importance of macroprudential regulation from the point of view of financial stability, while the banking regulatory departments stressed the systemic importance of large banks on China's financial system. Therefore, both sides need coordination and cooperation in macroprudential regulation.

4.3.3 Improvement of the financial support provision methods to the real estate industry and diversification of commercial banks' credit risks

The present housing financial system in China originates from a diversified cooperative, commercial, and policy-backed path exploration from 1987 to 1990, but finally a pattern of almost exclusive monopoly by the commercial housing financial institutions has developed. At present, there is only one cooperative housing financial institution, namely, Sino-German Bausparkasse (SGB), whose role is almost neglected; policy-backed housing finance accounts for a market share of 15.3% for personal housing loan, while commercial housing finance accounts for 84% of personal housing loan. The strong position of commercial housing financial institutions and their high loan concentration are not only shown for personal loans, but also housing development loans. With the financial sources of real estate developers, the proportion coming from a bank loan directly and indirectly is up to 50%. As the housing construction and consumption in China relies too much upon the support from commercial housing financial institutions, the hidden risk is self-evident. Therefore, it is necessary to give diversified financial support to the real estate economy and spread the financial risks of the bank effectively.

(i) Prudential development of MBS and diversification of bank risks

The personal housing mortgage loan issued by the Chinese banks features a long term of 10 years, or 30 years at the longest. The liabilities of commercial banks are all types of deposit dominated by the time and current deposits of not more than 5 years, which has led to an unmatched period of assets, liabilities, and irrational structure. With the rapid development of the real estate industry, the personal housing mortgage loan has become a major business for commercial banks. However, in the face of a complex and volatile market environment, the hidden danger of default risk is also coming to the fore with each passing day (Shang & Jing, 2011). If under such circumstances MBS is launched, the bank can convert the loan with low fluidity to the securities with high fluidity, and recover ahead of time by way of true sale and get profits appropriately. While the fluidity of bank assets is increased, the risk that is concentrated in the bank can also be transferred and spread to the investors with different risk preferences. The MBS that has gone through such links as government body guarantee, credit enhancement and rating is characterized by high security, good profit and strong accounting liquidity, and is conducive to attracting funds otherwise idle in society. The funds recovered after MBS can continue to give financial support to the house purchasers. Ordinary investors will also be provided with an opportunity to participate in real estate industry investment indirectly and steady fund support will be offered for the development of the industry. At the same time, as a channel linking direct financing to indirect financing, MBS will play a major role in the development of the bond market and promotion of the capital market's coordinated development.

With the rapid development of the real estate industry over recent years, a large number of bank loans have been injected in the real estate industry. Up until the end of June 2011, the real estate loan balance of the major financial institutions across the country stood at 10.26 trillion *yuan*, including 6.26 trillion *yuan* for the personal housing loan balance. The risks of the real estate industry are largely concentrated in the banking system and it is urgently necessary to promote MBS. Recently, the China Banking Regulatory Commission "has studied conditioned, restricted and premised MBS," and under the precondition of guarding against risks, China's MBS will have a new development space. To push forward MBS, the following four problems must be solved first.

First, a suitable mode of MBS must be selected. The modes of MBS can be divided into three types: government-guided off-balance-sheet; market-guided off-balance-sheet; and on-balance-sheet modes.

(i) The MBS in the United States, Canada, and Hong Kong, China, adopt the mode of the government-guided off-balance-sheet, and the process is developed with the agency set up by the government separately as the core. The government body purchases a mortgage loan from the loan initiator to form an asset pool and then set up a special purpose entity to issue MBS; or the government body determines the qualification of the securities issuer through examination and approval, and the loan initiator issues MBS as an issuer. In the course of MBS, the government plays the role responsible for organization, coordination, and supervision, and simultaneously guarantees payment of MBS principal and interest with the state credit. Thereby, the risk and cost of securitization are reduced and it is made easier for the market investors to accept MBS as a financial derivative instrument for investment, hence the name of "government-guided off-balance-sheet mode." After the asset is transferred through securitization, bankruptcy remote will be achieved from the loan initiator, which also transfers the risk and income of the mortgage loan together.

(ii) Britain and Australia adopt the market-guided off-balance-sheet mode and the emergence and development of their MBS relies fully upon market operation. The government does not set up any special agency to participate in the securitization directly and only provides a legal framework. The commercial bank, in light of the financial market conditions, delivers the securitized asset to a special purpose trust company by way of trust; or a securitization company is set up to directly operate the MBS. As no government credit is introduced in the securitization, to raise credit rating, it is necessary to take some credit enhancement measures to increase the credit rating of MBS.

(iii) Germany adopts the on-balance-sheet mode for the MBS. The housing mortgage loan in Germany adopts a housing savings incentive or mutual-aid cooperative financing system. As the housing savings system is in a closed operation, the savings fund, and the interest rate of deposit and loan have no ties with the capital market, so the loan institutions have low fluidity pressure and interest rate risk, or any risk of loan early repayment. People are not active in securitization. Even if MBS is implemented, they tend to select the on-balance-sheet financing mode. The MBS issued by the loan-initiator is referred to as a mortgage secured bond, which is issued and secured by an asset pool made up of the house mortgage loan. If the value of the asset pool is insufficient for debt repayment, the bondholder is entitled to get repayment from the other asset of the issuer on the balance sheet. As the risk of the mortgage secured bond is not fully isolated, the loan initiator has still to bear its repayment obligation. Therefore, it is an on-balance-sheet mode.

Based on the analysis of MBS development modes abroad, the German on-balance-sheet mode is not in accord with the actual condition of China and we should adopt the off-balance-sheet mode. The trial run of the Construction Bank of China's "Jian-Yuan 2005-1 Personal Housing Mortgage Loan Support Securities" adopts the market-guided off-balance-sheet mode and the government body takes no direct part in the process of MBS and only provides a legal framework of securitization. No government credit is introduced in the trial run, nor does any external supervising agency control the quality of the asset pool at the source. Therefore, it is necessary to carry out the MBS in an active, yet prudent, way after making improvement based on the trial run of Jian-Yuan 2005-1.

Second, a standardized operation to regulate house mortgage loan should be applied. All financial institutions should pay attention to the unified standardized management of house loan products. First of all, the procedures for making a loan available should be standardized and each bank should unify the requirements for loan application, with examination of the borrower and appraisal of the mortgage value, and the unified regulations for the loan percentage worked out from there. Then, the loan contract should be standardized and unified regulations deliberated with respect to the duration of house mortgage loan, calculation of interest rate, mode of repayment, loan insurance, earlier repayment, disposal of the mortgage, as well as alteration or termination of the loan contract. Finally, the loan information should then be put under standardized management. Information coverage and management quality should be increased at a time when attention is paid only to the information about the repayment of the borrower. More information about the borrower's age, location of the real estate and so on should be collected, classified and coded scientifically under standardized management, so as to provide more information quickly and conveniently. The unification and regulation of the aforementioned procedures, contract clauses, and information will facilitate packing loan combination with the same features for securitization operation.

Third, a standardized intermediary service agency should be fostered. Credit enhancement and objective credit rating are the key links in the securitization of government mortgage loans, in which an intermediary agency plays an important role. Based on the experience in the securitization of government mortgage loan abroad, a credit enhancement agency can mainly fall into two types: one is the initiator of securitization, namely, the commercial bank itself; the other is an external credit enhancement agency, which can be either a commercial agency like an insurance company, or a government body with state credit. In light of the actual condition in China, the government should set up a state-owned agency to perform the function of credit enhancement. To maintain neutrality of a credit rating agency, the state should legally stipulate that a credit rating agency may not participate in the business activity of an enterprise, and there should be no common interests between a credit rating agency and an applicant. Simultaneously, the accuracy of the securities rating should be improved by drawing lessons from the rating standards and procedures of well-known credit rating agencies abroad.

Fourth, the risk prevention mechanisms in the securitization of government mortgage loans should be improved. The outbreak of the subprime mortgage crisis has warned us that in developing the MBS, prevention and control of financial risks should not be ignored (Zhang & Chen, 2011). To guard against the risk of MBS, first, the source risk of the house mortgage loan should be prevented and controlled. The establishment of the house mortgage loan security and insurance system can reduce the default risk of the loan itself and increase loan safety. At the same time, the risk can be spread and transferred to the guarantor and insurer, which will be more conducive to the development of the house mortgage loan securities market. Stress should be laid on regulating supervision over the whole course of securitization, tightening oversight, and creating a complete oversight system. An attempt can be made to set up a house financial supervision office that can coordinate all the functional departments and handle asset securitization specially, to meet the demands of the mutually integrated development of the credit market and the securities market. We should draw fully on the mature practical experience available in the world and carry out careful and continued oversight over the MBS.

(ii) Realizing diverse financing channels for real estate businesses and lowering dependence upon the bank credit channels

Currently, the major financing mode of the real estate businesses in China is the traditional bank credit loan and issuance of stocks, bonds, and trusts accounts for a low proportion. It is estimated that about 50% of the financial source for real estate developers comes from bank loans, directly or indirectly. It is necessary to create a new channel of financial source and lower reliance upon bank credit loans. As a special fund for financing the real estate industry, a REIT is a mature MBS mode after accumulation of scores of years of experience in the developed countries in the West and will be of great significance to the expansion of financing channels for China's real estate industry.

A REIT is a collective and non-specific investor and organization for real estate financial investment and specializes in raising money, making real estate investment, and business operation, and shares income from real estate investment. From the angle of the real estate industry, a REIT is a securitization investment fund most suitable for commercial real estate and can open up a new financing possibility for real estate businesses, while reducing bank risks by effectively lowering the real restate businesses' dependence upon bank loans. From an investor's perspective, REITs are conducive to opening up investment channels and investment in real estate that can be made with lower threshold and higher fluidity. Compared with an annual return of about 4% from an infrastructure trust product, small and medium investors can usually have an annual return of about 5–6% from investment in a real estate trust product. Relative to the stock, its price fluctuation is lower and income is more stable. This feature of REITs is evidently compatible with the market situation, in which an insufficiency of funds exists in the domestic real estate industry, while the investment and financing channels for non-governmental funds are deficient.

At present, the REIT is still in its exploration phase in China. At the end of 2005, the Yuexiu Investment under Guangzhou Yuexiu Enterprise (Group) established a trust fund with the property of Urban Construction Building and was issued to the public Guangzhou Yuexiu REITs (0405. HK) in the Hong Kong main board market. The pooled fund was mainly used for repayment of the loan. As the first REIT of its kind in the mainland and listed in Hong Kong, the investor's return reached 6.54–7.05%. At the end of 2009, the pilot program for the Shanghai Pudong Edition REITs was submitted to the competent department at the higher level. For this, four large-sized small open economies (SOEs) were selected, properties with an annual rent income up to 0.47 billion *yuan* would be provided, and the right to the rent income in the subsequent 10 years would be used for the establishment of trusts. Then the issuer of securities would entrust a major underwriter to issue a rent income voucher of the trusts to the qualified institutional investors in the interbank market. It is estimated that the raised fund would total 3.5 billion *yuan* or so.

To promote the development of REITs in our country, first, we should improve relevant laws and regulations concerning the REIT funds with reference to their counterparts of the United States and other countries. The management systems for real estate title registration and transaction should be supplemented and revised. Tax incentives should be given to REITs and the necessary law and policy environment should be created for their implementation and operation. Next, tighten oversight over the trust agency, trust personnel and business, strengthen the self-discipline mechanism of the trust industry, introduce a supervision mechanism over the principal and beneficiary, and ensure orderly and regulated development of REITs. Enhance the building of the REIT fund organizations, including the management committee, supervising body and specific operation establishment. Train as soon as possible a contingent of management talents that are both proficient in the investment trust fund business, and who are familiar with the real estate market and operation of real estate projects. At the same time, be active in strengthening the building of a contingent of service talents including lawyers, accountants, auditors, and asset appraisers that are indispensable for the business of REIT funds. Finally, it is also necessary to improve the system of making information known to the public, so that all the information about real estate, state policy, finance, and securities may be passed to the information requesters promptly and accurately, and start to push forward the development of REITs in China.

4.3.4 Other measures to stabilize real estate prices and maintain financial stability

Adoption of the aforementioned measures, such as selective monetary policy, macroprudential supervision, and improvement of the methods for financial support to the real estate industry may, to a certain extent, eliminate the role of credit funds in promoting the rise of real estate price, diversify the risks of the real estate industry assumed by the bank system, and maintain financial stability of the real estate industry in China. The source of the rise of real estate price since 1998 is the insufficiency between supply and demand arising from the land system and the real estate sector development mode; real estate regulation will result in the drop of real estate price. Therefore, under the present situation of rigid regulation, we should handle the magnitude flexibly, improve the mode of real estate development, promote steady and sound growth of the real estate sector, and provide financial stability with a good industry environment.

In 2010, when the price of real estate remained stable, policy regulation proceeded in an all-round way. In 2011, the "Eight Real Estate Market Regulation Measures" house purchase quota policy, trial real estate tax in Shanghai and Chongqing, an interest rate hike by three times and a deposit reserve rate hike by six times were implemented completely. As a result, the momentum of price rise was eased initially. By the end of 2011, the monthly data on the real estate price published by the National Statistics Bureau showed the price of commodity housing across the country had began to drop month on month. The Central Economic Work Conference suggested the real estate regulation policy should be adhered to without any wavering, house prices returning to reasonable levels promoted, construction of ordinary commodity houses accelerated, effective supply expanded, and the sound development of the real estate market advanced. Real estate regulation should be deepened continuously, and the realization of house prices returning to reasonable levels was the major task of the real estate regulation in 2012. If there is no other impact factor, the real estate regulation policy will not undergo any radical change in the short term. The continued rigid regulation has caused some changes in the psychological expectation and behavior of the real estate market players. In terms of the relationship between supply and demand in the market, influenced by a series of policy measures like the Housing Restricting Purchase Order, home buyers may adopt an attitude to wait and see for some time, thereby resulting in slow market demand. It becomes increasingly common for the real estate businesses to undersell at a reduced price. Simultaneously, the target of 36 million suites of social housing (10 million for 2011, 7 million for 2012) during the 12th Five-Year Plan period will inevitably give rise to strong expectation of shorter supply of the medium and high-grade commodity houses and significant increase in the supply of low-grade houses. The marketing of a large quantity of security houses will result in a reduction of the average house price that is included in the statistics of security houses. If the real estate regulation policy remains unchanged, the price in the real estate market will decrease year on year.

The drop of real estate price at an appropriate level is the prerequisite for house prices to return to reasonable levels, but the magnitude and speed of house price fall will determine the method of crushing the bubble. If the house prices fall significantly in a short time, it may lead to bankruptcy of real estate businesses due to fund chain breakage; if the magnitude of the fall is in excess of 20%, some mortgage lenders may stop supply due to the probable change of real estate into negative assets. The *Statistical Report on Loan Orientation of Financial Institutions 2011*, published by the People's Bank of China, revealed that the balance of the real estate loan in RMB of the major financial institutions and rural cooperative financial institutions, urban credit cooperatives, and foreign-invested banks stood at 10.73 trillion *yuan*. This was including 3.49 trillion *yuan* for real estate development loan and 6.24 trillion *yuan* for mortgage loan. The significant fall of housing price will bring risks to the mortgage loans granted after the year of 2009. Since the second half of 2008, the debt scale of China's local governments' financing platform has expanded noticeably and the overall credit risk has gradually increased, bringing about a certain systemic risk to the development of the macroeconomy (Ge & Gou, 2011). The slump of the real estate market led to a reduced auction price and quantity of land for local governments and a significant decrease in the fiscal revenue, which resulted in the rise of bad loan ratio by local financing platform.

In consideration of the close relationship between the safety of large bank credit fund and the real estate price, as well as the need for investment and GDP steady growth due to the shortage of external demand and lack of consumption growth, the real estate regulation should be fine tuned at the right moment. This is so that the price of newly built commodity housing will fall after a rise, gradually and steadily Xia (2010), and the ratio between housing price and income return to a reasonable range.

(i) The measures of administrative adjustment and control-like house purchase limitation will fade out at the right moment

In this round of property market regulation, administrative measures such as limitations on property purchase, loan, and price were introduced in succession, of which the policy for house purchase quota drew the most attention. On February 16, 2011, "Beijing Fifteen Real Estate Market Regulation Measures" were introduced in Beijing, which stipulated that non-locals were eligible for house purchase only after paying tax for over 5 years successively; for personnel with registered permanent residence in Beijing, those who owned more than two properties may not purchase any other house. After Beijing started to impose limitations on house purchase, 46 cities across the country introduced the Housing Restricting Purchase Order. The limitations on house purchase, loan, and price inhibited speculation demand for investment in real estate, eased the contradictions between supply and demand in the real estate market, and stabilized real estate prices.

However, such qualification restraint and restrictions on price and quantity will reduce the general level of social welfare (Hu & Sun, 2011). With the gradual visualization of real estate regulation effect and improvement of other economic measures, administrative measures such as restrictions on housing purchase and loan should be relaxed in good time and eventually be faded out, to release the purchasing power of the cities that implement these restrictions. Simultaneously, the withdrawal of administrative measures, such as house purchase restrictions, can change the expectations of house price fall in the overall society, maintain the investment in the real estate industry at a reasonable level, promote sound development of the real estate market, and fuel steady growth of the economy.

(ii) Supply of security houses and low- and medium-priced commodity houses should be increased

Urban social housing includes low-rent housing, affordable housing, public rental housing, housing of limited price, alteration of urban shanty area, alteration of shanty area in coal mines, forest areas, and reclamation areas and renovation of dilapidated houses. Structural defects still exist in the housing supply in China and coverage of social housing is not in excess of 10%, very different from meeting the necessary demand of low- and medium-income people. During the 12th Five-Year Plan period, 36 million suites of social housing will be built in our country, so that its coverage for urban residents may reach 20% or so. The establishment of housing purchase security can, to a great extent, hedge the investment in real estate development in the future, especially when the investment in residence may meet with a negative impact of contraction due to a fall of house price. It can also give support to the industries related to the real estate sector for steady growth of investment, and play a positive role in stabilizing the real estate market. In the real estate market, a structure based primarily on social housing, low- and medium-grade commodity housing and supplemented by high-end commodity housing is developed. In the construction of social housing, we should see to it whether the government policy support will bring about a debt burden and ensure the government will not be in a dilemma as to whether to face housing security or fiscal risk (Lin & Guo, 2011).

(iii) Long-term steady and sound development of the real estate market should be established

Since the start of the real estate market in China, its social housing is underdeveloped for want of a base for steady development and too much reliance upon the market. From the standpoint of a short-term view, overheating of the real estate industry can be solved through government regulation, but it is necessary to establish a long-term mechanism that is conducive to the sound development of the real estate market to guarantee its long-term development. The starting point of long-term development lies in satisfaction of the demand for independent-living housing, so that housing can return to being a basic living requirement. The policy on the supply of urban residence land is to expand the total amount, make structural adjustment, and optimize the layout. The scale of residential land supply will be increased and supply structure will be optimized. The housing security system will be improved and a security decision-making mechanism will be rationalized. A decision-making mode, with actual demand as the base and security effect as the guide, will be developed and the ratio between the social housing and commodity housing will be determined rationally by considering the regional difference. The social housing security system will be improved and the establishment of a legal system for commodity residence and social housing will be accelerated. A plan for the construction of urban housing will be worked out and improved; the establishment of housing information system will be sped up; and pilot work of real estate tax will be pushed forward based on housing information registration. The central and local fiscal systems will be improved gradually and reliance of local government upon the income from the real estate industry will be lowered, so that the locality may be endowed with the necessary conditions to discover the property market and its laws (Han & Jiang, 2011). Market management, including the development and construction of the real estate market, sale, and property management will be regulated. We should avoid a major impact upon the supply and demand of housing due to great changes in the macro policy and financial credit policy in a short term.

In this chapter, policy measures are proposed to stabilize the real estate price and maintain financial stability, in line with the present situation of real estate finance and real estate sector development. In theoretical circles and in the opinion of monetary policy formulators, a great divergence still exists as to whether the monetary policy maker should carry out prior reaction to the fluctuation in the property price. The conventional monetary policy instruments have great limitations in regulating the fluctuation in the real estate price. However, as the change in the housing market from prosperity to collapse contains serious financial risks, the monetary policy maker should consider property price fluctuation and its effect with expectation. This expectation involves stabilizing prices to an extent that is acceptable by economy and society by using selective policy instruments, such as control of the main body of borrower and lender, restriction on fund ratio, control of the repayment period and control of the fund price, so that the real estate bubble may recede slowly. In view of the limitations of monetary policy interference in the fluctuation of housing price, counter-cyclic supervision over the real estate market should be exercised by adjusting such macroprudential instruments as the capital requirement/risk weight, dynamic provisioning, and proportion of down payment for the mortgage loan and monthly installment/income ratio. The real estate price and financial stability will be maintained jointly in coordination with the monetary policy.

China's excessive reliance upon credit fund support by commercial financial institutions for house construction and consumption is a major impact factor for the real estate price fluctuation and for financial stability.

It is necessary to give diversified financial support to the real estate economy and spread the financial risks of banks effectively. First, MBS should be developed prudentially. The long-term mortgage loan should be converted to short-term circulating capital through securitization in the securities market to increase the fluidity of the assets of the lender and spread the risks of banks. Second, the financing channel of real estate businesses should be diversified and REITs explored positively to lower dependence upon financing through the bank's credit channel.

Realization of steady and sound development of the real estate industry and provision of a good industrial environment are prerequisite to avoid a threat to financial stability by real estate price fluctuation. The regulation intensity should be handled flexibly, so that the price of newly built commodity houses will fall after a rise insignificantly and steadily. The supply of social housing and low- and medium-priced commodity houses should be increased, and investment in the real estate and relevant industries should rise steadily. Administrative measures, such as restrictions on house purchase and loan should be relaxed at the right moment and eventually faded out. An exploration should be made to establish a long-term mechanism for the sound and steady development of the real estate market, so that the ratio between house price and income may return to a reasonable range and the operation system of social housing should be improved.

Chapter 5

China's Financial Stability: Standards and Methods of Measurement

The rapid globalization of the world economy and the increasing openness of China's financial industry have lent more leverage to capital, which makes a growing contribution to China's economic development. It also reveals the negative externalities of finance. As the high risks and unstable factors within the national financial system grow, financial stability has become one of the key issues facing China in its economic development. Therefore, the establishment of a financial stability index (FSI) and its measuring methods have great realistic significance for China.

5.1 MEASURING FINANCIAL STABILITY

The content of financial stability marks the starting point of study on financial stability and its nature. It is also the foundation of financial stability measurements. Due to the extensiveness and complexity of scales and fields involved in financial stability, there is no agreement on the content of financial stability among academics so far. A review of the literature shows that the understanding of financial stability is mainly based on the stable characteristics and specific performance of financial markets and financial institutions. The content is considered to include the steady operation of the financial market, controllable risks in financial institutions, and the effective allocation of savings and investments in the financial market (Crockett, 1997; Mishkin, 1991; Zhong, 2004). With the rapid integration of the world economy, some researchers believe that the content of financial stability should also include tolerance of major exogenous shocks and a stable currency that is not affected by changes in the relative prices of physical assets and financial assets (ECB, 2008; Hui, 2010; Schinasi, 2003). Based on past studies and aforementioned researches, this chapter defines financial stability by three dimensions: (i) steady operation of financial markets and controllable risks in financial institutions; (ii) effective tolerance of major exogenous shocks; (iii) relative stability of comparative prices of physical assets and financial assets.

The quantification of financial stability is hard to measure it due to its manifold connotations. In previous studies, the quantification of financial stability is realized by a comprehensive index compassing several basic indicators. Since 1999, the International Monetary Fund (IMF) has been trying to compile an index for financial stability based on chosen basic indicators. The index has been used to measure and evaluate the health and soundness of international financial institutions and their clients, including enterprises and household sectors. In 2004, the IMF published the *Financial Soundness Indicators: Compilation Guide* after further revising the index. Based on the IMF index, the European Central Bank (ECB) compiled a macroprudential index in 2006 to evaluate the soundness of financial systems of its member countries. Many scholars have also discussed the index of financial stability, typical examples include: Gersl & Hermanek (2008) compares the IMF indicator with the ECB's macroprudential index and further simplifies them into a financial soundness index containing six basic variables. Miguel & Estrada (2010) established an index with seven basic indicators based on past researches, measures, and analyze the financial stability of financial institutions in Colombia by weighted equal variance, principal component analysis, and quantitative reaction.

It can be seen that most of the researches conducted by overseas academics and ECB are supplements and revisions of the Financial

Soundness Indicator compiled by the IMF. Therefore, the IMF indicator has a high authority.

Domestically speaking, study on the measurement of financial stability has been making progress, thanks to the increasing openness of China's financial market and deepening reform of its financial system. Wang (2005) constructs a system for financial soundness measurement by taking banks' stable macro cost-control as a proxy variable of financial stability. Meanwhile, Wan (2008) measures China's financial stability by banks' soundness index; the financial stability working group's analysis of the People's Bank of China evaluated the country's financial stability in 2008 through four aspects, including macroeconomic environment, development of financial institutions, financial infrastructures, and financial risk management. Huo & Liu (2009) establish an indicator system of macro financial stability based on the ECB's macroprudential index. Measuring the weight values of indicators by state–space model, Wang (2010a, 2010b) constructs China's Financial Stability Condition Index. Hui (2010) sums up financial stability in two dimensions, including the stability of basic factors in financial institutions, and the ability to deal with major shocks. Hui establishes an index on financial stability. These academics have done much valuable work to explore China's FSI from various perspectives, based on the achievements of overseas studies.

It can be easily found from past researches that although the Financial Soundness Indicator compiled by the IMF is a representative method to quantify financial stability, the indicator cannot be applied indiscriminately for China. This is a result of the different accounting criteria, indicator systems, and statistical standards in different countries. Moreover, the ratio of Tier (one regulatory capital against risk-weighted capital), the proportion of loans distribution by sectors against total loans, the proportion of non-interest expenses against total revenue and other data required by the IMF Financial Soundness Indicator are hard to acquire in China. The existing studies in China have made some helpful and pioneering explorations and reflected on some aspects of China's financial stability. However, they failed to comprehensively measure the country's overall financial stability due to difficulties in obtaining data and differences in research methods. It is safe to say that so far there is no agreement in the academic community, both at home and abroad, on how to construct China's FSI system, which still remains to be explored and improved. Therefore, this chapter attempts to establish China's FSI system and explore financial stability indicators that fit China, with the achievements of Chinese and international scholars as references.

5.2 FINANCIAL STABILITY INDICATORS

Taking the characteristics of China's financial market and institutions into consideration, this chapter aims to select the basic financial stability indicators based on their basic connotation to financial stability, namely the steady operation of financial markets and controllable risks in financial institutions, effective tolerance of major exogenous shocks, and stability of comparative prices for physical and financial assets.

As regards to financial institutions, steady operation means that the institutions function well and perform their duties. This is mainly reflected in capital security and steady operation of financial institutions in the banking industry, securities industry, and insurance industry. For capital security, the ECB, Gersl & Hermanek (2008), and Miguel & Estrada (2010) all take the non-performing loan ratio (NPLR) as the basic indicator for financial institutions. The higher the NPLR grows, the more likely the institutions will suffer from loss. In addition, they are more likely to suffer from higher risks of bankruptcy and lower financial stability. Like studies conducted by overseas scholars, this chapter will also include the NPLR into China's FSI system and take it as a basic indicator in measuring the capital security in financial institutions.

For smooth operation, almost all the domestic scholars including Wan (2008), Huo & Liu (2009), and Wang (2010a, 2010b) take the quantity of new loans as the basic indicator of financial stability. This may be a result of the characteristics of the operation of China's financial institutions. Originating from the traditional government-dominated banking system, many financial institutions in the banking industry remain administrative. The four largest commercial banks in China have long played a role as the second government fiscal institution. Therefore, the quantity of new loans usually depends on the monetary policies. China has carried out proactive fiscal policies and relaxed monetary policies in 2009 to deal with the financial crisis. The value of new loans that year reached 9.6 trillion *yuan*, 2.31 times of the value in 2008. The new loans that appear in a short period without full examination will undoubtedly cause high risks of bad debts, pose threats to financial institutions, and influence national financial stability. Therefore, this chapter will draw upon lessons from the past researches and take new loans as one of the basic indexes of financial stability.

The smooth operation of financial institutions is also reflected in interbank lending rates and drastic fluctuations of the rates will affect financial stability. During the accounting process, this chapter has found strong correlation between the interbank lending rate and the interbank rate for pledge-style bond repurchase (with a correlation coefficient of 0.93). The two also have similar curves. Therefore, this chapter will include only the former (the interbank lending rate), to avoid repeating a large amount of information.

Besides, like the researches by the Gersl & Hermanek (2008), and Miguel & Estrada (2010), this chapter will use financial enterprises' circulating liabilities/liquid assets to measure the debt paying ability of financial institutions.

The smooth operation of the financial market is mainly reflected in the stability of assets price. Excessive prices will inevitably bring mass assets bubbles, which will eventually burst. Therefore, excessively high assets prices will endanger financial market stability. With the indicator system of Wang (2010a, 2010b), this chapter takes the price-to-earning ratio of the stock market and sale price of commodity houses as basic indicators of the state of the financial market. In addition, classical economics holds the idea that the financial stability and stability of currency value share the same goal. A high inflation rate will cause drastic fluctuations in the market, hinder the transformation from savings to investments, and cause financial instability (Schwartz, 1995a, 1995b). Actual interest rate is selected in this chapter to measure the inflation factors in the financial market, because when the rate is low or minus, residents and enterprises will withdraw their savings from the bank. The capital then flows to real estate or the stock market, blowing assets bubbles, and causing financial instability. Learning from the IMF financial soundness indicators, this chapter selects M2/GDP ratio as one of the key indicators of liquidity. The increase in this indicator can help to keep high liquidity in both financial institutions and financial markets. However, if the ratio gets too high, it may cause inflation and have a negative influence on financial stability.

In terms of shock tolerance, the financial system's ability to deal with exogenous and indigenous shocks mainly depends on the security of the macroeconomy, the openness of the financial system and the coordinated development of financial structure. The healthy and rapid growth of the national economy provides sound material foundation for financial stability. Financial stability suffers more pressure from exogenous shocks in an open financial system. A coordinately developing financial structure is the intrinsic requirement of financial stability. Most of the studies done by overseas scholars show that a country's financial stability may also be influenced by factors of external entity economies, which will affect the operation of the financial system and induce instabilities (IMF and WB, 2003). Based on the accessibility of related financial theories and data, this chapter selects variables including foreign exchange reserve, real effective exchange rate (REER), and foreign debt/exchange reserves as basic indicators of a certain financial system's ability to deal with major shocks.[1] Therefore, the indicators for financial stability selected in this chapter are as following in Table 5-1.

---

[1]The foreign exchange reserve is an important guarantee for foreign debt repayment and the stable operation of the national financial system. Foreign debt/exchange reserve is an important indicator of capital security in China. Too much foreign debt will increase the repayment pressure, and the liquidity of external capital can endanger financial stability by affecting allocation of resources. The REER will significantly influence the national economy. For China, a country deeply dependent on export, fast growth in REER will weaken its products' competitiveness in the global market and thus hinder the growth of the macroeconomy. Moreover, changes in expectations and directions of internal capital liquidity will threaten China's financial stability.

Table 5-1. The composition of financial stability indicators.

Comprehensive indicator	Classification indicator	Basic indicator	Attribute of indicator	
			Positive indicator	**Negative indicator**
Stable operation of financial system	Financial institutions	New loans of financial institutions		√
		NPLR in major commercial banks		√
		Interbank lending rates Circulating liabilities/liquid assets in financial enterprises		√
	Financial market	Real interest rates in financial market		√
		Price-earning ratio in stock market		√
		Price of commercial housing M2/GDP		√
Tolerance of major shocks	Foreign exchange risks	Quantity of foreign exchange reserve	√	√
		REER		√
		Foreign debt/exchange reserves		√

5.3 CHOOSING A METHOD FOR SYNTHESIZING AN FSI AND ITS ROBUSTNESS

5.3.1 Definition of FSI and choosing a method for synthesizing financial stability

Financial stability, with its rich connotation, involves multiple aspects including financial institutions, financial market, and international and national macroeconomic development. Therefore, financial stability is not a simple economic category but a comprehensive reflection of a series of factors, which means that the FSI should be a comprehensive system of multiple aspects and basic indicators. The FSI compiled in this chapter is used to measure the financial stability of a country by calculating the various basic indicators of financial institutions, financial market, external shocks, and macroeconomic development, and calculating their deviations from the long-term average values. Then the weights of different basic indicators will be decided by principal component analysis to compile a comprehensive FSI, which will be used to measure a country's financial stability.

This chapter, learning from the variance-equal weight method by Miguel & Estrada (2010), defines the FSI as:

$$\mathrm{FSI}_t = \sum w_{it} \times \frac{X_{it} - \overline{X_{it}}}{\acute{O}_{it}}.$$

FSI_t is the FSI for the t stage. ω_{it} is the weight of the variable at t stage. X_{it} is the value of X_i at t stage. The middle and long-term trend of X_{it} at t stage is represented by $\overline{X_{it}}$. σ_i stands for the standard deviation of No. i basic indicator. $(X_{it} - \overline{X_{it}})/\acute{O}_{it}$ is the X_{it}'s degree of deviation at stage t compared with its middle and long-term trend value's standard deviation. The FSI_t economically means the financial stability of financial stress (among sample data) at stage t in the comparatively long term.

If FSI_t is above zero (long-term average financial stress), it means that the financial stress at stage t is greater than the average financial stress level. The higher FSI_t gets, the greater the financial risks grow and the lower financial stability the economy has. If FSI_t is below zero (the long-term average financial stress), it means that the financial risks at stage *t* are lower than the average financial risks. The lower the FSI_t becomes, the lower financial risks the country suffers, and the better financial stability the country enjoys.

Technically speaking, there are basically three methods to determine the weights of the various basic indicators in the comprehensive indicator system.

(i) Weighted mean

The method of weighted mean grades the original indicators based on background information, evaluates the weight of each indicator, and compiles the indicators into a comprehensive index. The advantage of this method lies in its convenience. However, it fails to recognize the possibly high correlation among the indicators, which will make the weight structure problematic. Moreover, the evaluation of weight is lacking in objectiveness as it is influenced by researchers' subjectivity and randomness.

(ii) Analytic hierarchy process (AHP)

The AHP is the process where the thinking process on a complicated question is turned into a model and quantified. This method can break a complicated question down to several layers and factors. It determines the weight of the significance of different formulas by comparing and calculating various factors. The result will work as the basis for selecting the best formula. However, this method requires the researchers to assign values to indicators according to their significance, which is heavily dependent on personal experience and thus subjective. Although the method can avoid serious inconsistency in the thinking process, it fails to avoid the possible one-sidedness and subjectivity.

(iii) Principal components analysis

Principal components analysis compiles multiple interrelated basic indicators into several comprehensive indicators, which are independent from each other and contain the majority of information from the original indicators. The principal components will receive a weight automatically during the process. This will effectively avoid the interference of artificial factors. Therefore, the comprehensive evaluating theory based on principal components analysis can guarantee the objectivity of the evaluation and reflect realistic problems. Comparatively speaking, this method is scientific and objective; it perfects the comprehensive evaluation system and offers objective evidence for the management and decision-making process. Considering its advantages, this chapter determines the weights of basic indicators by this method.

5.3.2 Dealing with basic data

The 11 basic indicators included in the FSI system are all measured by their deviation degree of standard variance from the long-term average and have the same dimensionality, so the compilation of an index can be realized. Nevertheless, when it comes to the attributes of the indicators, some of them are positive indicators, i.e., the higher the indicator, the better the financial stability and the lower the financial risks. On the other hand, some of them are inverse indicators, i.e., the greater the indicator, the lower the financial stability and the higher the financial risks. The result cannot be comprehensive and reflective of different acting forces if the indicators of different attributes are simply added up. In order to reconcile the indicators' influence on financial stability, this chapter changes the attribute of inverse indicators by taking their reciprocal values.

The time sequence of a certain month or season usually consists of four factors, namely T (Trend, the long-term tendency of the time sequence of economic indicators); S (Seasonal, seasonal fluctuations repeated yearly); C (Cycle, the cycle and movement of business, economy or others, indicating the variation in a certain economy or industry); and I (Irregular, which is caused by unpredictable factors). The overall movement and characteristics of the economic indicators' time sequence are jointly shaped and influenced by these four factors. In economic analysis, the Seasonal and Irregular usually conceal or confuse the objective changes in economic development and bring difficulties to the study and analysis of economic development, as well as estimation of the current economic situation. Therefore, it is necessary to discompose the economic time sequence and remove the Seasonal and Irregular factors before conducting economic analysis. Many methods can be used to remove the factors, for example, moving average, TRAMO/SEATS, and X-12. X-12, put forward by the United States Census Bureau, is the most common one.

The data processing procedures of the basic indicators in the financial stability system are as follows: if a basic indicator is a minus, its reciprocal will be taken. Then the basic data sequence will be checked with the X-12 method to remove seasonal factors and irregular factors. Then the H-P filtering method will be adopted to calculate the middle and long-term $\overline{X_{it}}$ of every basic sequence and the difference between the basic sequence X_{it}, the seasonal factors, and irregular factors of which have been removed. Last, the chapter calculates $(X_{it} - \overline{X_{it}})/\acute{O}_{it}$, the comparative standard variance deviation of X_{it} from its middle and long-term trend.

With principal components analysis, both the correlation matrix R1 and the covariance matrix R2 can be adopted. The correlation matrix can avoid the influence of the different dimensions on the compiled indicators and the principal components' overdependence on large magnitude variables. Nevertheless, this will result in the underestimation or overstating of the indicators' comparative degree of dispersion in analysis, because every indicator has a standard deviation unit. The covariance matrix can not only eliminate the differences on dimension and magnitude, but also maintain the indicators' features in dispersion, thus avoiding the underestimation and overstating of dispersion degrees. Therefore, this chapter chooses the covariance matrix in the principal components analysis.

The data used in this chapter, covering statistics from January 2000 to July 2010, are acquired from the CEIC China Premium Database, China Economic Information Network's Macro Economic Statistical Database, and the Support System for China Statistics Application.

5.3.3 Results of the financial stability measurement

The weights of indicators (Table 5-2) are achieved by Eviews with the aforementioned methods.

Table 5-2. Weights of basic indicators of China's FSI system.

Basic indicator	Weight of basic indicator	Basic indicator	Weight of basic indicator
New loans	−0.27728	Effective interest rate	0.2422
Interbank lending rate	0.05981	M2/GDP	0.40197
Circulating liabilities/ liquid assets of financial enterprises	0.38397	Price-earning ratio of Shenzhen stock exchange	0.24016
REER	0.10259	Foreign debt/ exchange reserves	0.46641
Price of commercial housing	−0.25681	NPLR in major commercial banks	0.44750
Foreign exchange reserve quantity	0.10228		

Characteristic value of the first principal component $\lambda_1 = 7.579608$; proportion = 0.68906; cumulative proportion = 0.68906; characteristic value of the second principal component $\lambda_2 = 0.859001$; proportion = 0.07809; cumulative proportion = 0.76715.

Note: The weights were calculated according to the grades of the indicators.

5.4 AN ANALYSIS OF CHINA'S FINANCIAL STABILITY

According to calculation, China's FSI from January 2000 to July 2010 is presented in Figure 5-1. It can be seen from the chart that the financial stability in China has gone through obvious fluctuations and can be divided into three phases.

5.4.1 January 2000–April 2008

In this period, China's FSI had decreased continuously from its highest point of 4.16 in January 2000 to the lowest point of −2.39 in April 2008. This shows that the financial risks in China had been gradually weakened and the financial stability strengthened. For macroeconomic factors, this was a result of Asian countries' recovery from the financial crisis in 1998. As the global macroeconomy recovered, China's economy entered a

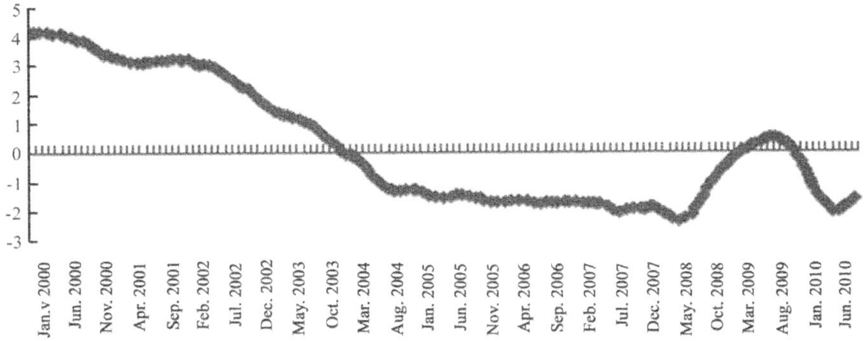

Figure 5-1. China's FSI from January 2000 to July 2010.

phase of rapid growth with the growth rate of GDP increasing from 8.3% in 2001 to 14.2% in 2007. At the same time, the foreign exchange reserves also grew quickly from $165.574 billion in 2000 to $1.528 trillion in 2007, an increase of 823%. This had laid a solid material foundation for China's financial stability. Besides, the non-performing loan rates of China's commercial banks had been decreased constantly from 23.6% in early 2000 to 6.3% in 2008, reflecting improvement in the quality of assets in banks. Moreover, the REER, price-earning ratio in stock markets, circulating liabilities/liquid assets and new loans remained stable during this period. China's macroeconomy had maintained a fast-growing and stable momentum with the smooth development of financial institutions and market, decreasing financial risks, and improved financial stability.

5.4.2 May 2008–July 2009

In this period, China was met with growing financial risks and decreasing financial stability. Internationally, due to the global financial crisis, the macroeconomy took a downturn as the financial crisis in the United States expanded. The industrial-added value and exports of China had been decreased. The exports growth in particular, had dropped to negative growth from 30%. Domestically, the main reason lay in the financial risks brought up by the government's macroeconomic stimulus plan. In 2008, the central government rolled out the 4-trillion *yuan* investment economic stimulus plan to reduce the impact of the international financial crisis. In order to get financial assistance from the central government, local governments had carried out various major projects. The necessity and feasibility of some were not fully checked. This not only worsened the overcapacity in China, but also further broke the balance of the economic structure. In addition, the quantity of new loans in commercial banks reached 9.6 trillion *yuan* in 2009 and the debt ratio of some local governments climbed to 300%. This led to a huge number of non-performing loans in commercial banks, which increased financial risks for this period and broke the balance of financial stability.

Due to the lack of alternative effective investment channels, capital from home and abroad entered the real estate market, which resulted in roaring housing prices and rampant speculation. According to the annual report by the China Index Academy in 2009, the prices of commercial housing in 12 cities had skyrocketed to near historic highs with growth rates above 50%. A report by Midland Realty showed that the sales and rental ratio in Beijing in 2009, at 1:546, renewed the historic record and exceeded 1:500 for the first time. In some regions, the number reached 1:700, much higher than the 1:200 warning line in overseas countries.

According to the calculation of Golden Keys Real Estate in 2009, the housing price-to-income ratio in Beijing reached 27:1 in 2009, much higher than the international average of 5:1. It can be seen from statistics that the real estate market in China had accumulated a huge amount of bubbles. Once the high housing prices fall, the breaking bubbles would bring strong shocks to the stability of China's financial market and financial institutions, as well as the country's overall financial stability.

5.4.3 July 2009–July 2010

Since the later half of 2009, the government had gradually strengthened its management of financial risks by tightening monetary policies and cleaning up financial platforms at local government levels. At the same time, the management and regulation of real estate market had been increased, which weakened the financial risks and improved financial stability. However, it is worth mentioning that China's FSI had increased dramatically since May 2010, indicating greater financial risks, and weakening financial stability. This trend appeared to further continue. According to initial estimation, China's FSI would continue to grow during the following period and its financial stability would be weaker. The reasons were:

(i) Prices. Due to the possible persistence of growth of structural prices including food prices, salaries, and prices of resource products, it was possible that structural upward pressure would suddenly occur in the future. In addition, the frequent natural disasters since 2010 had resulted in crop failures in some parts of the country. The influence of natural disasters usually lags. This, combined with changes in international market including Russia's ban on grain export, had caused great upward pressure in commodity prices since the later half of 2009.

(ii) Interest rates. Since the second half of 2009, China's consumer price index (CPI) had been much higher than the banks' interest rates, or rather, negative interest rates. Although short-term negative interest rates may stimulate economic growth, long-term negative interest rates would have an adverse impact on national financial stability and security. On the one hand, negative interest rates are actually a punitive tax on household savings and investment is one way to evade this taxation. For ordinary people, the channels of investing in China are quite limited so the investments will be focused on real estate and the stock market. This would blow the bubbles in the housing market and the stock market. On the other hand, negative interest rates would lead to unwise investments in capital-intensified industries, such as heavy industry and real estate, from entrepreneurs. These projects are sensitive to interest rates. Bubbles in the stock market caused by excess liquidity would further heat the investments on fixed assets and lead to the overexpansion of investments. Eventually, there will be more overcapacity and twisted resources allocation. Moreover, negative interest rates would worsen the imbalance in national income distribution, so as the enterprises get richer, while the residents become poorer. The nature of negative interest rates is subsidizing state-owned enterprises with household savings. As the CPI continued to grow, the interest rate was expected to increase, which would be a serious threat to the huge amount of debt at local governments and a real estate market full of bubbles. China's financial stability would also undergo change.

(iii) The REER. By the end of 2009, China's foreign exchange reserves had exceeded 2.399 trillion US dollars, well above other countries in the world. The number was 1.93 times that of the G7 member countries and 2.2 times of Japan's foreign exchange reserves. China's foreign exchange reserves grew by 25.25% during the first quarter of 2010. The huge amount of foreign exchange reserves led to complaints from many countries. Countries and regions including the European Union, Japan, and the United States, and international organizations including the World Bank and IMF, had exerted pressure on the Chinese government and forced the renminbi (RMB) to appreciate. Since the RMB appreciation plan was restarted in June 2009, the RMB had gone through minor appreciation and renewed record highs repeatedly. Judging from the middle and long-term trend, the appreciation of RMB cannot be avoided. However, the appreciation would lead to losses in China's foreign exchange reserves and threat to the country's financial stability due to rapid inflow and outflow of foreign capital.

Born in the real economy, finance serves the real economy and gradually turns into a comparatively independent power. It plays a significant role in the allocation of resources in the market. A stable financial system will promote economic growth by directing capital to sectors with higher effectiveness. Therefore, financial stability is the important foundation and precondition of economic development. However, the factors leading to financial instability are on the rise and becoming more complicated due to the further globalization of economy and finance, finance liberalization, and the appearance of various financial innovations. The financial tsunami caused by the subprime crisis in the United States had caught the world economies off guard and inflicted negative impact on the real economy. It led to severe fluctuations in the international financial market and slower growth in global economy. Therefore, all the governments and international organizations paid close attention to safeguard the stability of the financial system. They all need to analyze and make decisions by a proactive index, which reflects the potential risks and instability in financial institutions and financial market.

Aiming to establish an index to comprehensively reflect the fluctuations in financial stability of a certain economy, this chapter tries to compile a FSI for China based on existed achievements by the IMF and others. The index indicates that during early 2000 to the first half of 2008, China's financial stability had been reduced and financial stability strengthened gradually. From the second half of 2008 to the first half of 2009, financial risks had been increased and financial stability weakened. From the second half of 2009 to the first half of 2010, financial risks had been reduced and financial stability improved. However, the potential financial stabilities could not be ignored. Close attention and prudent measures should be taken when dealing with prices (assets prices included) and changes in interest rates and exchange rates. This index can reflect the current financial stability of a certain period. It can also be taken as a forecast and analysis of future financial stability, as it includes related information on the future development of finance and macroeconomy. It may provide reference for regulators in making and implementing financial stability policies and measures. Investors and consumers can also benefit from the index when estimating the trend in finance and economy.

As just mentioned, it is extremely difficult to reflect financial stability by a single index considering the multi-dimensions of financial stability. Although this chapter has made beneficial attempts in establishing the FSI, there are obviously questions that need further research. For example, how are we to construct financial or economic variables more scientifically in order to correctively and comprehensively reflect the behaviors of financial institutions and changes in the financial market, as well as their impact on financial stability? If the index is too complicated, it will be difficult to measure financial stability by this index. If too simple, the index will not be able to precisely reflect financial stability. Therefore, it remains to be discussed how to compile an FSI that can comprehensively, precisely, and timely reflect development in finance.

APPENDIX CALCULATION RESULTS

Principal components analysis
Date: 10/31/10 Time: 15:51
Sample: 2000M01 2010M07
Included observations: 127 after adjustment
Extracting 11 of 11 possible components

Eigenvalues (Sum = 11, Average = 1)

Number	Value	Difference	Proportion	Cumulative Value	Cumulative proportion
1	7.579608	6.720607	0.68906	7.5796	0.68906
2	0.859001	0.159542	0.07809	8.4386	0.76715
3	0.699459	0.188268	0.06359	9.1381	0.83073
4	0.511191	0.091106	0.04647	9.6493	0.87721
5	0.420085	0.042473	0.03819	10.0693	0.91539
6	0.377612	0.181136	0.03433	10.4470	0.94972
7	0.196476	0.051813	0.01786	10.6434	0.96753
8	0.144663	0.018903	0.01315	10.7881	0.98074
9	0.125760	0.063683	0.01143	10.9139	0.99217
10	0.062077	0.033549	0.00564	10.9759	0.99781
11	0.028528	—	0.00259	11	1

Eigenvectors (loadings):

Variable	PC1	PC2	PC3	PC4	PC5
Y01	−0.27728	−0.047411	0.129387	−0.241410	0.038978
Y02	0.05981	0.422385	−0.015039	−0.480777	0.345805
Y03	0.38397	0.199049	−0.221545	−0.032767	0.097380
Y04	0.10259	−0.550748	−0.163683	0.004779	0.157060
Y05	−0.25681	0.322173	0.343107	−0.140338	−0.165134
Y06	0.10228	−0.018319	0.569314	0.314675	−0.150216
Y07	0.24202	0.035020	−0.276945	−0.046598	0.125147
Y08	0.40197	0.326880	0.236655	−0.162170	0.168888
Y09	0.24016	0.454197	−0.149962	0.666327	−0.071569
Y10	0.46641	−0.114021	0.315088	0.295167	0.840332
Y11	0.44750	0.211887	−0.459178	0.176570	0.198621

Eigenvectors (loadings):

Variable	PC6	PC7	PC8	PC9	PC10	PC11
Y01	0.416549	0.322136	0.477795	−0.068981	0.403896	−0.250721
Y02	−0.331289	−0.270124	0.472958	0.175020	−0.038735	0.016374
Y03	0.087044	0.297869	−0.028964	−0.483077	0.433006	0.422899
Y04	−0.189066	0.488405	0.395742	0.041655	−0.401847	0.105058
Y05	0.582952	0.169438	0.024061	0.084169	−0.509013	0.138579
Y06	−0.222683	0.146572	0.158216	0.460175	0.392151	0.191830
Y07	0.145129	0.211457	−0.233931	0.377044	0.175549	−0.630676
Y08	−0.406279	0.593776	−0.387360	−0.073815	−0.125131	−0.084962
Y09	−0.094383	0.086611	0.385343	−0.210990	−0.161093	−0.293810
Y10	0.221903	−0.146572	−0.098117	−0.111866	−0.026996	−0.021748
Y11	0.199293	0.139762	−0.045536	0.553194	0.018990	0.446341

Chapter 6

Financial Safety Net and Financial Stability

The global financial crisis in 2007 brought profound damage to economic development and social stability, provoking thoughts about crisis prevention. Financial risks are endogenous concerning the intermediary nature, position, functions, and internal vulnerability of financial organizations. The panic caused by a crisis, in particular, strengthening the power of financial contagion and of destruction. Given these factors, financial safety is considered a great concern by nations and regions. In order to tackle financial risks, governments are initiatively taking steps, among which the financial safety net, an active and systemic mechanism, attracts much attention from authorities and academia.

Many scholars regard a financial safety net as a contract relationship for financial organizations, which can help them deal with crises and other economic impacts (Diamond & Dybvig, 1983; Kane, 1995). Demirguc-Kunt & Huizinga (1999) believe that the financial safety net is an institutional arrangement for the sake of the financial system and a measure to avoid the breakout and spreading of financial crisis. Kane (2001), in his in-depth research, points out that every financial safety net is a multi-dimensional policy framework to balance costs and profits generated under such circumstances. This framework exists to protect clients from the danger of bankruptcy, to set limits to excessive risk-taking behaviors of financial organizations, to prevent and mitigate the bad consequences of a bank run, to organize and deal with non-performing organizations, and to share the loss caused by shutdown of non-performing organizations within the whole society. White (2004) coins the term "safety net" to refer to a system that minimizes the damage of issues in the financial system by making use of governmental instruments or methods. Tang (2009) emphasizes that a financial safety net is a set of policy systems that governments resort to in their efforts to prevent financial industries from suffering shocks and further infectious bank run. It has mainly two functions: one being crisis prevention, which is to reduce or control over the disclosure of financial organizations to financial risks, and the other being crisis management, that is to hold up or relieve the destructive effects posed by financial crises. In a word, the financial safety net is an institutional system and policy framework that governments use to address financial risks and as a precaution to financial crises.

However, the pity is that up until now consensus has not yet been reached as to the constituents of the financial safety net. Hoening (1998) holds that the financial safety net involves deposit insurance, Federal Reserve's lender of last resort function, and Federal Reserve's large dollar interbank settlement system. Demirguc-Kunt & Huizinga (1999) point out that the financial safety net usually includes the deposit insurance system and the central bank's lender of last resort function. On the other hand, White (2004) believes that there are both micro tools (such as deposit insurance, government guarantee, short-term liquidity support to organizations, crisis coordination, and exit policy) and macro ones (such as tolerant monetary policy and support from International Monetary Fund (IMF)) that a government may adopt to lower the impairment induced by defects in the financial system. Schich (2008) sorts out four fundamental elements that make up a financial safety net, namely: prudential regulation; lender of last resort; a deposit insurance system; and a bankruptcy exit mechanism. Briefly, academics are holding different opinions regarding the elements of the safety net, because of diversified perspectives and emphases of their thoughts, and the institutional environment they focus on. The situation is the same with international organizations for the identical reason (Table 6-1).

As early as 2001, within the Financial Stability Forum (FSF) was an idea regarding the components of the financial safety net. It distinguished the financial safety net in a narrow sense from the one that was widely

Table 6-1. Opinions on the constituents of international organizations' financial safety net.

	Elements				
International organizations	**Prudential supervision**	**Lender of last resort**	**Deposit insurance system**	**Inferior financial organizations' exit mechanism**	**Secure payment and settlement system**
IADI	★	★	★	—	—
International Monetary Fund (IMF)	—	★	★	★	—
Bank for International Settlements (BIS)	★	★	★	—	★

★ refers to the constituent an organization agrees with; the data are sorted out according to Johnson C. S. Chen (2007): "Cooperation among Safety-Net Members in Bank Resolution Practical Considerations."

accepted. The former includes the deposit insurance system and lender of last resort; while the latter, apart from the two elements mentioned, adds prudential supervision to its understanding. Based on previous studies, Marinkovic (2004) put forward a more systemic, well-rounded and scientific opinion, regarding the financial safety net as a net where all kinds of organizations, rules, and programs are involved to act as protectors to a safe and sound operation of financial intermediate system. Marinkovic also thinks that the financial safety net should be redesigned to better deal with shocks and to cope with economic climate changes. In other words, it requires that the constituents of the financial safety net should be evolving in this dynamic financial world, in accordance with the variation of economic and financial development.

Nowadays, both the ideas in academia and the practices of governments regarding the constituent issue vary from one another. Nonetheless, the literature shows a trend of analyzing single constituents. In fact, it is necessary to look at the interior operating mechanism of the financial safety net in an objective manner and to have an accurate knowledge of it. Only in this way, we can make the best out of each element and adjust in accordance with actual situations during operation. Moreover, the in-depth analysis of the operating mechanism will lay a solid foundation for optimizing the design of the financial safety net. This chapter discusses the prudential supervision, lender of last resort, deposit insurance system,[1] and the financial organizations' market exit mechanism in the context of the general economic institutional environment. Of course, some of the procedures can be omitted but some should be strengthened in the light of each nation's economic state.[2]

6.1 LINKS AMONG CONSTITUTIVE ELEMENTS OF THE FINANCIAL SAFETY NET

From the process aspect, the financial security network includes preventive management, emergency management, and market exit management. Preventive management is mainly about financial institutions' market access, supervision management, and stability and security alert mechanisms. Emergency management aims mainly to stabilize the financial system by helping those financial institutions who are in trouble; market exit management is about financial institutions withdrawing from the market, which is mainly to handle those financial institutions which have failed in business operation and either rescue is no longer an option, or the cost is too high. Prudential supervision, lender of last resort, deposit insurance system, and financial institutions' market exit mechanism are the system tools of the financial safety net. These elements constitute the closely coordinated, organic combination of the whole (Wang & Li, 2007).

In general, the regulatory authorities implement prudential supervision in this way. It safeguards the financial system's security through the

[1] Deposit Insurance has two kinds, one being of covert and the other overt. Speaking of covert deposit insurance, governments offer guarantee for deposits but without arranging specific organizations or systems. On the contrary, the deposit insurance with clear arrangements of organizations and systems is called overt deposit insurance. And the Deposit Insurance System being discussed in this book is the overt one.

[2] It is acknowledged that the Deposit Insurance System embodies the design of market exit in the bank-based financial system, so it seems unnecessary to repeat the exit mechanism in the discussion. However, given its significance and relative independence, the book takes it as an independent element in theoretical analysis.

risk supervision measures of market access, capital adequacy, on-site and off-site supervision — it is a kind of preventive measure.

Lender of last resort is controlled by the central bank, mainly to provide liquidity assistance to safeguard the financial system's security through discount window and open market purchase. It is a preventive measure, which becomes intervention in the event of shock, and takes shock absorption measures afterwards.

The implementation of deposit insurance (by the deposit insurance agency) mainly provides supervision and insurance payments to protect the interests of depositors and to keep public confidence. In this way, it safeguards financial system security, is a kind of prevention before shock happens, intervention when it happens and takes shock absorption measures afterwards.

The market withdrawal mechanism for financial institutions via the market exit actuator (such as deposit insurance agency) happens mainly by the reorganization, liquidation, and other financial means to block the infection of financial risks and maintain the financial system's safety. It is a kind of preventive measure[3] and to block the crisis afterwards. Obviously, these elements have different characteristics, and through different ways and channels to maintain financial system security, in practice there is the possibility and necessity of mutual cooperation.

6.1.1 The internal relation among prudential supervision, lender of last resort, and the deposit insurance system

Fratianni (2008) considers that the financial security network[4] and prudential supervision are like two sides of a coin; the government provides a protective "umbrella" to the financial industry and meanwhile monitors institutions' behavior to reduce risks. The lender of last resort, the deposit insurance system, and prudential supervision in the process of financial system development are complementary to each other. In the past few

[3]The market exit system augments the probability for financial organizations to lose concession, so the organizations are avoiding high-risk businesses as much as possible, in which way the exit system is endowed with the function of prevention in advance.

[4]Here, it refers to the lender of last resort and the deposit insurance system.

years, just like prudential supervision, the lender of last resort and deposit insurance systems have also been constantly extended or expanded. For example, after suffering the most severe banking crisis, the United States began various aspects of reform, including the introduction of the Glass–Steagall Act in 1993. Not only was the Federal Deposit Insurance Corporation (FDIC) established, but restrictions were also placed on banks' regional and functional expansion (to separate the activities of commercial banks with investment banking operations), limiting the competition in banking through interest rates. In fact, the endogeneity of financial risk, lender of last resort and the deposit insurance system itself cannot overcome the moral hazard, and need prudential supervision to alleviate some of the negative effects. Similarly, regulatory loopholes produced by information asymmetry also need to be made up by lender of last resort and the deposit insurance system. Generally speaking, the lender of last resort and the deposit insurance system are easy to encourage bearing of excessive risk, and that is why prudential supervision should play a complementary part of it, or at least provide risk control. Prudential supervision has its inherent unsoundness; the evidence shows that it tends to block the "loophole" as a hysteresis behavior, appearing due to financial innovation and financial industry, circumventing regulatory motivation. The result is related to the regulatory mechanism of asymmetric information and the quality differences of supervisory staff, and may relate to regulators reaching an agreement with their controlled industry; moreover, during a crisis it becomes more tolerant due to the political pressure. Therefore, whether in theory or in practice, prudential supervision, the lender of last resort, and the deposit insurance systems are complementary, the intrinsic link between them being difficult to separate.

At the same time, it should be noted that the functions of prudential supervision, lender of last resort, and the deposit insurance system overlap in terms of function, and the latter two have some regulatory functions. Moreover, of course, their supervising function is for protecting the interests of this sector and is a voluntary regulation to the beneficiary, which refers to the banks that gain deposit protection or financial institutions that obtain the final loans. Besides, regulation can effectively reduce the moral risk of recipient institutions and produce less principal agent problems. It is particularly notable that, due to the responsibilities of lender of last resort and deposit insurance systems, when the problems for financial institutions really occur, they will implement bailout. From this perspective, the supervision is not thorough. It is difficult to truly put an end to moral hazard, and therefore to conduct mandatory prudential supervision is a necessity. However, prudential supervision, as the system the government uses to prevent systemic financial risk, is backed up by national force, but is also prone to arouse principal/agent problems[5] and regulatory tolerance[6] in regulators. Therefore, if we can make good coordination of the regulatory functions of prudential supervision, lender of last resort, and deposit insurance institutions, then national compulsory force and self-regulation as double advantages will produce good regulatory effect.

6.1.2 Internal relations between lender of last resort and deposit insurance system

As the core means of rescuing the troubled financial institution, the lender of last resort and the deposit insurance system's main object is the commercial bank. When the financial institution encounters crisis, both of these aforementioned rescue means have the function of providing emergency loan assistance, therefore have the basis of mutual complement and cooperation. In extreme cases, for example, when the deposit insurance institutions lack funds, the lender of last resort can also provide emergency loans to them; and the deposit insurance system is in fact reducing the burden of lender of last resort.

Although the lender of last resort and the deposit insurance system both have the function of protecting the interests of the depositor and maintaining financial stability, they still have differences in terms of rescue target, rescue conditions, rescue object, rescue timing, and the resulting economic effects. From the view of the rescue target, the lender of last resort focuses on financial institutions' temporary illiquidity problems (i.e., a lack of liquidity, but still has solvency), and the deposit insurance system focuses on solving commercial banks' lack of solvency problems

---

[5]In order to protect their own profits and authority, supervision organizations may resort to approaches that are subjective and unfavorable to the public interest.

[6]Regulatory tolerance means the supervision agencies' slack and tolerant attitude towards the problems of financial organizations so as to maintain their authority. It is likely to cause adaptive expectations of financial organizations and then moral hazard.

(i.e., the liabilities exceed the financial institutions' net assets). From the view of the rescue conditions, the lender of last resort requires the financial institutions to provide qualified collateral and accept punitive interest rates; deposit insurance institutions require member banks to pay the premium. From the view of rescue object, the lender of last resort provides aid to all financial institutions with a liquidity crisis, while the deposit insurance institutions only provide assistance to the membership bank that conforms to the conditions. From the view of rescue timing, as long as the bank is in operation, the function of lender of last resort remains, while the deposit insurance agency only implement the payment function when insolvent member banks close (Schich, 2008). From the view of economic effect, the lender of last resort is indirect (more on decision with the central bank), prevents bank runs, and maintains confidence by providing liquidity; while the deposit insurance system is direct, legal (Wang & Li, 2007), prevents bank runs, and maintains confidence through commitment to protect the interests of depositors.

These are the differences that compose the function of the lender of last resort and make the deposit insurance agency more feasible. In fact, when the central bank implements the function of the lender of last resort, it often conflicts with monetary policy, and although the deposit insurance system can prevent bank runs, it cannot avoid other forms of liquidity shocks (such as interbank loan, the extension of due commercial paper and other short-term debt requirements). This also shows that single institutional arrangement cannot effectively safeguard financial security, and the relationship between the lender of last resort and the deposit insurance institutions must be sorted out in order to deal with the banking crisis, and their coordination and cooperation strengthened to make the funded rescue time and sequence clear (Yan, 2005). At this point, Repullo (2000) points out that, faced with smaller liquidity shocks, the lender of last resort should be the main rescuer; otherwise, it should be the deposit insurance agency instead. Kahn & Santos (2005) expanded the study of Repullo under the condition of asymmetric information, emphasizing both with no information sharing incentive; crisis assistance and supervision power distribution should be carried out according to information advantage. Obviously, the cooperation of the lender of last resort and the deposit insurance agency is inevitable and necessary, but should be allocated properly.

Here are also inconsistencies in theory and practice for the functional distribution of the lender of last resort and the deposit insurance agency. For example, in theory, their distribution of functions is direct and clear, but in practice, the boundaries of the two are blurred, because it is often difficult to distinguish between liquidity risk and settlement risk. In this regard, Goodhart's proposal in 1988 on the distinction between liquidity shortage and insolvency is ridiculous; Frydl & Quintyn (2000) also pointed out that, in principle, the lender of last resort only provides support to banks that have reimbursement ability, but in the short-term encounter liquidity problems. And in the early stages of crisis, it is difficult to distinguish liquidity and solvency because banks often seek support from the lender of last resort due to lack of liquidity. Over a period of time, it creates insolvent institutions. This situation often occurs. Based on this, they proposed that people should note that the lack of liquidity may portend insolvency, and may even quickly transform into liquidity crisis. This is because the banks need to immediately repay their debts, and sell their assets at a very low price, and high loss of assets may lead to negative net assets. Therefore, in practice, based on the difference between liquidity risks together with a comprehensive consideration of the rescue target, rescue conditions, rescue object, rescue timing, and the resulting economic effect, a decision should be made to determine specifically who should implement the rescue.

6.1.3 The internal relations between financial institutions' market exit mechanism and prudential supervision, lender of last resort, and the deposit insurance system

Market exit mechanism as the last defense line of financial security is an important supplement of prudential supervision, lender of last resort, and the deposit insurance system. In practice, even though the effective implementation of the various means still cannot completely avoid financial risks, it is still possible to rescue invalid financial institutions — but sometimes the rescue cost is too high or prone to systemic risk afterwards. Therefore, a market exit program needs to be implemented for the troubled financial institutions in a timely manner. This will not only block the further spread of financial risk, but also can lighten the burden of the deposit insurance institution and the lender of last resort, and mitigate the bad influence caused by weak supervision. In particular, the existence of the financial institutions' market exit mechanism has formed a hard constraint on financial institutions, which is conducive to reducing their problems of moral hazard, thus better to carry out their functions of prudential supervision, lender of last resort, and the deposit insurance system. In addition, through the liquidation process of the withdrawal mechanism, it can provide compensation to the lender of last resort and the deposit insurance agency for the loss of rescuing.

From the functional perspective, the deposit insurance system is also related to the market exit mechanism design of the troubled financial institution. Therefore, it is very important to reasonably define the boundaries of the two kinds of exit mechanism and enhance their cooperation. The reason is: firstly, the exit mechanism of the deposit insurance system is a kind of market-oriented means, and the market withdrawal mechanism for financial institutions can adopt either administrative means or market means. Secondly, the deposit insurance system targets insured banks, while the market exit mechanism targets all financial organizations. Thirdly, due to different exit objectives, there are two different exercise operation procedures. Fourth, the deposit insurance system's exit mechanism is to fortify the management of insured banks (exit means loss of concession[7]) and to safeguard the interests of deposit insurance agencies, while the financial institutions' market exit mechanism is a measure taken by governments to stop financial risks from expanding for the sake of the public interest. In spite of the discrepancies, it is undeniable that both — involving financial organizations' market exit — have an internal

[7]Concession refers to the rights particularly authorized to specific persons or organizations by the rightful owner. Concession allows the franchisors to use, under some agreed terms, industrial property or intellectual rights of the owners, including a single business element like a trademark or a potent as well as a combination of several elements. The concession for financial organizations is the franchise rights conferred by the central government. The value of the concession equals the price of the franchise license. The higher the value, the more costs banks will have to pay for when losing the franchise due to bankruptcy. Thus to raise the concession value of financial organizations is an effective measure to mitigate moral risks and enhance stability of the financial system.

coherence. For instance, the two adopt similar exit methods such as merger, reorganization, and liquidation, and both are helpful in blocking the extension of financial risks.

Generally speaking, the market exit of commercial banks is taken care of by deposit insurance organizations so that the interests of the latter can be ensured, for they can use liquidation first to supplement their loss. Moreover, it is also helpful in enhancing efficiency, for the reason that the deposit insurance organizations have set up a series of proactive supervision, process interference, and shock absorbing afterwards for insured commercial banks. On the other hand, it is also worth noticing the deposit insurance organizations' dominance in operating market exit. For example, the problem of internal role conflicts[8] is likely to occur when deposit insurance organizations should have closed problem agencies if liquidation income is less than the insurance premiums, but they do not, for the sake of their own profits and instead leave financial risk to spread.

As the analysis above shows, the constitutive elements of the financial safety net are different in their inherent features and design goals, but in the meantime, their functions overlap to some degree owing to the complicated nature of financial risks. These elements promote, supplement, and interact with each other so that they work together to facilitate financial safety. Specifically speaking, the powerful prudential supervision shares its burden on the shoulders of deposit insurance organizations, lender of last resort, and market exit mechanism, as well as mitigates possible negative impact on deposit insurance system and lender of last resort. In return, the deposit insurance system and lender of last resort not only make up for the mistakes made because of loopholes in the supervision system, but also reduce the losses caused by problem financial organizations. Furthermore, a rational financial organizations' market exit mechanism can solve the problems left untouched by the first three elements, so that the negative impact coming along with a financial crisis is reduced to being as little as possible. On the other hand, market exit

[8]Internal role conflicts occur when the dual functions of an organization are contending against each other. Here, the internal role conflicts refer to the fierce clashes between the protectors of depositors and the persons in charge of the liquidation of problem financial organizations within a deposit insurance agency.

mechanism should be used in a proper way with the efficient operation of the first three elements as the premise, instead of just closing down the organizations any time they are beset by problems. The inner logics of the elements are demonstrated in Figure 6-1.

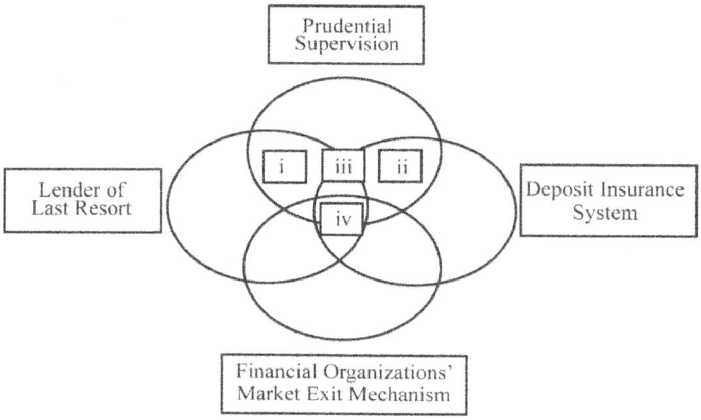

Figure 6-1. Logic system of the financial safety net.

Note: (i) means the mutually owned functions or complementary nature of prudential supervision and the lender of last resort. Both of the two elements perform regulative functions, which are complementary and share information.
(ii) means the mutually owned functions or complementary nature of prudential supervision and the deposit insurance system. Both of the two elements perform regulative functions, which are complementary and share information.
(iii) means the mutually owned functions or complementary nature of the lender of last resort and the deposit insurance system. The former is targeted at general financial organizations, while the latter serves member banks only. Their functions may overlap when it is hard to distinguish liquidity from liquidation risks. They can share information and collaborate with each other. The latter can provide liquidity assistance to the former.
(iv) means the mutually owned functions or complementary nature of the previous three elements and financial organizations' market exit mechanism. The market exit mechanism is employed to block up crises that the three elements failed to solve and to provide compensation of liquidation for the lender of last resort and deposit insurance agencies. Some of the functions possessed by the exit mechanism are the same as those of the deposit insurance system. The two can learn from and integrate with each other. When it comes to dealing with actual situations, the prudential supervision sector may sometimes do the job of enforcing market exit.

In brief, the constitutive elements of the financial safety market are complicatedly interrelated, fitting in with the complex economic environment and rapid financial development. Since the financial safety net is a sophisticated logic system, we should balance the use of those elements according to specific situations.

6.2 OPERATING PRINCIPLES OF THE FINANCIAL SAFETY NET

The financial security network is a large and complex system in which the components compliment and coordinate with each other through clear rules, formulating the inherent logical order and unique operation mechanism.

6.2.1 The implementation of prudential supervision

Prudential supervision is the most important barrier to prevent financial risk. It focuses on advance prevention. Thus, essentially it is a kind of proactive institutional arrangement. Typically, governments' prudential supervision to the financial system will refer to the provisions of the Basel Capital Accord, then formulate a set of regulations and policies, which present with the domestic situation needs such as strict market access system, capital adequacy requirements, etc.

(i) Setting the market access threshold

Market access acts as an important part in the financial regulatory system. It is the first step of prudential supervision, which is helpful for controlling the generation of financial risk from its source under strict market access policy. The threshold of market access mainly focuses on granting license issued by the financial industry, and meanwhile regulates a clear business scope of financial institutions. The Basel Capital Accord II regulates that when issuing the practice license, such things need to be reviewed: bank ownership structure; the qualification of members of the board of directors and senior management the bank's business strategy and plan the bank's governance assessments; internal control and risk management; and financial status expectation, including the capital scale, etc. Through strictly censored, institutions of poor quality can be excluded from the financial system, so as to maintain the steady and good qualification of the main financial body and avoid failure due to individual financial institutions affecting the entire financial system. By placing restrictions on financial institutions' business scope, the engagement of excessive financial institutions in risky activities can be avoided. Therefore, this measure can not only filter qualified financial practitioners, but can also increase the financial institution's franchise value, increasing the cost of bankruptcy closure, and reducing its engagement in risky business incentives.

(ii) Capital adequacy rate

A bank's capital adequacy ratio management is a general way for the financial regulatory authorities to carry out supervision. Capital adequacy ratio is an important indicator of solvency and liquidity.[9] National regulatory authorities generally define the supervision measurement within the framework of the Basel Capital Accord. Under enough capital as a guarantee, financial institutions can carry out business, reverse accidental damage, stabilize depositors' confidence, and thus can realize stable operation. As a result, the financial regulatory authorities will enforce capital adequacy rules, limit the substandard financial institutions of their capital expansion, restrict the establishment of branch offices, and limit profit distribution and other measures as severe punishment. Practically, capital adequacy requirements have been widely used, mainly because capital adequacy ratio has become an important measure to guarantee bank prudential management. At the same time, capital adequacy ratio follows clear rules, thus it is easier to facilitate the operation of the parties involved.

(iii) Information disclosure mechanism

Due to the existence of the problem of asymmetric information, moral hazard and adverse selection are always problems in the process of financial development, which hinders the progress of the financial industry and easily becomes a risk booster. Therefore, accurate, timely, and sufficient information disclosure is a basic requirement to financial institutions' regulatory authorities. This requires the establishment of a mandatory information disclosure mechanism, and regulatory authorities should confirm the

---

[9]The Basel Capital Accord III requires that the bank capital adequacy ratio should reach 8% and the core capital adequacy ratio should reach 6%.

credibility of financial institutions' information disclosure in order to eliminate the occurrence of false information. In the process, checking information disclosure is also an important means of risk prevention, to urge financial institutions to adopt self-inspection and risk avoidance.

(iv) Internal risk management of financial institutions

Strengthening the supervision of financial institutions' internal risk management is an important task for financial regulatory authorities. If financial institutions have possessed good risk management mechanism, the whole of society's ability to cope with the financial risk will be greatly enhanced. According to the requirements of Basel Capital Accord II, financial institutions should carry out a set of risk management procedures, including: possession of their own internal control and audit system; pay close attention to liquidity risk, market risk, credit risk, interest rate risk, operation risk, etc.; focus on distressed assets in business activities, rainy-day reserves, related party risk exposure, etc.; and regulate the limitation of large exposure.

It is necessary to point out that the Basel Capital Accord provides a model for the financial regulatory authorities, thus national regulators must be combined with its domestic characteristics and the financial system's development trend to design regulate patterns. This includes, for example, the United States's change from the original multiple regulatory model into umbrella regulation and functional regulation; Japan moving from original administrative guidance regulation into single-mixed regulation; the British separation of a self-regulatory mechanism into a single regulatory model. Meanwhile, Germany supervised under the universal banking model; China also faces to the transformative trend of separated regulation to mixed regulation. Thus, it can be seen that the financial supervision mode is not fixed, and it will be subject to change along with the development of the financial system. Under the post-financial crisis era, in particular, the financial system faces new adjustment, and financial supervision should make corresponding changes. From the glimpse of the developing trends, modern financial regulation will rush to strengthen and unify regulation. The financial regulatory framework will be further improved, and an effective financial supervision coordination mechanism will be established. Financial innovation products will be regulated with specific rules. Cross-border supervision of international cooperation and the regulation of financial institutions would be strengthened, too. Admittedly, to keep up with the pace of the financial development and to meet the needs of the financial situation changes, prudential supervision can maintain and play their roles.

6.2.2 Lender of the last resort

Despite the fact that prudential regulation is the cheapest financial safety net with the biggest impact, the existence of asymmetric information makes the regulatory loopholes possible and it will be difficult to accurately predict and avoid all the risk. Especially after the outbreak of the financial crisis, its regulatory function is very limited, which requires the financial safety net to play a bigger role.

As is commonly known, when some solvent financial institutions have a temporary liquidity shortage, the central bank can grant emergency loans to these institutions through discount windows or open market operations (i.e., the central bank acts as the lender of last resort). However, they need to provide a good collateral and pay a penalty rate (higher loan interest rate). The central bank can ease the public's fear of cash shortages, curb public panic, and avoid some of the public's excesses by financing financial institutions lacking liquidity. Of course, every action of the lender of last resort starts with solvency assessment of those financial institutions.

(i) Solvency of financial institutions

Only when a financial institution is solvent and there is only a problem because of temporarily liquidity, lenders will eventually help, since the lender of last resort will face the possibility of a great loss of assets from rescuing financial institutions in a solvency crisis. The central bank's lender of last resort function often contains many risky loans. Even though in practice it is difficult to distinguish between a financial institution's liquidity and solvency problems, the central bank will take all measures to determine the solvency of financial institutions to reduce the loss as much as possible.

(ii) Supervision and management

The supervision by the lender of last resort usually continues throughout a financial crisis. Through sharing information with financial institutions to evaluate whether there is liquidity risk, to decide whether to rescue, what rescue package to use and when is the best opportunity to grasp the final loan, it avoids waste of loan resources. To determine the optimal size of the loan collateral through on-site inspection and evaluation, the lender of the last resort can save resources and cooperate with regulatory work to ensure the security of the assets in that department through post supervision. After the central bank's bailout of problem financial institutions, it will conduct continuous supervision to safeguard assets against moral hazard. Once it finds that the problems of financial institutions have further deteriorated, the lender of last resort has the right to take strict security measures.

(iii) Financial resource

The central bank, as the lender of last resort, will rescue with a big pool of capital. This capital mainly comes from various kinds of deposit (including fiscal deposits, office and postal savings deposits, etc.), the deposit reserve, currency, central bank bills, and liquidation of collateral from member banks, etc. At the same time, the central bank as the lender of last resort is supposed to bear certain risks, especially for the insolvent financial institutions, because the value of the collateral value may be lower than the loan. Therefore, when the central bank bails out financial institutions with uncertain insolvency, it is likely to suffer bigger losses and cause many adverse consequences. Goodhart (1999) argues that large bailout loans ruin the balance sheet of banks and will weaken the central bank in independence and flexibility of monetary policy. In view of this, many central banks are reluctant to assume this risk alone. Normally, they demand fiscal and financial support from the government.

(iv) The final loan

Commercial banks facing short-term liquidity shortage will apply for the rediscount of discounted but not due commercial drafts to the central bank. In this way, the central bank provides financing support; the central bank also can pass on the open market purchase of central bank bills, treasury bonds, and debt-finance, etc., to inject liquidity to financial institutions. When financial institutions are in serious liquidity difficulties, the central bank will also provide emergency loans to qualifying financial institutions in trouble. By implementing loan aid to help problem financial institutions out of the predicament, the central bank ensures the safety of the entire financial system. After providing loans, the central bank will supervise the recipient operation and management behavior to ensure the safety in its own assets.

6.2.3 Deposit insurance system

When a creditor provides a loan for a financial institution in a temporary liquidity crisis, they should have eligible collateral and bear the penalty rate; which means that banks mired in an insolvency crisis will pay a high price. At the same time, if the lender of last resort can distinguish between liquidity and liquidation, it should only provide financial relief to those with a liquidity problem. Therefore, when the bank is trapped in liquidation crisis, the rights and interests of depositors will be threatened. In order to protect the depositors' interests and to stabilize economic and financial operation, the deposit insurance system arises at the important moment. A well-designed deposit insurance system is a means of relief for problematic banks and a means of guarantee to depositors. This helps to enhance the confidence of the depositor, stabilize financial institutions and even the entire financial system.

(i) Membership

The deposit insurance system adopts a membership policy, which can be mandatory or voluntary. Mandatory requirement helps to reduce the adverse selection problem.[10] In this way, those participating in deposit insurance institutions will be weak and highly risky. However, problematic agencies with moral hazard favor risky activities.[11] Voluntary membership

[10] Since well-run institutions will be unwilling to bear the additional premium cost and give up joining the system otherwise.

[11] For they can get high yielding and when facing a crisis, the deposit insurance institutions will have to "pay" for it.

is problematic at the same time. In practice, banks will weigh out the costs and benefits, with some joining the deposit insurance system, because this means that there is a safety net to the depositors that it is conducive to the absorption and retention of deposit. Some others will choose not to join the deposit insurance system, because it will mean bearing additional premium costs and being subject to deposit insurance institutions' supervision and manipulation. For big banks, because of their strong ability to cope with risks, even if there is one, the state is willing to help, for as the saying goes, they are "too big to fail." Therefore, they are generally not willing to join the deposit insurance system. At this point, in order to maintain the stability of the financial system and to create a fair competition environment, the government usually adopts compulsory membership for the deposit insurance system.[12] No matter which way to take, deposit insurance institutions should have a proper system in place to refine the members into a standard procedure and time schedule to finally determine the membership of the deposit insurance system.

(ii) Charging and managing the insurance fee

In order to maintain daily operation and compensate depositors' losses, deposit insurance institutions must have enough money as a guarantee. Money usually comes from the premiums paid by member banks, debt interest, asset management income, clearing agency fee, emergency assistance from the lender of last resort, etc. Because the member banks are the main favorite, their insurance premium constitutes the main source of funds. Charging a premium requires settling an insurance premium rate. In practice, deposit insurance institutions implement a unified insurance premium rate to every insured bank. This way, although simple, boasts a problem, because it does not distinguish between different risk preference and the insured banks of different quality. It is easy to make the risk preferential or poor quality banks produce moral hazard adverse risk, or good quality banks suffer an adverse selection problem. At the same time, it is unfavorable to motivate banks engaged in

[12] International Association of Deposit Insurance Institutions (IADIs) also suggests compulsory membership.

spontaneous low-risk economic activity. Some academics have found that people's willingness to have the same premium rate is subject to the conditions of asymmetric information (Freixas & Rochet, 1998). Due to a lack of necessary information, deposit insurance institutions tend not to correct for the differences between the characteristics of banks. Now, it is still a technical problem yet to be solved. Therefore, it is necessary to strengthen the cooperation of the deposit insurance system and prudential regulation, reducing the premium collection problem of moral hazard and adverse selection. Here, it should also be noted that when the economy is in a good state, deposit insurance institutions do not need to pay compensation, so they need to manage their internal accumulation assets and achieve value growth. This not only can enhance the strength of the deposit insurance institution itself, but also can reduce the burden of member banks and enhance the liquidity of the society as a whole. Of course, in the asset management, deposit insurance institutions would invest in low-risk and high liquidity assets to ensure the safety and around-the-clock availability of funds.

(iii) Supervision and management

To join the deposit insurance system, a member bank must accept its supervision and management. Deposit insurance institutions in this way can prevent the moral hazard of member banks, and protect depositors and their interests. Usually, laws of all states give the deposit insurance institutions the right to monitor these banks on-site and off-site. There is a reasonable and lawful system of rules, including monitoring rules, index evaluation system, operating procedures, etc. By these rules, the deposit insurance agencies can monitor each member bank on their capital state, assets operation, and daily business activities, etc. Through daily supervision and management, deposit insurance institutions can discover the problems of financial institutions and urge banks to rectify them.

(iv) Prevention rescue and management

When the deposit insurance institution finds signs of risk via its monitoring system, it can ask the necessary questions and offer hints and warnings, advising them to adhere to these. When the problems of financial institutions erupt and the capital adequacy ratio is lower than the standards set by the Basel Capital Accord or in violation of prudential supervision requirements, a deposit insurance institution shall exert its rescue and processing functions. At this point, the deposit insurance institution's approach is to provide emergency aid to troubled banks, in various ways that include providing emergency loans to insured banks, or to buying toxic assets, to help the banks back to business and to stable their activities. When problematic banks cannot be rescued, deposit insurance institutions would implement compulsory merger and restructuring measures, which entail choosing good financial institutions that have the intention of merger and acquisition and carrying on the direct subsidy or purchasing their non-performing assets to indirectly finance them. When the problem is very serious and has a big impact, deposit insurance institutions must respond to it by closing those banks. At this time, deposit insurance institutions should compensate depositors, paying them directly within the compensation limit. Agent banks could also be used to pay in forms of cash or deposit.

6.2.4 Financial institutions' market withdrawal mechanism

When the problem is so serious that it even poses a great threat to financial system stability, financial institutions are required to take market exit measures. A financial institution's market exit usually happens when funds have deteriorated to a certain degree (such as capital eroded by more than 60%, bad assets have reached more than 60%, three consecutive losses of 10% and is unable to repay debts, etc.) and is in payment difficulties. It should then be required to merger and acquisition or to bankrupt on its own order or by regulatory authorities, in accordance with market principles: open, fair, fair treatment of creditor's rights debt, the final cancellation process of the legal person status (Yan, 2006). The existence of this market withdrawal mechanism is a warning to heed the excessive crisis of financial institutions and to avoid their reliance on the idea of "too big to fail." The withdrawal mechanism is not only an effective means to end the problem of adverse effects, but is also a protection for the financial safety net, which avoids unnecessary burdens, and freezes costs.

(i) Setting up a threshold for market withdrawal

Making clear market exit criteria is the precondition of its effective implementation. Over the years, financial institutions exiting the market have followed these general principles: the troubled financial institutions cannot be rescued; rescue cost is far greater than the benefit, or will cause the occurrence of systemic risk and regional risk after the rescue. From the view of the present situation, while it is difficult for financial institutions to agree to a common standard of market exit, national regulators still have to develop the market exit criteria suited to the characteristics of the domestic financial system. It should be noted that financial institutions' market exit criteria are no determination of finality; the development of financial industry and economic environment change should be constantly revised, improved, and perfected.

(ii) Making procedures for market withdrawal

After making clear market exit criteria, problem financial institutions are supposed to take corresponding exit programs. Financial institutions heading for market exit take the main path of merger, reorganization, and bankruptcy liquidation. The selection of specific market exit should also take into account the following principles: (i) social cost minimization; (ii) stabilize market confidence; (iii) limited to related departments to provide funds. When a financial institution meets market exit criteria, the market exit actuator should takeover in time to avoid more problems. After the takeover, the problem can be further inspected and the seriousness of the problem is taken into account, which way to take depends on the specific circumstances. Countries tend to prefer mergers and acquisitions (M&A) rather than easily liquidation, because the impact caused by M&A on the entire financial system is much smaller. If the problem can be resolved in this way with a well-run institution willing to take over, the market exit actuator can help them complete the restructuring. If the problem cannot be resolved through consolidation, or no financial institutions are willing to take over the market exit actuator, liquidation is the only way left.

(iii) Allocation of liquidation

A market exit actuator should implement a lawful and objective liquidation procedure on problem financial institutions to ensure their orderly exit and minimize social losses. The bankruptcy and liquidation of problem financial institutions can create income that can be used to recover the investment and make up the loss of the main channel. Therefore, in accordance with the principle of the final loan and deposit insurance mechanism, income distribution will be implemented. Reasonable distribution of liquidation income ensures the rights and interests of the final loan and deposit insurance agencies, helping them to implement other packages, which can also aid the financial safety net into a virtuous cycle.

Figure 6-2 intuitively shows the logic of the financial safety net. Prudential regulation, the lender of last resort, the deposit insurance system, and financial institutions' market withdrawal mechanism have their own internal operation mechanism, and there is a certain logical order and

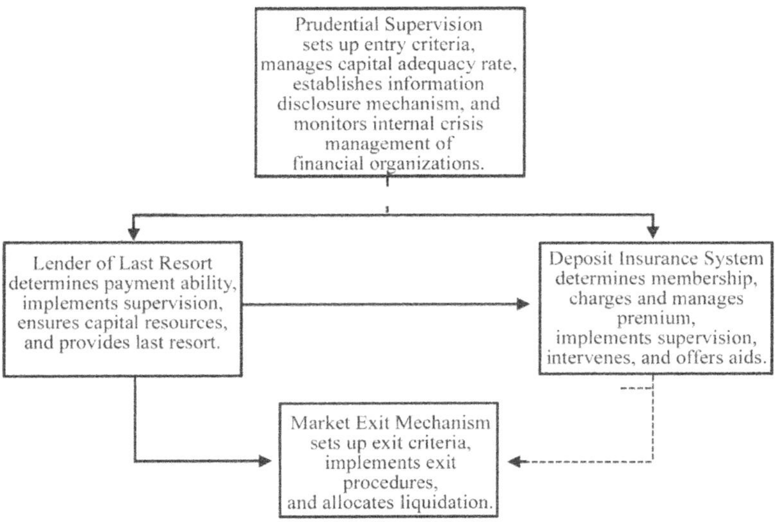

Figure 6-2. The logic of the financial safety net.

Note: The dashed lines in the graph indicate that this kind of transfer may not be needed.

delivery mechanism among them. Each transfer of elements has its specific conditions and order arrangement.

From the view of the individual elements, each element in financial risk focuses on different functions. Their different advantages and functions complement each other, thus forming the basis of cooperation. From the view of the financial safety net system, it is a system going all the way down the course of financial risks. Under a reasonable system design, the financial safety net can run an orderly and effective response to the risk.

According to above analysis, the author makes the following suggestions on the construction of China's financial safety net:

(i) It is necessary to determine the elements of a financial safety net according to the characteristics of China's economic system in order to build a reasonable and complete financial risk coping mechanism. On this basis, the financial safety net elements should be further clarified in internal relations.
(ii) It is necessary to optimize design of the financial safety net and to further improve the function of the financial safety net. This should be done according to the relation of the elements of the financial safety net and its system characteristics.
(iii) Define the scope of functions of the financial safety net elements, such as prudential regulation of the financial system as a complete regulatory measure, and the final loan and deposit insurance agencies responsible for the supervision and administration of financial institutions within its own system. Given that banks occupy absolute primary position in the financial system in China, an exit program can be performed by the deposit insurance agency. When enough experience has accumulated and great changes have taken place in China's financial structure, we should set up special financial institutions to perform market withdrawal mechanisms.
(iv) Due to the different objectives and priorities of function elements, overlapping is inevitable and reasonable. We should pay attention to the various elements in cross function, labor division, and cooperation among all the departments.

(v) A reasonable distribution of power among all the financial safety net departments, which is not only beneficial to coordination, but helps to establish responsibility, and checks and balances mechanism.
(vi) The orderly operation of the financial safety net must handle the financial risks, reduce human intervention, and improve the efficiency of processing.

6.3 CHOOSING THE RIGHT PATH FOR CONSTRUCTING CHINA'S EXPLICIT DEPOSIT INSURANCE SYSTEM

In view of the importance of the financial safety net, it is necessary for China to establish an explicit deposit insurance system. China's deposit insurance system is different from other countries in many ways. However, there are also many similarities in the operation mechanism after the establishment of the deposit insurance system. Therefore, in designing the deposit insurance system, not only the specific national conditions in China, but also the internal operating mechanism of the deposit insurance system should be considered to choose the advancement path that accords with China's practice.

6.3.1 Set the advancing mechanism

In general, the government provides implicit deposit insurance so that financial institutions and their managers do not have to bear the due cost of their poor operation and management, as well as worry about the lack of deposit sources due to poor management. Because of government credit guarantees, depositors generally do not focus on the management and risk profile in their choice of depositary bank. The establishment of an explicit deposit insurance system pushes banks to pay insurance premiums and face multiple regulations from the regulatory functions of the deposit insurance agency, adding additional costs. The monitoring from large depositors will become an important binding force on its business activities. This could also be one of the important reasons why banks are more reluctant to spontaneously establish the deposit insurance system.

The government provides implicit deposit insurance and depositors hardly take any risks. After the establishment of the deposit insurance system, part of the large depositors' assets will lose protection. In order to protect their own assets, they must bear the cost of implementing supervision. For other small depositors, the establishment of a deposit insurance system has little effect, but they must pay the time and waiting cost in the situation of bankruptcy. Thus, depositors also lack the intrinsic motivation to promote the establishment of the deposit insurance system.

According to the research results from Demirgü-Kunt *et al.* (2006), the establishment of the explicit deposit insurance system in China lacks private pressure. While there is a need for the reference and following the deposit insurance system in developed countries, this is far from enough to constitute the establishment of the explicit deposit insurance system in China. After excluding these factors, the establishment of the explicit deposit insurance system can only be promoted by the government for reasons of public interest.

After determining the main body of the deposit insurance system implementation, a corresponding advancing mechanism should also be set.

(i) Establish the advancing institutions and ensure the promotion responsibilities

After the decision is made to establish an explicit deposit insurance system, a special department needs to be set up to facilitate its implementation. Members of this department should be familiar with the functioning and development of macroeconomic, financial system reform practice, banking system operation, and legal environment in China. Therefore, experts from the People's Bank of China (PBOC), the China Banking Regulatory Commission (CBRC), the National Development and Reform Commission and the Ministry of Finance, as well as legal experts can constitute the Commission to Promote Explicit Deposit Insurance System.

(ii) Conduct situational research and serve the system design

In order to develop a practical promotion plan for the explicit deposit insurance system reference, the Commission needs to investigate national situations, including: analyze the economic environment (the macroeconomic development, financial system, and banking structure, etc.) and institutional conditions (bank credit evaluation system, internal governance, prudential supervision and cooperation, and legal framework, etc.); grasp a detailed deposit accounts structure (deposit types, amount distribution of different deposit types, deposit terms, depositors, and the relationship between GDP and revenues, etc.) to find the best warranty range and the lower limit of deposit insurance fund; understand the attitude of relevant institutions and individuals toward the establishment of the deposit insurance system and the impact they may suffer; and conduct stress tests for premium collection to find the upper limit of deposit insurance fund size.

(iii) Popularize public education and strengthen microfoundation

Public education includes the education for depositors and deposit-taking financial institutions to change their negative attitudes toward the deposit insurance system. Through education about the long-term benefits, they will recognize the inevitable trend of financial market-oriented reform and the benefits to establish the explicit deposit insurance system, as well as define their respective rights and obligations. Radio, television, and the Internet can be fully utilized to do extensive marketing, as well as regular and irregular notification by various media and public visits.

(iv) Clarify institutional responsibilities and establish coordination mechanisms

The establishment of the deposit insurance system will reallocate the mandate of existing relevant departments. For example, there is a need to reconfigure the supervision and information-access rights of the central bank, the CBRC, and the deposit insurance agencies on banks, and the rights of the CBRC and deposit insurance agencies to participate in the implementation of market exit mechanism on problematic banks. Regulatory affiliation of deposit insurance agencies also needs to be acknowledged. These relationships should be first defined in the establishment of the deposit insurance system, where the mechanism of power distribution and coordination should be detailed and operational.

(v) Coordinate all resources and optimize the mechanism design

Based on the research of a country's situation, a deposit insurance system that balances the interests of all parties, constrains costs, and minimizes risks should be designed. At the same time, professionals in the relevant fields should receive good training to ensure the smooth implementation of the deposit insurance system.

(vi) Conduct simulation experiment and provide the implementation

After the completion of the deposit insurance scheme design, the system simulation test should be conducted and representatives of relevant institutions and individuals be invited to participate. Their opinions and suggestions need to be solicited widely to identify defects in the system, conduct investigations, and constantly improve by considering the participants' opinions.

6.3.2 Improve the external conditions

(i) Improve the banking credit rating system

A credit rating is an important part of the information disclosure system, a means to do scientific and objective evaluation on bank credit conditions and an important indicator for depositors and the bank regulatory agencies to understand banking risks. China should accelerate the establishment and improvement of the relevant laws for banks' credit rating, clarify responsibilities, power and conduct codes of credit rating agencies, orient credit rating agencies with policies, increase the training of professionals and assess their professional literacy and ethics strictly.

(ii) Improve the governance structure of the banking sector

Banking governance structure consists of external management and internal control. External management mainly refers to the external audit and supervision that regulatory authorities like the central bank and the CBRC conduct to urge commercial banks to improve and perfect their internal management system. Internal governance mainly refers to a clear separation of responsibilities in banks among shareholders, board of directors, board of supervisors and managers, and the establishment of a reasonable cash compensation and equity incentives mechanism. At the same time, banks should also establish a corresponding internal audit system to enhance self-monitoring and self-correction capabilities.

(iii) Continue to enhance the effectiveness of prudential supervision

Strongly prudential regulation is very important to the smooth functioning of the deposit insurance system. With a lack of strongly prudential supervision, deposit insurance agencies will not only lose financial stability, but also face huge risks, increasing the instability of the financial system. China's central bank and the CBRC have accumulated rich regulatory experience and played very important roles in the maintaining financial stability before. However, with the deepening financial reform and increasing financial openness, financial regulation will face situations that are more complex and the task will be even more important and arduous. Therefore, a dynamic regulatory mechanism must be established to constantly improve the supervision and its efficiency.

(iv) Establish a long-term cooperation mechanism

There is no doubt that the deposit insurance system cannot solve the systemic financial crisis. It must cooperate efficiently with the central bank, the CBRC, the Audit Commission and the Ministry of Finance, and establish a close cooperation and information sharing mechanism in its everyday work. This should include: establishment of the information sharing mechanism and major events reporting system of relevant parties, and standardize information collection, collation, dissemination and transfer; when commercial banks face liquidity risks and deposit insurance agencies cannot afford to support banks or pay depositors, central banks (or directly to problematic financial institutions by the central bank) should provide an emergency loan to avoid a bank run and maintain the financial system's stability; in order to fundamentally reduce the damage caused by bank failures, the deposit insurance agencies should strengthen the cooperation with the CBRC on the regulation of the banking industry market access, business scope, capital adequacy ratio, information disclosure, senior management personnel qualifications, risk management, internal control, and market exit to promote the sound operation of commercial banks. It is noteworthy that China's banking industry will accelerate the pace of opening up in the process of globalization, as well as face the risks of globalization. Thus, it will be very difficult for the deposit insurance agencies in China to complete the tasks of financial stability involved in the global risks alone. Therefore, under the premise of secrecy, the deposit insurance agencies in China can exchange information with foreign deposit insurance agencies or other financial security departments, and expand extensive international cooperation (e.g., the coordination of the problematic financial institutions processing, etc.), "the uncoordinated policy will lead to too little regulation and excessive deposit protection" (Hardya & Nieto, 2010). Through bilateral or multilateral cooperation agreements set down, some cooperation can be institutionalized to facilitate coordination timely during the financial crisis and reduce the crisis transferred into China from strongly regulated countries (Buch & DeLong, 2008).

(v) Provide legal support

Laws and regulations of the deposit insurance system should be introduced as soon as possible to clearly define the deposit insurance institutions' setup, functions, powers, warranty, funding sources, premium collection, disposal, compensation. They should also cover the recovery of problem institutions, and personnel protection, leaving a legal basis for the deposit insurance system in its implementation, protecting prudential behavior by law and enhancing the credibility of the deposit insurance system.

6.3.3 Improve internal environment

(i) One-step process or in-stages process

From the perspective of institutional settings, Fu & Zhu (2009) proposed that the establishment of a deposit insurance agency should be in two stages: (i) an agency should establish within the PBOC; (ii) once up and running well, the agency can operate independently from the PBOC. Meanwhile, from the perspective of the members of a deposit insurance system, Meng (2010) also advocates establishing a deposit insurance system in stages: (i) design the deposit insurance system to optimize its function. However, large commercial banks should temporarily not join the deposit insurance system when first established. (ii) Bring the large commercial banks into the deposit insurance system. Although, it is easy to establish a deposit insurance institution within the PBOC, monetary mechanism and credit independence of the central bank will be interrupted, without the participation of large commercial banks, the scale and fund of the deposit insurance system would be small and the function of the system is limited, which is harmful to fair competition in the banking industry. Overall, a more realistic option is that China should build an independent deposit insurance institution, establish a fair deposit insurance mechanism, and improve the system during the process.

(ii) Single function or integrated functions

It is the policy makers' decision on establishing a deposit insurance institution as a "cashier box" or "risk minimization manager." A "cashier box" executes only single payment functions, while a "risk minimization manager" is multifunctional. The current central bank can achieve the single function as a "cashier box" but the other advantages of the deposit insurance system cannot play. Therefore, China's deposit insurance institution should be an integrated function institution to minimize the risks. These integrated functions include protecting depositors, supervising and inspecting member institutions, dealing with the institutions' problems and maintaining financial stability. When problems occur in one of its member institutions, the deposit insurance institution should take timely warning, intervention, treatment, and other measures to stabilize public confidence and the financial market, as well as to ensure depositors will be paid. It is worth noting that the deposit insurance institution has the power to perform its functions, including: the right to inspect its member institutions' basic business conditions, accounting and financial statements, business activities, risk profiles and non-performing loans (on-site inspection and off-site check included); the right to make recommendations or warnings to its member institutions according to the different conditions, as well as the right to report to the central bank when the risk exceeds the safety line. A deposit insurance institution helps the central bank to strengthen its market supervision and to promote industry self-regulation of depository institutions. Moreover, it also has the right of approval for deposit insurance system entry or exit, of participating contract cooperation, of designing the bank's internal budget and program, and of timely intervention of the banks and getting the right information to ensure that they fulfill their obligations to depositors. When dealing with the market exit mechanism, the subrogation priority[13] of the deposit insurance institution has a solid legal theoretical foundation. To award the deposit insurance institution, the right of subrogation is beneficial to the safety and stability of deposit insurance fund, and to the fulfillment of functions of the deposit insurance system, which is very helpful to protect depositors' interests and maintain financial stability (Chen, 2006).

(iii) Compulsory membership or voluntary membership

Many scholars (such as Li & Jiang, 2009) argue that the deposit insurance system should be compulsory rather than voluntary, concerning the actual situation of China. Here are the reasons. (i) If large commercial banks are excluded from the deposit insurance system, it will be difficult to standardize and legalize the deposit insurance system as well as supervise the risk behaviors of large commercial banks. What is worse, the lack of large commercial banks that hold a large proportion of the deposits will directly affect the size of the deposit insurance system in China. (ii) Small and medium commercial banks competing with the large commercial banks within the deposit insurance system also have to accept additional oversight and fees, which is bad for fair competition in the financial system. (iii) Regional commercial banks, city commercial banks, and urban and rural credit unions are small in terms of scale. Their ability to withstand financial risks is weak and their business space is narrow. Therefore, if

[13]The subrogation priority means when the deposit insurance institution has indemnified for the loss of depositor according to the law, it has the right to be repaid before the other ordinary creditor.

voluntary membership is selected, many banks are likely to reduce costs and not participate in the deposit insurance system. Thus, the risk of these bodies cannot be eliminated and the system will be useless. (iv) The deposit insurance system is associated with many aspects of society, shouldering the task of financial system revolution and financial stability. Therefore, it is necessary to implement compulsory membership to ensure that all deposits of qualified domestic financial institutions are required to join the deposit insurance system and automatically be assigned membership. Members should take the initiative to pay the premiums, the initiative to provide relevant information, receive regulatory from deposit insurance institution and actively cooperate with the deposit insurance institution. Because the total assets of overseas-funded banks account for a relatively small RMB deposits, showing limited influence, they are subject to strict regulation in the absorption of RMB deposits of depositors strong risk tolerance. Therefore, overseas-funded banks are temporarily not performed within the deposit insurance system.

(iv) Limited coverage or full coverage

Hardya & Nieto (2010) think that the deposit insurance system should not only set the minimum guarantee range, but also try to determine a maximum one. Although it is hard to comply with the upper limit during the crisis, the principle is valid for dealing with individual bank failure. Some academics also recommended that the deposit insurance system only cover the savings deposits of residents, not corporate deposits, interbank deposits, and fiscal deposits (such as Li & Jiang, 2009). Because there is a U-shaped relationship between explicit deposit insurance coverage and risk-taking behavior of banks (Angkinand & Wihlborg, 2010), the deposit insurance coverage China should try to find ways to minimize banks' risk-taking behavior. During the initial stage of establishment of the deposit insurance system, the guarantee deposit type should include residents' savings deposits, which account for about 43% of total deposits. The implementation of effective protection of these deposits helps secure public confidence in the banking system during the financial reform process. In addition, as for corporate deposits, the deposits of small businesses that combine capital and labor should be included in the deposit insurance system. Small businesses play an important role to provide employment and facilitate people's lives. However, they lack the ability to prevent and control risks. As the foreign currency is not allowed to freely circulate in China, the proportion that foreign currency deposits take in total deposits is small and constantly changes according to the exchange rate, which is difficult to ensure its value. Therefore, at the beginning of the establishment of the deposit insurance system, the foreign currency deposits were excluded. Other forms such as high interest savings, enterprises deposits, interbank deposits, insider deposits, and fiscal deposits can be excluded from insurance coverage, since these depositors are economically powerful. This exclusion contributes to enhancing market discipline and reducing the insurance premiums for institutions. Taking the survey from PBOC in April 2005 as an example, if the amount of the deposit guarantee is limited under 100,000, a majority of deposit accounts can be covered. Since this part of the deposit only takes a small proportion of all deposits, the depositors lack the strength to supervise banks. The provision of full guarantees helps the stability of the banking system without impairing market discipline. The amount of the deposit that is not guaranteed accounts for 70.53% of all deposit amounts under investigation, and these accounts with large deposits can form a strong market binding power. If China's current deposit account structure has not changed essentially compared with 2005, deposits under 100,000 can be considered to provide full guarantees. This can help the transitional stabilization period, as well as not introduce any additional burden on deposit insurance agencies. Of course, the guarantee limit should be finally confirmed with the latest survey data and a comprehensive consideration of the optimal fund size in correspondence with different guarantee amount. In addition, during the operation of the deposit insurance system, the guarantee amount should be timely adjusted based on the economic development level, inflation, resident income growth, and changes in the deposit insurance fund.

(v) *Ex ante* or *ex post* financing

Since the establishment of the deposit insurance system will increase the costs of commercial banks, they will inevitably lack the internal motivation to promote the establishment of a deposit insurance system under external pressure from financial liberalization. The government shall provide the basic funding for the deposit insurance system; the supplementary funds for deposit insurance mainly come from the premiums paid by members. However, when the fund is insufficient in the case of crisis, the deposit insurance agency can issue financial stability funds or bonds to raise capital, or receive the capital from the Ministry of Finance and the central bank. The investment amount can be adjusted in various ways with different economic development situations, and ex post financing is required more during the crisis according to the circumstances. Overall, the country should use a mixed financing method, where ex ante financing is the main part. Of course, the justice problem should be noted during the design of the deposit insurance system in the choice of financing methods. Expected loss pricing theory can be used as the basis for the design of the deposit insurance system, especially as an effective tool to conduct the scale management and risk assessment of the deposit insurance fund (Ling *et al.*, 2007).

It is necessary to note that, in the absence of empirical data about bank failures, it is difficult to determine the capital raising size with historical data or survey data. Thus, the fundraising size can be assumed to be 8% of guarantee deposits (see the bank's capital adequacy ratio). In the 2005 survey data, for example, we estimate the size of the fund which matches different guarantee amount, calculate the proportion of the size to the total deposits, GDP and fiscal revenue and determine the optimal size of the fund through a comprehensive comparison (see Table 6-2). It can be seen that the greater proportion of the fund size to total deposits, the stronger stabilizing effect it will have; the smaller proportion of the fund size to GDP or fiscal revenue, the lighter the burden the economy will carry.

This requires finding proper conjunction points to have a comprehensive consideration of the guarantee limit, affordability, and other factors to determine the optimal size of the fund. For example, a fund size under 50,000 *yuan* brings low pressure to GDP and fiscal revenue, but the proportion to total deposits and the stabilizing effect on the banking system are naturally small. A fund size less than 50 million *yuan*, on the contrary, falls to the opposite extremes. A fund size with guarantee of between 10 million *yuan* and 20 million *yuan* can bring both pressure and a stabilizing effect in the middle as well. Under an extreme state of the economy,

Table 6-2. Fund size under different guarantee limit (Unit: %).

	Under 50,000 *yuan*	Under 10,0000 *yuan*	Under 200,000 *yuan*	Under 500,000 *yuan*
Fund size/total deposits	1.64	2.36	3.01	3.69
Fund size/GDP	2.57	3.68	4.70	5.75
Fund size/fiscal revenue	14.91	21.39	27.30	33.45

Source: China Statistical Yearbook 2006.

the first two fund sizes can be used depending on the circumstances and under the general state. The total amount and structure of GDP or fiscal revenue, and insurance premium stress test resulting from the research on the country's situation can be used to determine fund usage with a size of less than 100,000 or 200,000 *yuan*. In particular, in order to develop a practical guarantee limit and fund size, a current deposit account structure is needed to receive full investigation, in order to obtain the data as a basis to analyze and determine the amount that can be employed.

(vi) Fixed rate or risk-adjustable rate

China's banking system is led by oligopoly. Big, medium, and small financial institutions coexist and have administrative monopoly characteristics. Thus, "institutional category difference rates" can be adopted according to the risk resilience of different banks, based on determining the basic premium rate in accordance with the amount of the deposits. Premiums can be taken in accordance with the banks' risk rating when conditions are ripe (Fu & Zhu, 2009). At present, there is still obvious polarization in China's banking industry. Large commercial banks have the obvious advantage over small banks in terms of size, staff, competitiveness, and development trend. Thus, the classified levy rate could be considered, i.e., different levy rate toward large commercial banks and other small banks. There are big differences among small and medium banks in their risk profile, and risk-adjusted rates can be implemented in accordance with their capital adequacy ratio, non-performing assets ratio, internal control mechanisms, profitability, and liquidity. In general, due to the small size of the deposit, the total cost of the differential rates for small and medium banks is small. Large commercial banks have strict supervision and there is no big difference among their risk profile, so a modest flat rate can be imposed (the rate of low risk small and medium banks is lower than that of large commercial banks and the rate of high-risk small banks is higher than large commercial banks). This differential rate reduces the overall collection cost of deposit insurance premium. Additionally, the implementation of a moderate level of premium rates for large commercial banks can contribute to fair competition among commercial banks, and the implementation of differential rates for small and medium commercial banks can contribute to encourage small and medium commercial banks to improve their management levels and to reduce risk.

(vii) Administrative exit and market exit

The market exit mechanism of problematic financial institutions now is government-led. The lack of relevant laws about the exit of financial institutions makes these exit decisions often dependent on the subjective judgment of the authorities, which can be very random and does not meet the trend of the government's economic function transformation. After the establishment of the explicit deposit insurance system, market exit would be the ultimate means to address the problematic financial institutions, but also an important way to protect the safety of deposit insurance funds. In order to ensure deposit insurance agencies deal methodically and effectively with the problematic financial institutions, the establishment of market exit mechanism within the deposit insurance system should be an inevitable choice. Market exit mechanism can be conducted in the manner of merger or liquidation.

A merger entails the selection of sound financial institutions with the intention to combine these (merge) with problematic financial institutions. Of course, the deposit insurance agency must review the qualifications of these institutions and then select the most appropriate institution for this operation. In the process of merger, the deposit insurance agency can offer financial assistance to institutions that implement the merger, or offer indirect financing by purchasing the non-performing assets of troubled financial institutions. Liquidation means to dissolve the troubled financial institutions with serious problems that are costly to rescue and no other financial institutions are willing to take over, and to pay depositors. In the liquidation process, the deposit insurance agency should reimburse depositors promptly, properly and equitably, reduce processing costs, and prevent moral hazard by improving market discipline through the necessary legal means.

6.4 SUGGESTIONS FOR HOW TO PERFECT CHINA'S LENDER OF LAST RESORT INSTITUTION

(i) Specify function and position of lender of last resort

By learning from countries like United Kingdom, United States, etc., which possess mature and sound lender of last resort institutions, the self-united lender of last resort institution framework is built up to specify its intention, target, responsibility, scope, and modes,, so as to enhance assistance purposiveness, standardization, operability, and timeliness. To realize this, it is considered to specify the position and function of central bank's lender of last resort institution in the law of the PBOC, give the central bank the right to make decisions by themselves, and make the central bank more independent to make decisions.

(ii) Standardize assistance procedure of lender of last resort

Currently, one of the most prominent problems in the lender of last resort institution is that whatever happens in the financial institutions, the central bank always is the first to offer assistance. In this way, the lender of last resort becomes "lender of first resort," which goes against the original intention. Therefore, the central bank should specify assistance procedure to financial institutions, and simultaneously make it public and supervisory. When financial institutions are in trouble, they should first self-assist, assist each other, or find shareholder assistance. If these are not possible, then the central bank is involved for assistance.

(iii) Specify standard of assistance objects

The central bank should distinguish whether banks face crisis because of systematic risk, because of their own bad management and operation. As regards the latter, they should follow the market principle. Meanwhile for the former, the central bank needs to provide assistance to avoid more serious financial crisis. Of course, if some financial institutions that play a very important role are not capable of paying off debts when in financial crisis, the central bank also helps them out to avoid any social panic caused by their bankruptcy.

(iv) Improve assistance methods

Normally, the lender of last resort does not have to intervene into light liquidity shortage. If it is moderate or severe, the lender of last resort should intervene in good timing, or even provide direct liquidity to banks. In China, bank lending is the main financial system. Therefore, it is reasonable to choose reloaning as the method to assist problematic financial institutions, which is supposed to be more effective. However, the premise to assisting problematic financial institutions is that liquidity shortage occurs. Not all such institutions get the chance. Additionally, under the background of marking the financing ratio ramp up gradually, it is better for the central bank to diversify assistance methods, fully exerting the function of the discount window and opening market operation. More importantly, the methods are considered to be combined, based on the degree of financial crisis and the operation status of financial institutions.

(v) Charge a punitive interest rate

The current low interest rate of assistance loans ought to be improved. At the time of providing final loans assistance, the interest rate could be increased properly, which will raise the costs of financial institutions to ask for assistance from the lender of last resort, and decrease the actions of financial institutions to excessively seek for assistance owing to low interest rate. Besides, assistance loans duration should be shortened to encourage financial institutions to repay loans at the time of economic or bank operation turnaround. After all, the final loans from the central bank are not operative capital, but emergency capital. The requirement for financial institutions to return loans promptly will strengthen their confidence to operate strictly. Of course, other methods are also considered for use at the same time (e.g., attach stricter "supervisory clauses") to avoid negative effects resulting from a high interest rate.

(vi) Flexibly apply constructive fuzzy strategy

Normally in a good economic environment, if certain financial institutions are in trouble it will not lead to systematic risks. Such financial institutions mostly suffer self-operation problems. Consequently, the optimal strategy should be to reduce assistance to decrease moral hazard. Meanwhile, in a comparatively bad economic environment or even economic recession, financial institutions face difficulties mainly because of overall environment. In this situation, the central bank should take greater efforts to provide assistance, for which it is crucial to standardize central bank's decision-making mechanism for final loans.

6.5 RELATED IDEAS FOR BUILDING CHINA'S MACROPRUDENTIAL SUPERVISION SYSTEM

In China, financial supervision is comparatively effective and its financial system is comparatively stable, which do not create conducive conditions for developing systematic risks to financial crisis. However, a number of financial institutions are owned by the state, most of which possess homogeneity in their operation principle, behavior pattern, risk explosion, etc. This indicates a hidden danger of high systematic risk. Therefore, it is necessary to build China's financial macroprudential supervision in the long term to maintain financial stability.

(i) Further improve microprudential supervision system

The foundation of the macroprudential supervision system plays an important role and its further improvement is important and fundamental. To realize this, the increase of microprudential supervision capability and effectiveness is focused on more, and dynamic harmony is kept with the development of financial service and innovation.

Firstly, speed up the building of financial supervision provisions, institutions and mechanism to prevent severe "supervision hollow" and "supervision dead space."

Secondly, strengthen the building of supervision competence and talents to improve the supervisory capability of assets and liabilities, investment strategy and asset allocation, and the capability of risk warning, prevention, and control.

Thirdly, upgrade supervisory technology and method step by step by taking modern technology to identify, prevent, and deal with financial risks.

In particular, a coping mechanism has not yet been built to include factors such as liquidity injection, toxic assets disposal, financial institutions restructuring and bankruptcy, etc. In the case of financial crisis assistance, financial supervisory authority could take powerful action to prevent the spread of financial risk. Simultaneously, liquidity injection and problematic asset disposal have a good effect on the recovery of financial institutions and market function. In conclusion, it is crucial to build a powerful lender of last resort and a set of orderly and effectively operational mechanisms to deal with financial crisis and danger.

(ii) Build a supervisory mechanism framework suitable for China's situations

We now follow a separate supervisory framework set by "One Bank and Three Commissions." The three commissions, the CBRC, the China Securities Regulatory Commission (CSRC), and the China Insurance Regulatory Commission (CIRC), mainly take the microprudential supervisory responsibilities, with the central bank taking a small quantity too. It can be seen that this kind of supervisory framework is unlikely to make microprudential supervisory institutions plan a main role in the future macroprudential supervisory institutions. None of these commissions meet the conditions to stand in a leading position. The leading department of macroprudential supervisory system must control an overall situation, coordinate the common interests of each department, and solve the problems of a particular department or financial system to ensure safe and stable financial development. In this aspect, the central bank is obviously the best choice for macroprudential supervision. Nevertheless, since only the central bank grasps the function of lender of last resort, the government should specify it as the responsible macroprudential supervision authority. A microprudential supervisory authority mutually shares information with the central bank. The central bank supervises financial system risks and feeds analysis results and suggestions back to the microprudential supervisory authority. Then the microprudential supervisory authority can take proper action based on the suggestions. It has to be noted that the financial department, national assets management departments, and other departments also take responsibility for financial stability to some extent. Hence, the macroprudential supervisory framework must rely on a mechanism where each department is united and clearly positioned. Of course, when it is time, it is necessary to build a higher level financial commission on the basis of the current supervisory framework, which particularly concentrates on macroprudential supervision and financial stability maintenance to fully analyze and supervise all institutions, products, tools, markets and transaction behavior that may cause financial system risks. It should also develop and build tools, standards, and indicators related to macroprudential supervision, to prevent systematic risks.

(iii) Build and improve regulations related to counter-cyclical supervision as soon as possible

The main purpose to build a macroprudential supervision system is to eliminate any pro-cyclical effect on the financial system due to Basel Accord or accounting standard. Thus, further research of the financial system's inner pro-cyclical mechanism is required, and a proper counter-cyclical supervision mechanism built through counter-cyclical policies (e.g., counter-cyclical capital buffer mechanism, provision, counting, and drawing policy reformation, and fair-value accounting rules). It has to be admitted that the choice of rule-orientation or discretionary approaches will probably happen in such a situation. By connecting to the real situation in China, currently the reasonable choice should be mainly rule-orientation assisted by discretionary approaches. Regarding counter-cyclical supervision, leverage indicators, prospective provision, counting, and drawing policy and fair-value accounting rules, it is suggested to apply regular counter-cyclical supervision policy, while discretionary approaches are used when necessary.

(iv) Explore macroprudential supervisory indicators suitable for China's situations

Some achievements have been made on the research of systematic risk indicators and macroprudential supervisory indicators. However, the indicators are not suitable for all countries or all situations. Therefore, by learning from international experience, we design macroprudential supervisory indicators suitable for China's situation, and continuously supervise these, mainly focusing on the deviation of each indicator from the historical average value to perform continuous correction during supervision. Taking the banking industry as an example, a credit indicator (the ratio of credit to GDP, credit increase speed, the structure of credit to industry) can be sampled as judgment standard of asset price bubble; simultaneously, macro stress testing is applied to evaluate the possible loss to the economic system when crisis occurs. The macroprudential supervisory authority feeds the above indicators and expected loss back to the banking industry's supervisory authority, and puts forward relevant policy suggestions. The banking industry's supervisory authority then implements a concrete supervisory policy based on these indicators and suggestions. Additionally, the rapid financial innovation and development of China's financial institutions while self-risk management capability is far from being enough needs to be taken into account. The macroprudential supervisory authority need to consider the safety, liquidity, and profitability requirements of bank, security, insurance and other industries to design a supervisory indicator system which could both promote financial innovation and prevent financial risks by strengthening capital adequacy ratio, assets and liabilities, and the in-table and off-table business of financial institutions.

(v) Pay attention to the strengthening of risk management to large financial institutions

In other words, under the macroprudential supervision framework, it is always emphasized how important it is to supervise financial institutions that have a systematic effect. With the growth of power of large state-owned financial institutions and the formation of large financial holding groups, the pattern of mixed operation is formed, which means a kind of institutional contradiction similar to the United States's, between which separate supervision and mixed operation may emerge. Thus, the macro-prudential supervisory authority should strengthen the supervision to such institutions.

Firstly, reinforce assets and liabilities management of large financial institutions, prevent their leverage ratio over ramp, and ensure their safety.

Secondly, pay attention to the dynamic supervision of overseas investment and the assets of large financial institutions, coordinating the relationship between safety and profitability to prevent a big overseas risk.

Lastly, build relevant information collection, risk assessment, and warning systems for large financial institutions to assess their risks at regular or irregular intervals, to prevent systematic risks.

References

REFERENCES IN ENGLISH

Alesina, A. & Summers, L. H. 1993. Central Bank Independence and Macroeconomic Performance: Some Comparative Evidence. *Journal of Money Credit & Banking*, 25(2), 151–162.

Allen, F. & Gale, D. 1999. Bubbles, crises and policy. *Oxford Review of Economic Policy*, 15, 9–18.

Allen, F. & Gale, D. 2000a. Financial contagion. *The Journal of Political Economy*, 108, 1–33.

Allen, F. & Gale, D. 2000b. Bubbles and crises. *The Economic Journal*, 11, 236–256.

Amable, B., Chatelain, J. B. & Bandt, O. D. 1998. Stability versus efficiency of the banking sector and economic growth. Cepremap Working Papers.

Angkinand, A. & Wihlborg, C. 2010. Deposit insurance coverage, ownership, and banks' risk-taking in emerging markets. *Journal of International Money and Finance*, 29, 252–274.

Ba, S., Chen, H. & Niu, B. 2007. Financial globalization in an era of uncertainty: Prospect of global financial stability and supervision in 2007. *Western Forum*, 5.

Ba, S., Liu, X. & Niu, B. 2005. On interaction between local governance and banking reform during China's transition. *Journal of Financial Research*, 5.

Babus, A. 2007. The formation of financial networks. Discussion Paper 06-093, Tinbergen Institute.

Bai, Q, *et al.* 2001. *Introduction to Research on Sustainable Development of Finance*. China Financial Publishing House, Beijing.

Beck, T., Demirgü-Kunt, A. & Levine, R. 2006a. Bank concentration and fragility: impact and mechanics. In *The Risks of Financial Institutions*, M. Carey & R. Stulz (eds.). University of Chicago Press, Chicago.

Beck, T., Demirgü-Kunt, A. & Levine, R. 2006b. Bank concentration, competition, and crises: first results. *Journal of Banking and Finance*, 30, 1581–1603.

Bell, S. & Quiggin, J. 2003. Asset price instability and policy responses: the legacy of liberalisation. *Journal of Economic Issues*, 9, 629–656.

Bergman, U. M. & Hansen, J. 2002. Financial instability and monetary policy: The Swedish evidence. Working Paper.

Bernanke, B. 1983. Non-monetary effects of the financial crisis in the propagation of the great depression. *American Economic Review*, 73, 257–276.

Bernanke, B. 2002. Asset Price Bubbles and Monetary Policy. Remarks before the New York Chapter of the National Association for Business Economics. New York, NY, October 15.

Bernanke, B. 2008a. Financial Markets, the Economic Outlook, and Monetary Policy. Speech Delivered at the Women in Housing and Finance and Exchequer Club Joint Luncheon, Washington, January 10.

Bernanke, B. 2008b. Policy Coordination among Central Banks. Speech Delivered at the Fifth European Central Banking Conference, The Euro at Ten: Lessons and Challenges. Frankfurt, Germany, November 14.

Bernanke, B. 2009. *The Crisis and the Policy Response*. Speech at London School of Economics, London, January 13.

Bernanke, B. & Gertler, M. 1989. Agency costs, net worth and business fluctuations. *American Economic Review*, 79, 14–31.

Bernanke, B. & Gertler, M. 2000. Monetary policy and asset price volatility. NBER Working Paper No. 7559.

Bernanke, B., Gertler, M. & Gilchrist, S. 1996. The financial accelerator and the flight to quality. *Review of Economics and Statistics*, 78, 1–15.

Bhattacharya, S., Boot, A. & Thakor, A. V. 2004. Credit, intermediation, and the macroeconomy: readings and perspectives in modern financial theory. *Oup Catalogue*, 4(4), 1196.

Booth, P. & Currie, D. A. 2003. *The Regulation of Financial Markets*. Institute of Economic Affairs.

Bordo, M. & Jeanne, O. 2001. *Asset Prices, Reversals, Economic Instability, and Monetary Policy*. Annual Meeting of the American Financial Association, New Orleans, Lousiana.

Bordo, M. & Jeanne, O. 2002. Boom-bust in asset prices, economic instability, and monetary policy. NBER Working Paper No. 8966.

Bordo, M., Eichengreen, B., Klingebiel, D. & Martinez-Peria, M. S. 2001. Is the crisis problem growing more severe? *Economic Policy*, 16, 53–82.

Bordo, M. D. & Murshid, A. P. 2000. Are financial crises becoming increasingly more contagious? what is the historical evidence on contagion? NBER Working Papers.

Bordo, M. D. & Wheelock, D. C. 1998. Price stability and financial stability: The historical record. *Review*, 41–62.

Bordo, M. D., Dueker, M. & Wheelock, D. C. 2000. Aggregate price shocks and financial instability: An historical analysis. NBER Working Paper No. h0125.

Borio, C. & Crockett, A. 2000. In search of anchors for financial and monetary stability. *Greek Economic Review*, 20, 1–14.

Borio, C. & Lowe, P. 2001. To provision or not to provision. *BIS Quarterly Review*.

Borio, C., English, W. & Filardo, A. 2002. A tale of two perspectives: old or new challenges for monetary policy? BIS Paper No. 19.

Borio, C., Furfine, C. & Lowe, P. 2001. Proeye legality of the financial system and financial stability: issues and policy options. BIS Working Papers.

Boss, M., Elsinger, H., Thurner, S. & Summer, M. 2004. Network topology of the inter-bank market. *Quantitative Finance*, 4, 1–8.

Boyd, J. H. & De Nicoló, G. 2006. The theory of bank risk-taking and competition revisited. *Journal of Finance*, 60, 1329–1343.

Boyd, J. H., De Nicoló, G. & Smith, B. D. 2004. Crises in competitive versus monopolistic banking systems. *Journal of Money, Credit and Banking*, 36, 487–506.

Brock, P. L. 2000. Financial safety nets: lessons from Chile. *The World Bank Research Observer*, 15, 69–84.

Buch, C. M. & DeLong, G. 2008. Do weak supervisory systems encourage bank risk-taking? *Journal of Financial Stability*, 4, 23–39.

Burger, 2007. Rethinking financial stability from US subprime mortgage crisis: A perspective of German Central Bank (trans.). *China Finance*, 23, 31–33.

Calomiris, C. & Mason, J. 1997. Contagion and bank failures during the great depression: The June 1932 Chicago banking panic. *American Economic Review*, 87(5), 863–883.

Canoy, M. F. M., Van Dijk, M. F., Lemmen, J. J. G., De Mooij, R. A. & Weigand, J. 2001. Competition and Stability in Banking. *Social Science Electronic Publishing*, 13(2), 85–112.

Cao, R. 2004. *Risk and Financial Arrangement.* Social Sciences Academic Press, Beijing.

Carletti, E. & Hartmann, P. 2002. Competition and stability: What's special about banking? *Social Science Electronic Publishing*, 2.

Carlson, M. & Mitchener, K. J. 2005. Branch banking, bank competition, and financial stability. *Journal of Money Credit and Banking*, 35(2), 99–118.

Carter, M. 1989. Financial innovation and financial fragility. *Journal of Economic Issues*, 23(3), 779–793.

Castiglionesi, F. & Navarro, N. 2007. *Optimal Fragile Financial Networks.* Mimeo, Tilburg University.

Cecchetti, S., Genberg H., Lipsky, J. & Wadhwani, S. 2000. *Asset Prices and Central Bank Policy.* Geneva Reports on the World Economy No. 2. Centre for Economic Policy Research, London.

Chailloux, A., Gray, S. & McCaughrin, R. 2008. Central bank collateral frameworks: principles and policies. IMF Working Paper No. 08/222.

Chang, R. & Velasco, A. 2000. Financial fragility and the exchange rate regime. *Journal of Economic Theory*, 92, 1–34.

Chant, J. 2003. Financial Stability as a Policy Goal. Bank of Canada Technical Report, Ottawa, 95, 1–28.

Chari, V. & Jagannathan, R. 1988. Banking panics, information, and rational. Federal Reserve Bank of Minneapolis in its Series Working Papers with Number 320.

Chen Johnson, C. S. 2007. Cooperation Among Safety-Net Members in Bank Resolution Practical Considerations. IADI 1st Inter-regional Conference, Istanbul Turkey.

Chortareas, G., Stasavage, D. & Sterne, G. 2003. Does monetary policy transparency reduce disinflation costs? *Manchester School*, 71(71), 521–540.

Christopher, K. & Philips, L. 1997. Asset Price price bubbles and monetary policy. Reserve Bank of Australia Research Discussion Paper No. 9709.

Cifuentes, R., Ferrucci, G.H. & Shin, S. 2005. Liquidity risk and contagion. *Journal of European Economic Association*, 3, 556–566.

Claessens, S. & Laeven, L. 2004. What drives bank competition? Some international evidence. *Journal of Money, Credit and Banking.*

Cocco, J., Gomes, F. & Martins, N. 2005. Lending relationships in the interbank market. Working Paper, London Business School.

Coggins, B. 1998. *Does Financial Deregulation Work? A Critique of Free Market Approaches.* Elgar.

Crockett, A. 1996. The theory and practice of financial stability. *De Economist*, 144, 531–568.

Crockett, A. 1997. Why is financial stability a goal of public policy? *Economic Review*, 4, 5–22.

Cukierman, A. 1992. Central bank strategy, credibility, and independence: Theory and evidence. *General Information*, 1(4), 10.

Cummins, J. D., Doherty, N. & Lo, A. 2002. Can insurers pay for the "Big One" measuring the capacity of an insurance market to respond to catastrophic losses, *Journal of Banking and Finance*, 98–11-B, P2.

Dasgupta, A. 2004. Financial contagion through capital connections: a model of the origin and spread of bank panics. *Journal of European Economic Association*, 2, 1049–1084.

De Nicoló, G. & Loukoianova, E. 2007. Bank ownership, market structure and risk. IMF Working Paper.

Degryse, H. & Nguyen, G. 2007. Interbank exposures: an empirical examination of contagion risk in the Belgian banking system. *International Journal of Central Banking*, 3, 123–171.

Demirgüç-Kunt, A. & Detragiache, E. 1998. The determinants of banking crises in developing and developed countries. IMF Staff Papers.

Demirgü-Kunt, A. & Huizinga, H. 1999. Market discipline and financial safety net design. World Bank Policy Research Working Paper No. 2183.

Demirgü-Kunt, A., Kane, E. J. & Laeven, L. 2006. Deposit insurance design and implementation: policy lessons from research and practice. Working Paper No. 3969.

Diamond, D. & Dybvig, P. 1983. Bank runs, deposit insurance, and liquidity. *Journal of Political Economy*, 91, 401–419.

Diaz-Alejandro, C. F. 1985. Goodbye financial repression, hello financial crash, *Journal of Development Economics*, 19(1-2), 1–24.

Domaç, I. & Martínez Peria, M. S. 2000. Banking crises and exchange rate regimes: Is there a link? The World Bank Working Paper, No. 2489.

Dooley, M. P. 1996. A survey of literature on controls over international capital transactions. Staff Papers — International Monetary Fund, 43(4), 639–687.

Dowd, K. 1992. *The Experience of Free Banking*. Routledge, London.

Dowd, K. 2004. *Competition and Finance*. China Renmin University Press, Beijing.

Drees, B. & Pazarbasioglu, C. 1995. The Nordic banking crises: Pitfalls in financial liberalization. World Bank Working Paper 95/61-EA.

Duan, Z. & Zeng, L. 2007. Research review on relations between asset price fluctuation and financial stability. *Shanghai Finance*, 4.

Duisenberg, W. F. 2001. The contribution of the Euro to financial stability. In *Globalization of Financial Markets and Financial Stability–challenges for Europe*, Baden-Baden, pp. 37–51.

Dziobek, C. & Pazarbasioglu, C. 1997. Lessons from systemic bank restructuring: A survey of 24 countries. *Social Science Electronic Publishing*, 14(35).

ECB, 2008. EU Banking Sector Stability, European Central Bank.

Eichengreen, B. 1998. Exchange rate stability and financial stability, *Open Economies Review*, 9(1), 569–608.

Eichengreen, B. & Rose, A. K. 1998. Staying afloat when the wind shifts: external factors and emerging-market banking crises. NBER Working Paper No. w6370.

Eisenberg, L. & Noe, T. 2001. Systemic risk in financial systems. *Management Science*, 47, 236–249.

Evans, O., Leone, A. M., Gill, M. & Hilbers, P. 2000. Macroprudential indicators of financial system soundness. IMF.

E, Z. 2000. On correlation between capital flow and financial stability. *Journal of Financial Research*, 7.

Ferguson, R. 2002. Should Financial Stability Be an Explicit Central Bank Objective? Paper Presented to an International Monetary Fund Conference on Challenges to Central Banking from Globalized Financial Markets, Washington, D.C., September 17.

Filardo, A. 2000. Asset prices and monetary policy. *Economic Review, Federal Reserve Bank of Kansas City*, 3, 11–37.

Filardo, A. 2001. Should monetary policy respond to asset price bubbles? Some Experimental Results, FRB of Kansas City Working Paper, 7, 1–4.

Financial Stability Forum, 2001. Guidance for Developing Effective Deposit Insurance Systems. September.

Fischer, S. 1999. On the need for an international lender of last resort. IMF Working Paper.

Fisher, I. 1933. The debt-deflation theory of great depression. *Econometrica*, 1, 337–357.

Foot, M. 2003. *What is Financial Stability and How do we get it?* Roy Bridge Memorial Lecture, London, April 3.

Frankel, J. A. & Rose, A. K. 1998. The endogeneity of the optimum currency area criteria. *Economic Journal*, 108(449), 1009–1025.

Fratianni, M. 2008. Financial Crises, Safety Nets and Regulation. Invited Lecture at the Annual Meetings of the Società Italiana Degli Economisti.

Freixas, G. & Rochet, J.-C. 1997. *Microeconomics of Banking*, MIT Press., Cambridge MA.

Freixas, X. & Rochet, J. 1998. Fair pricing of deposit insurance: is it possible yes. Is it desirable? No. *Research in Economics*, 52, 217–232.

Freixas, X., Parigi, B. & Rochet, J. 2000. Systemic risk, interbank relations and liquidity provision by the central bank. *Journal of Money, Credit and Banking*, 32, 611–638.

Friedman, M. 1991. *The Counter-Revolution in Monetary Theory*. John Wiley & Sons, Inc.

Friedman, M. & Schwartz, A. 1963. *A Monetary History of the United States: 1867–1960*. Princeton University Press, Princeton.

Frydl, E. & Quintyn, M. 2000. The benefits and costs of intervening in banking crises. IMF Working Paper No. 00/147.

Furceri, D. & Mourougane, A. 2009. Financial crises: past lessons and policy implications. OECD Economics Department Working Papers No. 668.

Furfine, C. 2003. Interbank exposures: quantifying the risk of contagion. *Journal of Money, Credit and Banking*, 35, 111–128.

Gai, P. & Kapadia, S. 2008. *Contagion in Financial Networks*. Mimeo, Bank of England, March

Gavin, B. M. & Hausmann, R. 1996. The roots of banking crisis: The macroeconomic context. Inter-american Development Bank.

Gersl, A. & Hermanek, J. 2008. Financial stability indicators: advantages and disadvantages of their use in the assessment of financial system stability. *Prague Economic Papers*, 2.

Gilbert, R. & Vaughan, M. D. 1998. Does the publication of supervisory enforcement actions add to market discipline? *Research in Financial Services: Private and Public Policy*, 10, 259–280.

Goldfajn, I. & Valdes, R. 1997. Balance of payments crises and capital flows: The role of liquidity. Working Papers Central Bank of Chile.

Goldsmith, R. W. 1969. *Financial Structure and Development*. Yale University, New Haven, Connecticut.

Goldstein, M. 2008. *The Subprime Credit Crisis: Origins, Policy Responses and Reforms*. Peterson Institute for International Economics.

Goodhart, C. 1988. *The Evolution of Central Banks*. MIT Press, Cambridge.

Goodhart, C. 1995. *The Central Bank and the Financial System*. MIT Press, Cambridge.

Goodhart, C. 1999. Myths about the lender of last resort. *International Finance*, 2, 339–360.

Gorton, G. 1985. Bank suspension of convertibility. *Journal of Monetary Economics*, 15(2), 177–193.

Gorton, G. B. 1988. Banking panics and business cycles. *Oxford Economic Papers*, 40, 751–781.

Granger, C. W. 1980. Testing for causality: A personal viewpoint. *Journal of Economic Dynamics and Control*, 2, 329–352.

Greenspan, A. 1996. "Remarks", at Financial Markets Conference of the Federal Reserve Bank of Atlanta, Coral Gables, Florida, February 23.

Greenspan, A. 2001. Opening Remarks at a Symposium Sponsored by the Federal Reserve Bank of Kansas City, Jackson Hole, Wyoming, August 31.

Greenspan, A. 2002. Economic Volatility. Remarks at a Symposium Sponsored by the Federal Reserve Bank of Kansas City, Jackson Hole, WY, August 30.

Gruen, D., Plumb, M. & Stone, A. 2005. How should monetary policy respond to asset price bubbles? *International Journal of Central Banking*, 1, 1–31.

Guo, C. 2005. *Financial Tilt in Developed Countries*. China Financial Publishing House, Beijing.

Hahn, V. 2002. *Transparency in Monetary Policy: A Survey*. Ifo-Studien: Zeitschrift fr Empirische Wirtschaftsforschung.

Hardy, D. C. & Nieto, M. J. 2010. Cross-border coordination of prudential supervision and deposit guarantees. *Journal of Financial Stability*, 7, 155–164.

Hardy, D. C. & Pazarbasioglu, C. 1999. Determinants and leading indicators of banking crises: Further evidence. IMF Staff Papers.

Herrero, A. G. & Pedro del R. 2003. Financial stability and the design of monetary policy. *Social Science Electronic Publishing*, 1–62.

Hoenig, T. 1998. Financial Modernization: Implication for the Safety Net. Conference on Deposit Insurance Session on Deposit Insurance and Financial Modernization Federal Deposit Insurance Corporation, Washington, D.C.

Honohan, P. & Klingebiel, D. 2000. Controlling the fiscal costs of banking crises. World Bank Policy Research Working Paper No. 2441.

Houben, A., Kakes, J. & Schinasi, G. 2004. Towards a framework for safeguarding financial stability. IMF Working Paper WP/04/101.

Howells, B. F. & Mariscal, P. 2002. Central banks and market interest rates. *Journal of Post Keynesian Economics*, 24(4), 569–585.

Huang, S. & He, K. 2007. Property right, financial stability policy, and independece of central bank. *Research on Financial and Economic Issues*, 6.

IMF, 2008a. Sovereign Wealth Funds2A Work Agenda. February 29. Available at www.imf.orgPexternalPnpPppPengP2008P022908.pdf.

IMF, 2008b. The Recent Financial Turmoil-Initial Assessment, Policy Lessons, and Implications for Fund Surveillance. April. Available at www.imf.org.

IMF, 2010. *World Economic Outlook: Recovery, Risk, and Rebalancing*. Washington, DC.

IMF and World Bank, 2003. Staffs of the world bank and the international monetary fund analytical tools of the FASP. 2, 1–32.

Issing, O. 2003. Monetary and Financial Stability: Is there a Trade-off?" BIS Papers.

Iyer, R. & Peydro-Alcalde, J. 2007. The achilles heel of interbank markets: financial contagion due to interbank linkages. Working Paper ECB.

Jack, S. & Carolyn, W. 2007. Asset-price misalignments and monetary policy: how flexible should inflation-targeting regimes be? Bank of Canada Discussion Paper.

Jacklin, C. & Bhattacharya, S. 1988. Distinguishing panics and information-baked bank runs: Welfare and policy implications. *Journal of Political Economy*, 96, 568–592.

Kahn, C. M. & Santos, J. A. C. 2005. Allocating bank regulatory powers: lender of last resort. Deposit insurance and supervision. *European Economic Review*, 49, 2107–2136.

Kaminsky, G. & Reinhart, C. 1999. The twin crises: the causes of banking and balance-of-payments problems. *American Economics Review*, 89, 473–500.

Kane, E. J. 1995. Three paradigms for the role of capitalization requirements in insured financial institutions. *Journal of Banking & Finance*, 19, 431–459.

Kane, E. J. 2001. Financial safety nets: reconstructing and modeling a policymaking metaphor NBER Working Paper.

Kaufman, G. 1991. Lender of last resort: A contemporary perspective. *Journal of Financial Services Research*, 5, 95–110.

Kaufman, G. G. 1994. Bank contagion: A review of the theory and evidence. *Journal of Financial Services Research*, 8(2), 123–150.

Kent, C. & Lowe, P. 1990. Asset price bubbles and monetary policy. Research Discussion Paper No. 9709, Reserve Bank of Australia.

Keynes, J. M. 1936. *The General Theory of Employment, Interest and Money*, Macmillan Cambridge University Press.

King, R. G. & Levine, R. 1993. Finance and growth: Schumpeter might be right. *Quarterly Journal of Economics*, 108, 717–737.

Krugman, P. 1979. A model of balance-of-payments crises. *Journal of Money, Credit and Banking*, 11, 311–325.

Kydland, F. E. & Prescott, E. C. 1977. Rules rather than discretion: The inconsistency of optimal plans. *Journal of Political Economy*, 85(3), 473–491.

La Porta, R., Lopez-de-Silanes, F., Shleifer, A. & Vishny, R. W. 1998. Law and finance. *Journal of Political Economy*, 106(6), 1113–1155.

Lagunoff, R. & Schreft, L. 2001. A model of financial fragility. *Journal of Economic Theory*, 99, 220–264.

Large, A. 2005. A Framework for Financial Stability. Speech Delivered at the International Conference on Financial Stability and Implications of Basel II, Istanbul, March 18.

Leitner, Y. 2005. Financial networks: contagion, commitment, and private sector bailouts. *Journal of Finance*, 60, 2925–2953.

Levine, R. & Zervos, S. J. 1993. What have we learned about policy and growth from cross-country regressions? *American Economic Review*, 83(2), 426–430.

Levine, R. & Zervos, S. J. 1998. Stock markets, banks, and economic growth. *American Economic Review*, 88(88), 537–558.

Litan, R. E. 1997. Institutions and Policies for Maintaining Financial Stability. Federal Reserve Bank of Kansas City, Proceedings, pp. 257–297.

Liu, J. 2004. Tortuous struggle of Japan to deal with non-performing assets. *Economic Herald*, 11.

Liu, X. 2002. Vulnerability of Chinese financial industry needs more attention. *Modern Commercial Banking*, 7.

Lybek, T. 1999. Central bank autonomy, and inflation and output performance in the Baltic states, Russia, and other countries of the former Soviet Union, 1995–1997. *Social Science Electronic Publishing*, 99(6), 7–44.

Marinkovic, S. T. 2004. Designing an Incentive-Compatible Safety Net in a Financial System in Transition: The Case of Serbia, DP35 South East Europe Series.

Markowitz, H. 1952. Portfolio selection. *Journal of Finance*, 7(1), 77–91.

Martha, L. 2005. "House Prices and Monetary Policy in Colombia", Document presented at the First Monetary Policy Research Workshop in Latin America and the Caribbean on Monetary Policy Response to Supply and Asset Price Shocks, Santiago, Chile, November 17.

Martinez-Miera, D. & Repullo, R. 2007. Does competition reduce the risk of bank failure? Unpublished manuscript, *Rafael Repullo*, 23(10), 3638–3664.

Marx, K. 1887. *Capital* (vol. 1). Progress Publisher, Moscow.

McKinnon, R. & Pill, H. 1997. Credible economic liberalizations and overborrowing. *American Economic Review*, 87, 189–203.

Merton, R. C. 1992. Financial innovation and economic performance. *Journal of Applied Corporate Finance*, 4, 12–22.

Miguel, A. M. & Estrada, D. 2010. A financial stability index for Colombia. *Annals of Finance*, 6, 555–581.

Mill, J. S. 1848. *Principles of Political Economy*. John W. Parker, London.

Minguez-Afonso, G. 2007. Imperfect common knowledge in first generation models of currency crises. *International Journal of Central Banking*, 3(1), 72–81.

Minsky, H. P. 1972. "Financial Instability Revisited: The Economics of Disaster." Reappraisal of the Federal Reserve Discount Mechanism, 3, 97–136.

Minsky, H. P. 1985. The financial instability hypothesis: A restatement. In *Post Keynesian Economic Theory. A Challenge to Neo Classical Economics*, P. Arestis & T. Skouras (eds.).

Minsky, H. P. 1991. The Financial Instability Hypothesis: A Clarification, *General Information*.

Mishkin, F. S. 1991. Asymmetric information and financial crises: a historical perspective. In *Financial Markets and Financial Crises*, G. Hubbard (ed.). The University of Chicago Press, Chicago.

Mishkin, F. S. 1999a. Global financial instability: framework, events, issues. *Journal of Economic Perspectives*, 13, 3–20.

Mishkin, F. S. 1999b. Lessons from the Asian crisis. *Journal of International Money and Finance*, 18, 709–723.

Mishkin, F. S. 2007. Housing and the Monetary Transmission Mechanism. Finance and Economics Discussion Series, Federal Reserve Board, Washington, D.C.

Mishkin, F. S. 2008a. Monetary Policy Flexibility, Risk Management, and Financial Disruptions. Speech Delivered at the Federal Reserve Bank of New York, New York, January 11.

Mishkin, F. S. 2008b. The Federal Reserve's Tools for Responding to Financial Disruptions. Speech Delivered at the Tuck Global Capital Markets Conference, Tuck School of Business, Dartmouth College, Hanover, New Hampshire, February 15.

Nee, V. 1992. Organizational dynamics of market transition: Hybrid forms, property rights, and mixed economy in China. *Administrative Science Quarterly*, 37(1), 1–27.

Nier, E., Yang, J., Yorulmazer, T. & Alentorn, A. 2008. Network models and financial stability. Bank of England Working Paper No. 346.

Oosterloo, S. & Haan, J. D. 2004. Central banks and financial stability: A survey. *Journal of Financial Stability*, 1(2), 257–273.

Padoa-Schioppa, 2003. Banking, structure, financial dependence and growth: international evidence from industry data. *Journal of Finance*.

Peng, M. W. & Heath, P. S. 1996. The growth of the firm in planned economies in transition: institutions, organizations, and strategic choice. *Academy of Management Review*, 21(21), 492–528.

Plantin, G., Sapra, H. & Shin, H. S. 2005. Marking to Market, Liquidity and Financial Stability. Available at SSRN: http://ssrn.com/abstract=1186342.

Qiang, J. 2007. Degree of dependence on foreign trade, balance of trade, and China's financial stability. *International Economic Review*, 3.

Quintyn, M. & Taylor M. W. 2003. Regulatory and Supervisory Independence and Financial Stability. *CESifo Economic Studies*, 49. Available at www.cesifoeconomicstudies.de.

Radelet, S. & Sachs, J. 1998. The East Asian financial crisis: diagnosis, remedies, prospects. *Brookings Papers on Economic Activity*, 1.

Repullo, R. 2000. Who should act as a lender of last resort? An incomplete contracts model. *Journal of Money Credit and Banking*, 32, 580–605.

Research Group of National Bureau of Statistics, 2005. Preliminary analysis on the influence of real estate on national economy. *Management World*, 1.

Rossi, M. 1999. Financial fragility and economic performance in developing countries: Do capital controls, prudential regulation and supervision matter? IMF Working Paper.

Rothschild, M. & Stiglitz, J. 1976. Equilibrium in competitive insurance markets: An essay on the economics of imperfect information. *Quarterly Journal of Economics*, 90(4), 630–649.

Sachs, J., Tornell, A. & Velasco, A. 1996. Financial crises in emerging markets: the lessons from 1995. Working Paper No. 5576.

Saunders, A., Elizabeth, S. & Nickolaos, G. T. 1990. Ownership structure, deregulation, and bank risk taking. *Journal of Finance*, 45, 643–654.

Schaeck, K., Cihák, M. & Wolfe, S. 2006. Competition, concentration and bank soundness: new evidence from the micro-level. IMF Working Paper No. 06/143.

Schich, S. 2008. Financial Crisis: Deposit Insurance and Related Financial Safety Net Aspects. Financial Market Trends-ISSN 1995-2864-© OECD.

Schinasi, G. J. 2003. Responsibility of central banks for stability in financial markets. IMF Working Paper.

Schinasi, G. J. 2007. Private finance and public policy. IMF Working Paper.

Schwartz, A. J. 1988. Financial stability and the federal safety net. In *Restructuring Banking and Financial Services in America*, W. S. Haraf & G. E. Kushmeider (eds.). American Enterprise Institute, Washington.

Schwartz, A. J. 1995a. Systemic risk and the macroeconomy. In *Banking Financial Markets and Systemic Risk: Research in Financial Services, Private and Public Policy*, G. Kaufman (ed.). JAI Press Inc, Hampton.

Schwartz, A. J. 1995b. Why financial stability depends on price stability. *Economic Affairs*, 15, 21–25.

Sheldon, G. & Maurer, M. 1998. Interbank lending and systemic risk: an empirical analysis for Switzerland. *Swiss Journal of Economics and Statistics*, 134, 685–704.

Sims, C. 1980. Macroeconomics and reality. *Econometrica*, 48 (1), 1–48. (JSTOR 1912017)

Smith, B. 1987. Bank panics, suspensions, and geography. Some Notes on the Contagion of Fear in Banking.

Stiglitz, J. E. 1982. The inefficiency of the stock market equilibrium. *Review of Economic Studies*, 49, 241–261.

Stiglitz, J. E. 1985. Credit market and the control of capital. *Journal of Money, Credit and Banking*, 17(2), 133–152.

Stiglitz, J. E. 1989. Markets, market failures, and development. *American Economic Review*, 19, 197–203.

Stiglitz, J. E. & Weiss, A. 1981. Credit rationing in markets with imperfect information. *The American Economic Review*, 71(3), 393–410.

Stulz, R. M. (2000). *Does Financial Structure Matter for Economic Growth?* A Corporate Finance Perspective.

Tadesse, S. 2005. Banking Fragility and Disclosure: International Evidence. *SSRN Electronic Journal*, wp748.

Tang, X. & Zhang, W. 2002. On establishing early-warning system for financial crisis in China. *Economic Perspectives*, 6.

Tirole, J. 1996. A theory of collective reputations (with applications to the persistence of corruption and to firm quality). *The Review of Economic Studies*, 63(1), 1–22.

Upper, C. & Worms, A. 2004. Estimating bilateral exposures in the German interbank market: is there a danger of contagion? *European Economic Review*, 48, 827–849.

Vivier-Lirimont, S. 2004. Interbanking networks: Towards a small financial world? *General Information*, 2004.

Wallace, N. (1988). Another attempt to explain the illiquid banking system: the diamond and dybvig model with the sequential service constraint taken seriously. *Federal Reserve Bank of Philadelphia Quarterly Review*, Fall, pp. 3–16.

Walder, A. G. 1998. The local government as an industrial corporation. In *Zouping in Transition: the Process of Reform in Rural North China*, A. G. Walder (ed.). Harvard University Press, Cambridge.

Wang, Y. & Pan, S. 2006. Influence of FDI on balance of payments and financial stability: A theoretical and empirical study. *Economic Science*, 4.

Weller, C. E. 2001. Financial crises after financial liberalisation: Exceptional circumstances or structural weakness? *Journal of Development Studies*, 38(1), 98–127.

Wellink, N. 2002. Current Issues in Central Banking. Speech Presented at the Central Bank of Aruba, November 14.

Wells, S. 2004. U.K. interbank exposures: systemic risk implications. *Journal of Monetary Economics*, 2, 66–77.

White, W. R. 2004. Are changes in financial structure extending safety nets? BIS Working Paper No. 145.

White, W. R. 2006. Procyclicality in the financial system: do we need a new macro-financial stabilization framework? BIS Working Paper No. 193.

Wicksell, K. 1898. *Interest and Prices*, Augustus M Kelley Pubs.

Winkler, B. 2000. Which kind of transparency? On the need for clarity in monetary policy-making. European Central Bank Working Paper 26.

Xiang, X. 2005. New insight into the definition of financial stability. *Journal of Zhejiang Provincial Party School*, 4.

Yang, S. 2010. Talks of Deng Xiaoping on construction industry and housing problems. *Developing*, 5.

Yin, D. 2001. Local governments and variations of financial systems: Ways and efficiency. *South China Financial Research*, 2.

Ying, Y. & Liu, S. 2006. Mechanisms of action of financial structure to financial stability: A functional perspective. *China Economic Times*.

Yu, R. & Sun, W. 2007. Government action, systematic risk, and financial stability. *Economic Theory and Business Management*, 7.

Yuan, D. 2006. What is the optimum scale for China's foreign exchange reserve? *Shanghai Securities News*.

Zhang, H. & Duan, X. 2006. Research review on major issues in financial stability. *Studies of International Finance*, 5.

Zhang, X. 2004. On institutional factor of economic security. *Theory Journal*, 12.

Zhang, Y. & Sun, G. 2003. Theoretical and empirical studies on early-warning system for financial crisis. *Studies of International Finance*, 10.

Zysman, J. 2009. *Governments, Markets and Growth:Financial Systems and the Politics of Industrial Change*. Jilin Publishing Group, Jilin.

REFERENCES IN CHINESE

Cao, G. & Xu, G. 2010. Influence of banks' behavior on macrocontrol and countermeasures under the background of real estate market game. *Journal of Chinese Academy of Governance*, 5.

Cao, Q. 2011. Inflection point of finance' in macro control of real estate market. *Economic Theory and Business Management*, 3.

Chen, X. 2006. Study of legislation regarding the priority of subrogation of deposit insurance agencies. *Studies of International Finance*, 7.

Chen, Y. 2007. On government's control over the allocation of financial resources in countryside of Wuling area and its effect. *Journal of Enshi Technical College*, 4.

Cheng, C. & Zhang, X. 2011. Empirical analysis on the influence of asymmetric interest-rate policy on housing price in China . *Research on Economics and Management*, 9.

Feng, J. & Li, D. 2011. Research review on financial supervision and decision-making mechanism of monetary policies. *Economic Perspectives*, 9.

Feng, K. 2011. Research on the role of Chinese real estate market in conduction mechanism of monetary policy. *Economic Perspectives*, 4.

Fu, B. & Zhu, Z. 2009. On feasibility of establishing deposit insurance system in China. *China Business*, 20.

Ge, H. & Gou, T. 2011. Study of credit risks of local government financing platform in China. *Economic Perspectives*, 1.

Ge, Z., Jiang, Q. & Yan, Z. 2011. Cause of systematic financial risk in China, cases, and macro-prudential countermeasures. *Journal of Financial Development Research*, 4.

Han, P. & Jiang, D. 2011. Efficiency analysis of regulatory policies regarding real estate: based on dynamic consistency. *Research on Economics and Management*, 4.

He, D. 2007a. Building a long-term mechanism for post-WTO financial stability. *Modern Economic Science*, 1.

He, D. 2007b. The Role of the Bank of China in Financial Stability. Doctorate dissertation, Sichuan University.

He, D. *et al.*, 2004. Bond market surveillance: a comparative analysis. *Public Finance Research*, 7.

He, D. *et al.*, 2012a. *China's Financial Safety: A Multi-Dimensional Analysis.* Social Sciences Academic Press, Beijing.

He, D. *et al.*, 2012b. *Innovation, Risk and Safeguard: Financial Safety in China's Financial Development.* Social Sciences Academic Press, Beijing.

He, F. 2005. Efficiency analysis of the allocation of government-oriented financial resources. *Shanghai Finance*, 5.

Hu, T. & Sun, Z. 2011. House-purchase restrictions and social welfare: A theoretical approach. *Economic Science*, 6.

Huang, P. 2003. *Problems of Local Finance in China.* China Procuratorate Press, Beijing.

Hui, K., Ren, B. & Chao, X. 2010. The measure of China's financial stability. *Economic Survey*, 1.

Huo, D. & Liu, S. 2009. Study of indicator system for China's macro-financial stability. *Journal of Shanxi University of Finance and Economics*, 10.

IMF, 2006. *Financial Soundness Indicators: Compilation Guide.* International Monetary Fund, Washington D.C.

Jia, K. 2010. *Challenge to Financial Innovation in the Period of Strategic Opportunities: Where does China's Policy-Based Finance Go.* Economic Press China, Beijing.

Li, H. & Jiang, H. 2008. On issues regarding local governments and regional financial development. *Financial Theory and Practice*, 1.

Li, Y. & Jiang, H. 2009. Construction of China's financial safety net: theoretical review, international experiences and system design. *South China Finance*, 6,

Lin, B. 2000. National model and utility function under the background of institutional change of China's finance. *Journal of Financial Research*, 12.

Lin, P. 1999. Theories and policies regarding financial safety net. *South China Finance*, 11.

Lin, J. & Guo, H. 2011. Dilemma of housing finance market: taking the U.S.A. as an example. *Comparative Economic & Social Systems*, 4.

Ling, T., Du, Y. & Yang, M. 2007. Fairness problems in designing deposit insurance financing system. *Journal of Financial Research*, 5.

Liu, J. 2004. Twists and turns in Japan's efforts to resolve non-performing asset. *Economic Herald*, 11.

Liu, Y. & Shen, K. 2008. Behavior patterns of local governments in China and the influence of the patterns on local financial ecology. *China Finance*, 10.

Lu, W. 2011. Review on the first symposium on macro economy and real estate market. *Economic Perspectives*, 3.

Ma, R., Wang, H. & Liu, S. 1994. *History and Operational Mechanism of Township Enterprises in China.* Peking University Press, Beijing.

Meng, B. 2010. Thoughts on building deposit insurance system. *China Economist*, 1.

Meng, J. 2005. Making full use of monetary policy in maintaining financial stability. *New Finance*, 5.

Miao, W. 2007. Financial and monetary stability: analysis of independency of central banks based on information-constrained economy. *Journal of Financial Research*, 1.

National Bureau of Statistics of China, 2005. Analysis on influence of real estate on national economy. *Management World*, 1.

Ni, P. 2011. *Annual Report on Development of Housing Market (2010–2011)*. Social Sciences Academic Press, Beijing.

People's Bank of China 2009. *China Financial Stability Report 2009*. China Financial Publishing House, Beijing.

Peng, G. & Miao, Y. 2010. International reference and the choice of China under the framework of macro-prudential regulation. *Economic Theory and Business Management*, 11.

Shang, Y. & Jing, X. 2011. Influential factors for risk of home mortgage loan default and countermeasures. *Research on Economics and Management*, 1.

Shen, Y. & Zhang, X. 2011. Stability of payable ability for housing: theories and case analysis. *Finance and Trade Economics*, 2.

Tang, L. 2009. How to improve China's financial safety net. *Zhejiang Finance*, 5.

Tang, S. 2010. Local Finance, Local Governments, and Finance Industry: A Speech on the 10th Local Finance Forum. Available at http://www.ebchina.com/ebchina/htmlDocument/2010-09-28/detail_1188.shtml.

Wan, X. 2008. Judgement and measure of vulnerability of Chinese financial system from 1987 to 2006. *Journal of Financial Research*, 6.

Wang, H. 2010a. Local governments: from the perspective of financial development in China. *Financial Theory & Practice*, 2.

Wang, H. 2010b. The construction of Chinese financial stability state index: based on the analysis of state space model. *Contemporary Finance & Economics*, 5.

Wang, G. & Li, H. 2007. Financial stability, financial efficiency and institutional improvement of Chinese financial safety net. *Wuhan Finance*, 5.

Wang, M. & Li, Z. 2005. System of financial stability evaluation index: study of macro-cost control of bank stablity. *China Soft Science*, 9.

Wang, Z. 2007. Hindered financial intervention of local governments and welfare loss analysis. *Gansu Finance*, 12.

Wei, L. 2010. Thoughts on China's monetary policy and coordination mechanism for financial stability. *Huabei Finance*, 1.

Wu, J. 2002. Bank reform: top priority of China's financial reform. *China Economic News Weekly*, 30.

Wu, J. 2008. Difficulties in China's economic transition and solutions. *China Reform*, 2.

Wu, N. & Yun, H. 2005. Rethinking on China's financial stability. *Journal of Financial Research*, 2.

Xia, B. 2010. Reflections on regulation and control over housing market. *Economic Perspectives*, 2.

Yan, H. 2005. Deposit insurance system and the lender of last resort of central banks. *China Finance*, 11.

Yan, W. 2006. *Study of Market Exit of Financial Institutions*. China Financial Publishing House, Beijing.

Zeng, K. 2005. Allocation of financial resources in China. *Journal of Financial Research*, 4.

Zhang, H. & Chen, L. 2011. Risk prevention mechanism of MBS-mortgage-backed securitization in the U.S.A: review and reflection. *Comparative Economic and Social Systems*, 5.

Zhang, J. & Wu, Z. 2011. Study of functions of financial affairs office in Chinese local governments. *Shenzhen Finance*, 1.

Zhang, Q. & Lang, B. 2011. American housing finance market: operational mechanism, supervision reform, and reflection. *Comparative Economic and Social Systems*, 3.

Zhang, Y. 2010a. Frontier of research on the conduction mechanism of monetary policy: theoretical review from the perspective of new global financial crisis. *International Economic Review*, 5.

Zhang, Y. 2010b. Better to cancel the financing function of local financial affairs offices. 21st Century Business held on November 3.

Zhang, Y. 2010c. Analysis of intervention of local governments in financial development. *Securities & Futures of China*, 6.

Zhong, B. 2004. Theory, indexes and methods of monitoring financial stability. *Shanghai Finance*, 9.

Zhou, L. 2003. Changes of fiscal capacity and financial ability of China during Reform. *Finance and Trade Economics*, 4.

Zhou, X. 2011. Response of financial policy to financial crisis: formation background, interior logics, and major content of macro-prudential policy framework. *Journal of Financial Research*, 1.

CPSIA information can be obtained at www.ICGtesting.com
Printed in the USA
BVOW06*2320270916

463496BV00003B/3/P

9 789813 109056